Praise for *Confessions of ᴄ*

"To read *Confessions of a Hayseed DA* is to be reminded of what the law is really all about: It's about people. Robert Meehan was district attorney of Rockland County, New York for nine years ending in 1974. His posthumous memoir—it was discovered and edited by one of his daughters after his death—is part *Mr. Smith Goes to Washington*, part *It's a Wonderful Life*, and all rich with real life. Unlike the hard-boiled crime movies he grew up loving, Meehan's time as DA is filled with the kind of tight community connections that remind us that both victims and criminals have families, friends, and histories. Meehan's integrity leaps off the page. He may not have always been the most popular man in Rockland County, but it's easy to see why he was respected."

> — Amanda Bennett, Pulitzer Prize-winning author and investigative journalist, former Director of Voice of America, former Executive Editor of *Bloomberg News*, and former Editor of the *Philadelphia Inquirer* and *Lexington Herald-Leader*

"*Confessions of a Hayseed DA* is a captivating portrayal of the sorrow, tragedy, joy, goodness, sadness, and even humor of those who must answer for themselves before the law. The confessional of Robert Meehan is a testament to a man's steadfast principle of fairness in adjudicating the law with too rare compassion and understanding."

> — Joe Sestak, former US Congressman (PA-07) and Vice Admiral, US Navy

"A hayseed? While he may have lived in 'upstate' New York, this humble public servant was erudite and sophisticated. As the son of the county's Chief Medical Examiner and later as a prosecutor for then Assistant Attorney General Robert R. Meehan, I knew the players depicted and many of the featured cases. The graphic description of the train bus collision injected a level of detail I never knew and reignited many of the emotions from that tragedy. I am grateful to this great man for memorializing these historical events and providing a unique insight into our criminal justice system when placed in the hands of a man with unwavering ethics, integrity and compassion."

> — New York State Supreme Court Justice Thomas P. Zugibe, former Rockland County District Attorney, 2008–2019

"An entertaining and compelling account of the dynamic challenges facing the chief prosecutor of a small scenic county just thirty miles north of New York City as he deals with the vagaries and absurdities of crime in the community he cherished and called home. This book reminds us of the delicate decisions and balance required to ensure justice in our communities while protecting the rights of the accused as provided for in our constitution. In comparison to the polarizing times we live in today, DA Meehan's thoughtful, ethical and occasionally self-effacing approach to criminal justice serve as a profound reminder that 'justice for all' is only possible with the dedication of good public servants who respect and are committed to the search for the truth in all matters large and small."

> — Anne Crowley, former Press Secretary and Director of Communications for New York Governor Mario M. Cuomo, and former Executive Vice President, Corporate Affairs for Fidelity Investments

"Robert R. Meehan has published posthumously an unexpected gem in *Confessions of a Hayseed DA*, thanks to the perseverance of his daughter, who discovered the long-forgotten manuscript. Meehan takes readers behind closed doors of the Rockland County District Attorney's Office and delivers a narrative that is by turns a page-turning exposé of a fugitive homicide case, a frank examination of the politics of the criminal justice system, and a love letter to his loyal staff and supportive wife. The prose is lively, self-deprecating, and shot through with authenticity and a sly humor."

> — Paul Grondahl, author of *Mayor Corning: Albany Icon, Albany Enigma*, journalist, and director of the New York State Writers Institute

"I wish I could have met Robert Meehan. As a District Attorney, I love a good legal fight and I think we would have had a lot in common. DA Meehan fought fervently for the rights of both victims and the accused. And he refused to allow those rights to be subordinated to the political and social winds of the time. Although it was written more than forty years ago, this book is extraordinarily timely. The overarching message—that prosecutors have the obligation to represent all of their constituents with tireless fervor and conviction, regardless of win-loss records or popularity contests—should be shared with all those who aspire to represent the People in a court of law. I was particularly moved by DA Meehan's successful efforts to change the laws of New York State in regard to the rights of rape victims. This is a passion that we share. It was a privilege to read this book."

> — Summer Stephan, District Attorney, San Diego, California

Confessions of a
HAYSEED DA

Editor Kathleen Meehan Do with her dad, author Robert R. Meehan.

Confessions of a HAYSEED DA

Robert R. Meehan

Edited by
Kathleen Meehan Do

excelsior editions

AN IMPRINT OF STATE UNIVERSITY OF NEW YORK PRESS

Published by State University of New York Press, Albany

Excelsior Editions is an imprint of State University of New York Press

For information, contact State University of New York Press, Albany, NY
www.sunypress.edu

Library of Congress Cataloging-in-Publication Data

Names: Meehan, Robert R., 1930–2004, author. | Meehan Do, Kathleen, editor.
Title: Confessions of a hayseed DA / Robert R. Meehan ; edited by Kathleen
    Meehan Do.
Description: Albany, NY : State University of New York, [2022] | Includes
    index.
Identifiers: LCCN 2021061311 (print) | LCCN 2021061312 (ebook) | ISBN
    9781438488646 (pbk. : alk. paper) | ISBN 9781438488639 (ebook)
Subjects: LCSH: Meehan, Robert R., 1930–2004. | Public prosecutors—New
    York (State)—Rockland County—Biography.
Classification: LCC KF373.M415 A3 2022 (print) | LCC KF373.M415 (ebook) |
    DDC 345.74728/01262092 [B]—dc23/eng/20220204
LC record available at https://lccn.loc.gov/2021061311
LC ebook record available at https://lccn.loc.gov/2021061312

10 9 8 7 6 5 4 3 2 1

For all those devoted to upholding
and protecting the rule of law . . .
especially Laura

Contents

Editor's Note

Robert R. Meehan, my dad, took the Oath of Office as District Attorney of Rockland County, New York, on January 1, 1966. He served three, three-year terms, ending in 1974.

A couple of years later, my sister, Mary, and I recall learning that Dad was working on a book. All we knew about it was the title, *The Hayseed DA*. I hated that title. I didn't know if the book was a work of fiction or true-to-life, but I didn't like the idea that the book would be about some kind of hick.

That was where the story seemed to end. We never knew what it was about, and I always assumed that he never finished it. Life goes on, and I forgot about the book. I never thought to ask him what became of it. After Dad died in 2004, I started wishing I had.

My uncle, Tom Meehan, Dad's brother and the acclaimed Broadway book author of multiple musicals including *Annie*, *The Producers*, and *Hairspray*, died in August of 2017. About eighteen months later, I was planning on getting together in New York with his widow, my Aunt Carolyn, when she mentioned that she had a bag of my dad's papers that she had found while cleaning out Tom's office. The thought crossed my mind, could *The Hayseed DA* have found its way to Tom and Carolyn's Greenwich Village apartment? Did Dad ask his talented writer-brother to look at it?

The bag was heavier than I expected and appeared to be filled with legal pads and folders. I was dying of curiosity but decided to wait until I got home to see what was inside. That evening, I poured myself a glass of wine and started looking through the bag. I pulled out the legal pads filled with Dad's familiar script, written, as he always did, in black Flair pen. I pulled out some folders that had groups of papers stapled together. And then, at the bottom of the bag, I found a bound manuscript: *The Hayseed DA* by Robert R. Meehan.

It is hard to describe what a gift it has been to find and read this book. Dad had, in fact, finished it. It is a memoir of his nine years as district attorney, beginning when he was thirty-five years old. Reading this book is for me—and for all of my family and those who loved him—a chance to hear Dad's voice again: the young Dad, *Rockland's Fighting DA*, the Dad who gathered inspiration from his favorite characters of television and film. It brought back his passion for the rule of law, his belief that both victims and those accused of a crime deserved a fair chance to receive justice. He was driven, he was occasionally irreverent, he had a wry sense of humor, and he would walk through fire for his family and friends. All of that shines through in these pages.

Before I had even finished reading the first chapter, I knew I had to publish this book. I could actually feel Dad standing behind me, cheering me on. My sisters Mary and Pat immediately signed on to help.

It has been quite a project to first digitize the book and then edit it, being sure to maintain my father's unique voice while telling his story. There are only a couple of significant changes from his original manuscript. First, I changed the name of the book to *Confessions of a Hayseed DA*. The book is as much about what Dad was proud of as it was about things he wished he had done differently. It is a tribute to those he worked with and the lessons they taught him. It is not just a memoir; it is, in many ways, a beautiful confessional.

The other change happened when I found a short story, not included in the original manuscript, mixed in with all of the papers in one of the folders. It was about the nail-biting experience of November 2, 1965, the night Dad won the upset, squeaker election to become District Attorney of Rockland County. It had to be included. And so, with a little bit of editing magic, it was.

As much as anything else, this book is a love letter to Rockland County—its people, its history, and its character. As he makes clear in this book, Dad ruffled some feathers and was not always the most loved person in Rockland. In the end, however, I do believe he earned the respect of the people he served. For Dad, that was enough.

Preface

This book is a memoir of various incidents that occurred during my nine years as District Attorney of Rockland County, New York. Every case actually happened and all the events concerning my private and political life are based on truth.

Without exception, the names of all friends, judges, lawyers, policemen, and investigators are true. However, in most cases, the names of criminal defendants and witnesses or victims of crime, as well as some minor identifying details, have been changed.

I have relied totally on my memory of these events. For almost everyone, their memory is all they can rely on to recall the private events of a significant period in their life, but since there were transcribed records of all my trials, I could have used those to be exact and precise. I chose not to because it has been more interesting, more challenging, and, yes, more fun to try to remember rather than copying transcripts.

I have, however, tried my utmost to remember in an even manner, recalling the good days and the bad, the victories and the defeats, the triumphs and tragedies of a time in my life I shall never forget.

Chapter 1

Watching Haircuts on a Saturday Night

I was going on *The Barry Gray Show* one evening in early December 1970 and I must say I was pleased. I had been on local radio shows in Rockland County and I had even been on a Sunday morning talk show on TV in New York, but *The Barry Gray Show* was a highbrow radio talk show, targeted to late evening intellectuals who scorn TV. It was a definite first for me.

I had been elected District Attorney of Rockland County back in 1965 in what was considered locally a big upset. A Democrat hadn't held the office since 1911, so I became mildly famous in the county just for getting myself elected. However, this fame stopped very sharply at the county line. In fact, most people in New York City weren't quite sure where Rockland County was, and they certainly didn't know who I was.

There were two other guests on the show that night: Peter Vallone, a politician from New York City who planned to challenge Herman Badillo for Congress, and Giraud Chester, who had written a new book entitled *The Ninth Juror*, about his own experience as a juror on a murder trial in New York City.

I was introduced to the other guests and to Barry Gray just before we went on the air at 11:30 p.m. They all seem to know each other, or at least acted like they did, but I had never met any of them before and, although they were very pleasant, I got the impression that they wondered why I was on this New York City–oriented show—I did too.

We went into the small studio and I was impressed that the microphones looked like something out of *The Big Broadcast of 1938*. It was a semi-circular set up with Gray in the middle. Each of us had an individual microphone and we sat down at little tables facing each other. Gray had a headset on so he could hear his cues but other than that, it was all the same.

The show went on the air and the first thing Barry Gray did was introduce each of his guests and identify who they were. The other two were introduced first and after their introductions, Peter Vallone and Mr. Chester both said, "Good evening, glad to be with you," or words to that effect. When he got to me, Gray said, "And lastly we have Robert Meehan, who is the District Attorney of Rockland County." I was a little more nervous than I thought. My response was simply to nod at the microphone, which I suppose is not the best radio form.

Gray started his informal talk with Giraud Chester, asking many questions about his book and the actual trial he had sat on. Then he went to Pete Vallone and the problems of Queens and the South Bronx. After a few minutes of the ghetto problems, it was back to Chester. I thought he wasn't even going to get to me, but he did.

Right after the second commercial break, Gray turned, looked at me dead pan, and said, "What do you do up there in Rockland County?" A monumental question, but I was prepared to start an answer when he immediately broke in and continued, "You know I've had district attorneys on the show, but I never had a 'Hayseed DA' on before. I figure that up there in Rockland County you sit around and watch haircuts on Saturday nights, just for something to do!"

I thought to myself, "Holy mackerel, I should have stuck to my late night TV movies, which I so dearly love." But strangely enough, the rest of the show went rather well and when it was over an hour or so later, I liked Barry Gray and I kind of thought he liked me.

∿

I've always remembered those lines of Barry Gray and they never offend me, because after all, I suppose I am something of a hayseed. My clothes never seem to quite fit, my shoes are scuffed, my ears tend to stick out a bit, and my hair always appears a little in disarray, even after I comb it. In short, I lack the polish and manner that anyone would associate with a "Mr. District Attorney" figure.

However, I am writing now because I want people to know that even us "Hayseeds" do have our interesting moments. I suppose I could start with that very day of *The Barry Gray Show*. The day began with a phone call that woke me from my usual sound sleep at 4:30 that morning. But better yet, let me tell you how it all began.

One month earlier, at about 7:30 in the evening, a gas station in Sloatsburg, New York, had been held up at gunpoint. The twenty-one-year-old attendant, who was working alone in the station, had not only been robbed of the day's receipts but was kidnapped by the holdup man and his girlfriend (or "Moll," as we should call her). They put him in the trunk of their car and headed north on the New York State Thruway. Four hours later the young attendant's body was found lying face down a few feet off the shoulder of the Thruway, fifty-five miles to the north in Ulster County. Two .45-caliber bullets had entered the back of his skull. This was a brutal murder.

Four days after that, another young gas station attendant in nearby Mahwah in Bergen County, New Jersey, was held up and murdered by two shots from a .45-caliber weapon—according to ballistics, the same .45.

To the hardened citizens of New York City or Detroit or Los Angeles, this may be the type of news they have come to accept. In our corner of the world, it was a nightmare; a vicious killer was on the loose. The jurisdiction for prosecution was in Bergen County, New Jersey, for the Mahwah killing and Ulster County, New York, for the murder of the Sloatsburg attendant. In the state of New York, jurisdiction lies where the body is found if it is not known where the murder actually occurred, as was the case in the first days of the investigation. Hence, Ulster got the case.

An around-the-clock investigation went forward, led by the New York State Police from the Kingston Barracks in Ulster County, the Bergen County Prosecutor's Office, the Ramapo Police Department, and my office from Rockland County because of our deep involvement and concern.

∿

A break came several days after the Mahwah killing. One Laura Mancini, out of conscience or fear or both, came forward and said that she had accompanied one John Barkley, age thirty, of Mahwah, New Jersey, on his murderous junkets in both Rockland and Bergen counties. Barkley was described as a bearded, Caucasian man who was tall and heavy-set. She told authorities in graphic detail of the robberies and senseless killings. Yes, very senseless, because neither attendant had in anyway attempted to thwart the robbery.

The killing on the New York Thruway was the sorrier of the two. As Laura reported, John Barkley successfully robbed the station of $82 but then for no apparent reason, and in rather good spirits, insisted at gunpoint that the young attendant get in the trunk of the car. As they drove north, Laura said that John was in the best of humor and joking as she pleaded that they let the boy go free. They finally stopped on the Thruway shoulder just south of Kingston and John got out, opened the trunk, and let the young man out. With the gun in his hand, Barkley stood there with Laura and his victim in the dim light of his taillights and, with a broad smile, told the boy, "I guess I'd better kill you!" It seemed like such a joke that the boy smiled and kidded back and Laura felt surely he would let him go. But John turned away for a moment and the boy, who was not tied up in anyway, turned and ran south along the shoulder, away from the car. John, seeing this, turned and ran after him and just before he caught up with him, fired two shots into the back of his head.

The full meaning of Barkley's jovial, happy-go-lucky mood did not really have meaning to me until I was to come face-to-face with it, standing alone only a few short days later.

≈

Laura Mancini not only handed Barkley up on both murders, but she set in motion the biggest manhunt in the history of Rockland County. She told where John was hiding out, in a summer cabin in the foothills of the Ramapo Mountains in Hillburn, New York, near the New Jersey State line.

As the police closed in, John retreated into the rough terrain of the Ramapos on one of the first bitter cold nights of the season at the end of November.

Having made his initial escape into the mountains, the manhunt began in earnest with New York and New Jersey State Police and many local Rockland County police departments, led by the Ramapo Police, fanning out into the dark, cold, and rugged mountains.

The story was front-page news. The second day the banner head-line of the local Rockland daily paper, the *Journal News*, read, "KILLER

STALKED IN RAMAPOS." The third day the headline screamed, "POLICE CLOSE IN ON BARKLEY." The fourth day I received the telephone call.

When the phone rang at our house after 1 a.m. in those days, it was either 1) a police department reporting a serious crime, 2) the local press working on a morning deadline, or 3) and the most frequent, someone a little worse for alcohol, calling to let his district attorney know just what he thought of him. For this reason, my dear wife, Nancy, was assigned to screen all such calls. With the police and the press, she was great—with the tipplers, she was not.

"Bob, this one sounds like she really needs help," or "Oh, you've got to take it, he sounds desperate."

Nancy is a compassionate girl, but a judge of slurred speech she is not. After answering the phone at 4:30 that morning, Nancy said, "Bob, it's young Joe St. Lawrence and he says it's very important." Joe was then about twenty-one years old and owned his own motorcycle shop in Sloatsburg, but more important, he was the son of my high school football coach from days gone by at Suffern High School.

I took the call and Joe got right to the point. He knew John Barkley as a regular customer at his cycle shop and John had just called him to say that he wanted to surrender, but he would only surrender to me and I must be alone with no other law enforcement officers. My first thought was, "Why me?" But my first question was, "Where is he?"

St. Lawrence said he truly did not know, that Barkley had only told him he was more than two hundred miles away and that he wouldn't tell him unless Meehan accepted the deal to come alone. Barkley told Joe that he would call back in an hour for an answer. Without hesitation, I told him the deal of going alone was out, that as district attorney, I did not even have the power of a peace officer to make arrests and, besides, I wasn't a complete fool. I would, however, personally meet him with one of my investigators from the District Attorney's Office.

We then got to the issue of "Why me?" and why through St. Lawrence. The answer really surprised me. It seems without realizing it until that minute, I knew John Barkley and he knew and apparently liked me.

⁓

It had begun over eight years earlier. I had just bought my house on Cherry Lane in the little hamlet of Tallman. It was one of those development deals with practically nothing down and almost everything beyond a roof over your head was what they called an "extra." Since I had just passed the bar exam and had four daughters, the oldest age five, I could barely conjure up the $700 or $800 needed for the down payment and closing costs, so there would be no "extras." Unlike others who say that, and then get caught up in the world of a new house, I meant it. That meant that for landscaping we got the standard three scrawny little bushes and that was all. I told Nancy that all of those nice things would come in due time, and they did.

We still live in that house on Cherry Lane. Instead of eight rooms it has twelve, instead of a six-by-eighteen-foot deck made of two-by-fours, we have a twelve-by-twenty-two-foot closed-in and heated porch with a fourteen-by-twenty-foot swimming pool attached, and we must have fifty trees and shrubs in the yard. Nancy and I, along with the kids, did it all ourselves and, therefore, we love it all the more.

The improvement of Cherry Lane all began in the summer of 1961 when we went to Barkley's Nursery in Upper Saddle River, New Jersey, for a sale where they were selling shrubs and little evergreen trees at about $2 or $3 a piece. Barkley's was just south of the New Jersey border and not far from our house, and so we went there several times that summer and in the summers that followed. We always went in my beat up old Ford station wagon and the kids went with us, and it was a happy time, especially for Nancy. I was the carpenter, the electrician, the plumber, and the mechanic, but she was—and is—the gardener.

I can well remember that second summer when we went back and the owner's big handsome young son made a fuss over our newest addition. We had of course had our annual baby, but this one's name was Tommy. We were all so proud of our only boy. Mr. Barkley was proud of his son, too. His name was John.

∿

The twenty-two-year-old was now thirty and feared for his life; the happy days were behind him. He was sure that those police that stalked him in the mountains would kill him if he tried to surrender to them. He was wrong; I knew most of them on a first-name basis and they wouldn't have. But John in desperation had made his escape by crossing the mountains and heading west.

I told Joe to let John Barkley know that my word was good; that he must allow me to bring an investigator and let us know where he was. Joe believed me and he was sure that John would, too. Barkley had made St. Lawrence the middleman because he knew of the great friendship between the Meehans and the St. Lawrences. Joe was to call me back as soon as John Barkley returned his call.

I immediately called one of my investigators who lived only a mile away and asked him to come right away with no questions asked. Eric Vrhel arrived at the house about six minutes later; that's the kind of guy he is.

I explained the whole set up to Eric and damned if he didn't know the Barkleys, too. I should've realized it; he had worked several years before as a police officer in Upper Saddle River. Both of us felt a little ridiculous for not having realized who this arch-criminal from Hackensack was.

Eric had one disagreement with me. There must be two peace officers to bring in a fugitive and we must have someone from Ulster County where there was an open murder warrant. I knew immediately that he was right. I picked up the phone and called St. Lawrence and told him to tell John that I would have to be accompanied by *two* men. He didn't like it but would pass it on to John when he called.

Eric and I sat there and waited. Nancy had gotten up and made coffee. She didn't know what was going on, but she knew it was important and she knew enough not to ask. "Need to know" was a vital part of our business. In retrospect, I realize how hard that must have been for Nancy. But she understood my job and has always supported my decisions.

Sure enough, just after 5:30 the phone rang again. This time I answered it myself and it was Joe St. Lawrence. John had balked at two men, but would go along with one. He told Joe what city he was in under a pledge that Joe wouldn't tell us. Joe also had a phone booth number to call back and that was also to be kept from us. I didn't press St. Lawrence to break his word to Barkley but I was adamant, it must be on our terms with two men or not at all.

I suggested that Joe come to my house, place the call out of our presence, and then, after explaining my position, let me personally talk to John. Joe thought this was a good idea; he arrived at the house within fifteen minutes and the call was placed. Joe talked to John for about three minutes and then called me to the phone. John was willing to talk to me. Before I picked up the telephone, I looked Joe St. Lawrence hard in the eye and said, "One thing Joe, are you morally certain that's John Barkley's voice on the phone?"

"Absolutely, Mr. Meehan, I'd know it any place."

Alright, I'd talk to him. I knew that I must be firm but I tried to act casual. I explained the need for two men, gave my personal assurance as to his safety if he surrendered peacefully, and he quickly backed down and agreed to my terms. I then asked where he was and he still wouldn't say.

"John, how can we come get you if we don't know where you are?"

"Mr. Meehan, let me talk to Joe Saint again."

I put Joe back on the phone and he and John rather cleverly worked out a plan. When Joe hung up he said, "He's in Cleveland, that's all I'll tell you now. When we get to Cleveland, I'll call to make sure he's still there, and then I'll tell you his exact location. By the way, he also insists that I be there."

I was certain that Joe St. Lawrence was sincere and not part of any devious plan, but as a betting man I would have given long odds against John Barkley surrendering to us in Cleveland. It had first occurred to me that it might have been a desperate attempt by one of Barkley's friends to call off the massive manhunt in the Ramapo Mountains by convincing us he was far away in Cleveland. With Joe's assurance that it was his voice and further verification that the phone call had in fact been made to an area code 216 number, my fears of a complete hoax were somewhat relieved, but I was still very skeptical. It occurred to me that a man who had needlessly, and yes rather sadistically, ended the lives of two young men may not be trustworthy. He might also enjoy the prospect of making a fool out of the DA by sending him on a fruitless trip to Cleveland while he headed out of town. Worse yet, he could be waiting for us in ambush.

However, I was also certain that if John Barkley had truly managed to escape the human dragnet in the Ramapos, our chances of capturing him were getting slimmer. Some killers want to surrender—precious few, but we had to take the chance that this might be the one.

～

So I put the wheels in motion toward Cleveland, Ohio. First call was to my secretary or "Girl Friday," Ann Hickey.

"Annie, no questions asked, four round-trip tickets to Cleveland, one one-way ticket from Cleveland to New York, deal directly with the airline. Let's see, it's now almost 6 a.m., any flight after 8:30. Return flight time to be decided. Get back to me in twenty minutes."

"Yes, Boss."

I would have insulted her if I had said, "This is confidential," or anything of the kind. She knew it without me saying it.

Next call, Charlie Purcell, senior state police investigator assigned to Rockland County and one of the best cops I've ever met.

"Charlie, Bob Meehan. We just may have our boy, John Barkley, lined up. I need a man from Kingston Barracks to make the collar." Charlie wanted a few details; I gave him very few and left it at, "Trust me." He did.

I should have made one more call. I didn't. It was a mistake not to.

At 6:15, Ann called back. We were confirmed for United Flight 617 leaving LaGuardia at 9:42 a.m. to arrive nonstop Cleveland International at 11:14, return flight open.

"Thanks, Annie. Tell them at the office that I won't be in today. Something has come up on a wiretap and I've got to see Mr. Hogan in New York. Eric will be with me and, by the way, even though you don't know what the hell's going on, wish us luck." She did but not until she had gotten me to promise to call as soon as I could let her know what all the cloak and dagger was about.

At about 6:30, Senior State Police Investigator Charles Teelon called to say he had talked to Purcell, had cleared it with his boss, and was available. I told him to be at LaGuardia Airport by 9:15 and I would fill him in.

Eric went home to get dressed. I took a shower and got ready, and by 7:30 Eric was back to pick me up to head for LaGuardia. Joe St. Lawrence was also back at the house ready to go. Everyone was calm with the exception of one Nancy Ann Meehan.

"OK, Nance, wish me luck."

"Aren't you even going to tell me where you are going?"

"No."

"Well, when will you be back?"

"I don't know."

"Well, won't you at least call?"

"Yes, I'll call as soon as possible."

I bent down to give her a quick kiss on the cheek and then we headed for the airport, with no overnight bag, no briefcase, no toothbrush, just a copy of *The Ninth Juror*. If I could make it back in time for *The Barry*

Gray Show, I was damned if I was going to sit and be interviewed with that man without having finished his book.

We met Investigator Teelon at the airport at 9:10. I should have told him that the plane left at 9:42, not 9:15. That was just a meeting time. He had left Kingston Barracks in an unmarked radio car at 7:55 and with much assistance from Troop T, New York State Police Thruway Patrol, had made the 102-mile trip in one hour and twelve minutes, which is breaking par for even the police course.

The air trip was uneventful. The others did little talking as I sat and tried to read more of *The Ninth Juror*. My problem was that I couldn't keep my mind on the book. My thoughts kept wandering back to John Barkley. Hopefully, within a few hours I would be seeing this boy again, whom I had only known as a friendly young man. But now he was a killer and must be treated as such, and I was DA and must act accordingly.

My primary concern must be the safety and peace of mind of the people of my county, my state, and our neighboring state of New Jersey. It was a time to be firm but fair, tough but compassionate. I said a prayer that I would be up to it.

～

We arrived in Cleveland about five minutes ahead of schedule. Joe went directly to a phone booth, made the call, was back in three minutes, and said, "OK, he's in room 393 at the Cleveland YMCA on Prospect Street and he'll wait for us there."

The chances of a wild goose chase had diminished, the danger had not. I then told Eric and Charlie that we would now have to check in with the Cleveland Police Department. I purposely hadn't brought this up before because I didn't want to look foolish contacting the Cleveland Police Department if this had proven a wasted trip and I also didn't want St. Lawrence getting upset about more men involved. But as I explained to him, we would make the arrest and then immediately bring in the Cleveland men because they were necessary for a waiver of extradition from Ohio back to New York. Joe accepted this more easily than I would have thought.

We went to the substation of the police department at the airport and met with detectives George Monaghan and Peter Conklin. We identified ourselves, told our story, and gained their immediate and complete cooperation. Within twenty minutes we were pulling out of the airport parking lot in an unmarked radio car, heading for the YMCA downtown, and hopefully our meeting with John Barkley. We had devised a mutually agreeable plan that went completely according to plan—until it didn't.

We parked about a block from the YMCA and Detective Monaghan went alone to see the YMCA manager and get an idea of the floor plan and the exact location of room 393, as well as the exit stairs and fire escapes. Monaghan was back in about fifteen minutes; the setup was good. Room 393 was near the center of the hallway, about three doors from the elevator. There were no fire escapes out the window of Room 393, but there were fire exits at both ends of the hall.

It was decided that Monaghan would be at one fire exit and Conklin at the other. They would walk up the stairs to get to their location. Charlie, Eric, and Joe would go up on the elevator. Charlie would stay at the elevator door, then they would signal that they were all in place, at which time Eric and Joe would approach the door to Room 393. Joe was to station himself flat against the wall next to the door toward the elevator, away from the hinge of the door, and hopefully out of harm's way. Eric was to knock on the door and then step back against the wall in the other direction with gun drawn. If Barkley called out as to who was there, St. Lawrence was to identify himself and stand fast.

Since I was not a peace officer, I could not be in on the actual collar, so Eric and Charlie insisted that I wait downstairs at the desk in the lobby. I wasn't going to stand still for this until Eric, who is more than a friend, said, "What do you want to be, a fucking hero? Let us do our job. It's bad enough having St. Lawrence up there." I reluctantly agreed.

Five minutes later, we were pulling up in front of the YMCA. The Y is a big, ornate old building with a very large lobby, something out of the turn of the century. The two Cleveland detectives entered first and went directly to the stairways. Charlie, Eric, and Joe entered just ahead of me and headed for the elevator.

I entered and went straight to the desk and flashed my badge and credentials to the elderly clerk. I told him that this was a police emergency and I was to be handed the phone immediately when a call came in on the switchboard from Room 393. Eric had agreed to call from the room as soon as Barkley was in custody and I was to head right up. I then stepped back from the desk, lit a cigarette, and waited. I didn't have to wait long.

~

"Mr. Meehan?" I heard a voice right behind me. I turned quickly and stared right into the face of Big John Barkley—all six feet, four inches and 250 pounds of him.

I was momentarily stunned looking at his broad smile and outstretched hand. All I could think of was Laura Mancini's account of his smiling face and geniality moments before he fired two fatal shots into the head of the young gas station attendant.

I recovered quickly, gave him a very firm handshake, and said, "John Barkley, how the hell are you?"

"I'm fine Mr. Meehan, but after all that talk on the telephone, I'm surprised that you came alone."

I thought to myself, "God, this is ridiculous." My three armed men were a long, two stories above us while John and I were in the lobby along with about a dozen YMCA guests, mostly senior citizens, scattered about the large room, reading or dozing in their large heavy leather chairs, oblivious to the drama that was taking place a few feet away. The desk clerk, who was the closest to us, was perhaps the most senior of all and could not be expected to help.

I was unarmed. It was never my practice to carry a gun. I looked searchingly at John's rumpled, casual attire as we shook hands. I was looking for the telltale bulge of a .45. Seeing none, I relaxed slightly.

"Well, John," I continued with a fixed smile, "actually, I didn't come alone. Joe Saint and one of my guys just went up to the room looking for you. They should be back down in just a minute."

With the same set smile, I turned to the desk clerk and said, "Let me know when that call comes in."

John was telling me how happy he was to see me and asking about the family. In fact the conversation was eerily reminiscent of standing in front of Barkley's Nursery those many years before.

I thought to myself, I have no choice but to play the hand that's dealt me. I'll just continue this small talk and hope for the best. So for the next several endless minutes, John and I stood there and did just that, made small talk.

"How are the children? They must be getting big. How's the boy doing with all those sisters?"

I told him they were fine and growing and that young Tommy now had a little brother. John thought that was great—but still the desk phone didn't ring.

"How do you like being DA, Mr. Meehan? I bet it's a lot different than being a regular lawyer." I thought to myself, "It sure is!" The talk went on as the phone lay silent. I kept my answers short, my voice relaxed and friendly, but I stayed determinedly away from any reference to the reason I had come to Cleveland that day.

Anyone overhearing our conversation would have been certain that it was just two old friends meeting again. As the minutes passed I began to see the irony and maybe even the humor in the situation. John Barkley, crazed killer, wily eluder of the Ramapo manhunt, was surrendering peacefully to me alone—just as he had wanted to. I pictured the carefully planned operation on the third floor, the well-placed armed men, guns drawn, ready for any contingency. Except one that is—that John would be downstairs in the lobby chatting with me. All our *Dragnet* and *Adam 12* plans had gone up in the quiet afternoon smoke of the vintage YMCA lobby.

Finally, a long ten minutes later, the call came from Eric. His voice was tense. "Bob, he's not here. We finally managed to get into the room, but he's gone."

With Barkley standing only a few feet away and able to hear me, I acted like I was talking to Joe St. Lawrence, and said, "Joe, come on down, just you and Eric. I met John down here in the lobby just after you went up. He's fine and says he's looking forward to seeing you—OK, see you in a minute." I then whispered into the phone quickly, "No drawn gun."

Two minutes later, Joe and Eric got off the elevator and approached us. John was still smiling as I said, "Eric, you remember John Barkley?" Eric said sure and everyone shook hands all around, much like you would greet an old friend at the Elks Club.

Then Charlie and Detectives Monaghan and Conklin approached us and it was more good fellowship and smiling handshakes. But we now had a ring of men, arms concealed, surrounding John Barkley. I was feeling a hell of a lot better, and with a more genuine smile on my face said, "John, these fellows are from the Cleveland Police Department. They're going to help us cut through the red tape so you can go back to New York with us tonight." This was just fine with John so we all headed out the door of the YMCA. Eric and Detective Monaghan quickly frisked John on the sidewalk before the seven of us squeezed into the unmarked car and headed for police headquarters. As I suspected by that time, he was clean.

I'm sure that the desk clerk wondered later about my flashing the badge and the "police emergency" bit. Neither he nor anyone else in the lobby that afternoon could have realized the purpose of our brief visit to the Cleveland YMCA. Handcuffs were not in evidence until they were placed on John in the police car, but they then of course had to be used.

$\sim$

The booking and extradition process began immediately. Within two hours, we had been before a Cleveland city judge, all paperwork was done, and we were free to head back to New York.

We made no attempt to question John as to the homicides or to get a written statement. That was part of our agreement made on the phone that morning, and more important since John wanted it that way—part of the Constitution of the United States.

At the police station, I made four calls. The second was to the District Attorney of Ulster County, my friend Joe Toracca, who was pleased to hear the news. The third call was to the Prosecutor's Office in Bergen County, New Jersey, where the reception was less than friendly. They were burned up because they hadn't been in on the arrest.

The last call was to Ann Hickey at the Rockland County District Attorney's Office. She was her usual happy enthusiastic self as I started to tell the story, but when I finished with the scene in the lobby of the YMCA, I expected her to laugh, but she didn't. "Well, Annie, don't you think it's a little bit comical?"

"No, I don't think it's the least bit amusing when one of my men takes a chance on getting himself killed."

I thought to myself, she's saying, "One of my men." I'm the district attorney but that crazy Annie thinks she's the boss. The trouble is that she was right—she ran that office. Ann was the only one who knew all the cases in all the courts, and more important, when and where they were and who was supposed to be there. As far as administration, budgets, salaries, and such, forget it, Annie ran the whole thing. Although at that time just a few years short of being a grandmother, Ann was young in appearance and certainly young at heart. She loved the District Attorney's Office and it was mutual.

"Look, Annie," I continued, "calm down. We are all fine. As it turned out there was no real danger." I then told her that the matter was still confidential, but to be prepared to alert the local press and that I would call her again when we knew our flight arrangements back. The last thing

I said to Ann was, "First thing, call Nancy, tell her I'm fine, the case I'm working on is going well, I'll be home tonight, but that's all you tell her."

The first call I made from Cleveland that afternoon was the one I should have made before I left in the morning. Chief Joseph Miele of the Ramapo Police Department, a friend of a lifetime who graduated just a few years ahead of me at Suffern High School. I told the chief that we had Barkley in tow in Cleveland and that the search in the cold, dreary mountains could be called off. He wasn't mad, but I could sense that he was disappointed not to have been in on things; maybe even hurt that I hadn't trusted to call him. I explained that everything happened so fast that morning and that we couldn't call the search off in case it was a giant hoax. He knew and I knew that the explanation for not calling him personally was insufficient.

~

Detective Monaghan drove us back out to Cleveland International in the same unmarked car. On this trip, John was handcuffed. Our flight was leaving at 4:45 p.m. and was due at LaGuardia at 7:50 New York time. We arrived at the airport just past four o'clock and we all went into the police substation.

In the station, I told them to remove the handcuffs, and then I said, "John, you trusted me and I think it's fair to say that I didn't let you down, is that right?"

"Sure, Mr. Meehan, you've really been a friend."

I then said, to the dismay of my men and Detective Monaghan, "OK John, I'll trust you. You're going on that plane just like any other passenger with no handcuffs. You'll be sitting three abreast with Eric on one side of you and Charlie on the other. Remember they are both armed. Can you handle it, can I trust you, John?"

"Absolutely, Mr. Meehan. I'm relieved that this is over. There's no chance I'll make trouble."

"OK, then that's the way it will be." Eric's expression bespoke his disagreement, but the stubborn German knew the stubborn Irishman well enough by that time to know in fact that was the way it would be.

We boarded United Flight 426 a few minutes early and I informed the captain of who I was and that two of my men were armed. That was just before the days of metal detectors and we didn't have to tell him, but we wanted the captain and his crew to know that there were police officers on board with a prisoner in case trouble developed in flight. I made no mention of what the prisoner was charged with and the captain never asked.

It was a Friday afternoon and the plane, a DC-8, was full. But we arrived early enough that, without asking for preferential treatment, we were able to get the three seats abreast. I was in the aisle seat just behind Eric, with Joe St. Lawrence beside me in the center seat.

I guess it was a Friday afternoon, but the passengers and stewardesses appeared to be in particularly good humor, as was the passenger in seat M23, big John Barkley.

It was just getting dark and the lights of the city of Cleveland below, with its blanket of snow, made the city seem much warmer and friendlier that it had been when we approached in a midday overcast only a few hours before. Maybe it was the events of the day, but I felt so much more relaxed as we became airborne than I had in landing.

The "No Smoking" light had been out for about four seconds when the stewardesses started at the front of the tourist section taking orders for cocktails. Just before the stewardess got to the row head of me, Eric poked his head around the seat and said with a marked frown, "Hey boss, our friend here wants to know if he can have a drink."

I said, "What the hell, Eric, we only live once. It may be a long time between drinks for John. Let him have it." To which Eric responded with a smile, "I thought you'd say that." Since it was tourist, there were no free drinks, so I offered to buy a round for all of us. Eric and Charlie declined. Charlie is a hell of a nice guy and not the least bit stiff, but New York State Police regulations are, and he wasn't about to break them. As for Eric, I told him that it was OK with me, but he replied, "Come on boss, this isn't supposed to be a pleasure trip, I am on duty!" And so he was.

I started to settle back to complete *The Ninth Juror*, while sipping my drink, when suddenly John Barkley stood up, turned to me with his glass held high, smiling broadly, and said for all to hear, "Here's to you Mr. Meehan. You are a saint!"

I had to hold back a smile as I said, "Sit down, you crazy bastard."

When we arrived over the New York area there was heavy air traffic and we were in a holding pattern for about half an hour. By this time almost all the passengers seemed in good spirits and I guess several had downed a second or a third drink. While we were in the holding pattern, Eric again turned to me, "This son of a bitch wants another drink." I leaned forward and whispered, "Absolutely not, I'm not delivering a drunken prisoner to the barracks tonight." Eric grinned, "You're finally getting smart boss."

We landed at LaGuardia, waited for every other passenger to leave the plane, and then we left. We thanked the captain and as we did John piped up and told him what a smooth flight it had been and, with the usual smile, heartily shook the captain's hand.

A marked state police car was waiting for us. Charlie took his prisoner, John Barkley, in handcuffs with two uniformed troopers in the marked car. Eric, Joe, and I followed in the DA's car with both of us heading to the State Police Barracks at Stony Point in Rockland County.

I had called Ann Hickey from the airport in Cleveland and told her to alert the local press and radio to be at the Stony Point Barracks at 9 p.m. for a major announcement in the Barkley case.

～

It was raining when we arrived at Stony Point a little less than an hour later, but as we pulled in there was a small crowd of reporters and policemen waiting for us. The flashbulbs clicked in the rainy night and we immediately took John into the back room where he was formally mugged and printed.

I went out to the front desk where I talked to the reporters, all of whom I knew on a first-name basis. I told the story in a matter of fact way, starting with the call at 4:25 that morning. I did say that John wanted to surrender to me because he knew me from years before at the nursery, but as to his actual surrender, I only said, "John Barkley, after advising of his location, surrendered to us quietly in the lobby of the YMCA in Cleveland, Ohio, at 1:05 this afternoon."

There were a couple of hostile questions as to why I had allowed the men to continue to comb the Ramapo Mountains throughout the morning and early afternoon if I knew he was in Cleveland. I answered that I couldn't take a chance on the whole Cleveland adventure being a hoax and they readily accepted this.

Two detectives from Bergen County, New Jersey, were there along with Billy Sinclair, Chief of Detectives of the Ramapo Police Department, and two of his men. Sinclair, whom I've known for thirty years and greatly respect, was not happy nor were his two men, but they did treat me well, congratulating me and being generally friendly.

I learned more of the inner feelings of the police who had been on the mountain that day about ten days later from my eleven-year-old daughter, Kathleen. A police sergeant of the town of Ramapo had given a lecture to her sixth grade class on the workings of the police department. Apparently the subject got around to the Barkley case.

That evening, Kathy said to me, "Daddy, the policeman who talked to us today said that you were drinking martinis on an airplane while all the men were up in the mountains freezing to death looking for the murderer."

I said, "Kath, that's not true, I was drinking *one* Manhattan!"

～

The two detectives from New Jersey, neither of whom I had ever met before, were a different story. They were openly angry that they had not been called in and said so. I was mildly apologetic and said I did what I thought was best. But they would not drop it and continued their criticism and said of the Bergen County prosecutor, "Our boss is really pissed off!"

Then, as I do only five or six times a year, I blew. "Well, you tell him to go fuck himself. I loved your old boss, Guy Callissi, but I've called this new SOB six times in the last year and he's never even had the courtesy to return my call! Don't push it boys—you're in my territory now. In about two minutes, I'm going to have you thrown out of here."

At this point, Eric stepped between us and said to the New Jersey men, "Come on fellows, I think you better leave now." They did with no further words spoken.

As quickly as I get mad, I get over it and a few minutes later, over a container of coffee in the squad room, I was telling the Stony Point troopers the actual story of the arrest and they laughed like they thought it was as funny as I did. Maybe they were just being polite, but it really seemed humorous at the time. And besides, the troopers were feeling good that night. As unhappy as New Jersey and, to some degree, the Ramapo Police Department may have been, the state police were happy and proud to have been involved. The fact that it was a man from Kingston barracks, not Stony Point, made no difference—it was all New York State Police.

Charlie then came in and said they were going to leave for Ulster County with Barkley in a couple of minutes and Barkley wanted to thank me. I walked out to the holding cell and said goodbye to John Barkley. He was still smiling, but not so exuberantly as before. He thanked me for helping him and I said one last thing to him.

"John, I have friends who knew that boy from Sloatsburg that you killed and you're going to have to pay for that. But I did know you and your family in better times and for that reason this is a doubly sad case for me personally. I can't wish you luck, I don't want you to beat the rap, but somehow, someway, I hope you can find peace with yourself." We shook hands through the cell bars and then I kind of sadly went back into the squad room. That was the last time I ever saw John Barkley.

∾

Later, Joe shared some details he had learned in his conversations with Barkley. John had been hiding in the Ramapo Mountains for days—without socks or underwear—and almost froze to death while crossing a river. He came down from the mountains in the Sloatsburg area and saw a flatbed truck with a tarpaulin cover parked at a Hot Shoppes restaurant. He crawled under the cover and hid as the driver returned and proceeded to drive to Ohio. Once there, John decided he was just too tired to run anymore and called Joe. In addition to asking Joe to reach out to me, he also asked Joe to bring socks and underwear for him to Cleveland.

Joe also recalled that after I allowed him to have the drink on the plane, John turned to him and said, "I guess this is probably the last time I'll ever have one of these."

∾

Eric and I left Stony Point and headed to New York City for *The Barry Gray Show*. You've already heard about that, except I do remember during the show that the talk got around to air travel and I did say, "I flew to Cleveland today to pick up a prisoner, but I seldom travel outside of the county on business. My men do most extraditions without me." Barry Gray rightly saw nothing interesting in that statement and the subject changed.

∾

As I now sit in my den on Cherry Lane thinking of that day, I can look out at the little evergreens from Barkley's Nursery, which are now even with the second-story windows. John Barkley is in the seventh year of a life sentence at the New York State Prison at Attica. There is an open murder charge against him in Bergen County that has never been prosecuted. Very importantly, New Jersey had the death penalty; New York did not.

But as has been the habit of a lifetime, I look back on that day and I don't think of what I may have done right. Instead, I ask myself, what did I do wrong and how can I avoid making the same mistake tomorrow?

I should have called Chief Joe Miele that morning and told him of my contact with Barkley. One of his men didn't have to go; they had no open charge. He could've kept his men ringing the mountains until we were sure that the Cleveland story was true. But they would have been in on it, they would have been part of it. When my own hometown police department, my friends of a lifetime, had their pride on the line I let them down. Two and a half years later, when my life was on the line, they didn't let me down.

Chapter 2

Stop Writing Obituaries!

That fateful trip to Cleveland brought about an unexpected opportunity for a little reflection about how I had gotten to the District Attorney's Office in the first place.

After we took off from LaGuardia and I had settled back to read more of *The Ninth Juror*, a stranger in the seat directly across the aisle tapped me on the arm. "Excuse me," he said, "but when I was coming on board I heard a stewardess say something about a district attorney being on the flight. You look familiar to me. Are you the district attorney up in Rockland County?"

With a smile I acknowledged that I was. I guess I was pleased that someone recognized me outside the county. He then said, "I'm embarrassed, but I can't remember your name."

When I told him, he immediately responded, "That's it, I remember all those 'Meehan for DA' signs. Let me tell you the story. I am from Cleveland, Ohio, and I am in the wholesale chemical line. Well, this goes back about four years. I had business at Lederle Laboratories in Pearl River and my partner and I stayed overnight at a place called the Tappan Zee Inn in Nyack.

"We were sitting in the bar having a drink at about 10:30 that evening when we realized that some sort of a party was going on in the ballroom. So my partner and I walked in to see what was going on. Even when we saw the crowd watching a big tote board, it still took us a few minutes to realize it was Election Night and that the combination of cheers and moans were as new results were posted on the board.

"As God is my witness, we didn't know that it was Election Night. I've never been involved in politics before or since and I've always thought of elections as once every four years for president. At first, we didn't know what party it was, but the people were friendly and to tell you the truth, within an hour we were caught up in the excitement of the thing.

"There was some cheering about local officials and state legislators but in no time at all it seemed to boil down to one thing. Would this guy named Meehan win the race for district attorney?

"Now here you have two guys from Cleveland, Ohio, who never heard of you, cheering their heads off, rooting for a guy they never heard of to get elected in the county that we had never set foot in before."

At that point, I interjected about how well I remembered the night, and with a grin I thanked him for his moral support. "I'll tell you, I needed all the support I could get that night."

He then went on, "I remember you coming in at about two in the morning and the place going crazy. It was like Jack Kennedy walking in. I'll tell you, I'll never forget it. I never realized how exciting small-town politics could be!"

We talked for a few more minutes and he asked me if I liked the job and if it was going well. I of course said that I did. He then asked what I was doing heading for Cleveland.

"Well, we have a possible extradition out there in your hometown."

A few minutes later, after exchanging business cards and the usual, "If I ever get arrested in Rockland County, I'll look you up," the conversation ended and he went back to reading his newspaper as I again opened *The Ninth Juror.*

～

But my mind kept wandering back to that memorable night for me, November 2, 1965. Not to the Tappan Zee Inn at 2 a.m., but to my small law office in Tallman at about 11 p.m. The returns were mostly in and I was morally certain that I had lost. There were about twenty-five or thirty people at the office, all family and friends. The political pros were at the Tappan Zee Inn. I was not a political pro; in fact, this was my first run for political office. Don't get me wrong, those pros helped me get the nomination and they wanted me to win; it was just that they were all sure that I would lose.

Of course, they had strong reasons to believe this. In those days Democrats just didn't get elected to countywide office in the Republican stronghold of Rockland. We had elected a Democratic county judge for one term in 1938, but we had not elected a Democratic district attorney since 1911, and he too lasted only one term.

But that was when the Irish bricklayers of Haverstraw and Stony Point had been able, with an overwhelming Democratic vote, to counterbalance the Republican farm communities that made up most of the rest of the county.

Now the brickyards were gone, and most of the Irish that remained—my family a notable exception—had become affluent and with it, sad to say, had changed their registration to Republican.

So it was in the Rockland County of 1965 that the Democrats were still fielding "duty candidates" to keep the two-party system going. Someday we would break the Republican stranglehold on the courthouse, but as the evening wore on it looked like that day would not come in 1965.

However, despite what the pros may have thought I was, I was not a "duty candidate." I was running to win, not for exposure, as is the case with so many young lawyers making their first run for public office. I was convinced that winning would take a combination of three things: opportunity, timing, and probably most of all—luck.

The opportunity was easy. The party hierarchy was delighted to have someone who wanted to run and was willing to campaign hard. Although they privately didn't share my belief that I could win, they heartily endorsed my candidacy.

To me, the time was right. The farming community of the 1920s and '30s had become the exurbia of the 1940s and '50s. Rockland was becoming a getaway place for the artists, actors, and other well-to-do city dwellers seeking peace and serenity in the Ramapo Mountains, at the foot of High Tor, or along the majestic waterfront of the Hudson River. Then in 1955 the Tappan Zee Bridge opened, connecting to the New York State Thruway and cutting through the heart of our county. This was followed closely by the opening of the Palisades Interstate Parkway. Commuting became easy and a good portion of people from The Bronx moved in. It was a new wave of ethnics—Irish, Italian, and Jewish. Significantly, better than 60 percent were registering Democratic. The political scene was changing.

Add to that, the popular incumbent district attorney, Mort Silberman, was giving up the office to run for county judge. His first assistant district attorney, Robert Stolarik, became the heir apparent. A decent guy and a good attorney, Stolarik was tall, blonde, handsome, and politically well connected. His father-in-law had been a Republican judge in Suffern for twenty years. But although cut in the "Mr. District Attorney" image, he lacked flair and charisma, and as I thought he would turned out to be a better lawyer than campaigner.

In the course of the campaign, the luck seemed to break my way. A growing band of volunteers made up of friends, family, neighbors, clients from my law practice, students from the law course I taught at Rockland Community College, and a few political pros were working hard for me, and they were really beginning to make an impression. A few good issues developed, including the new problem of suburban drug abuse and consumer fraud, and they were fought out in the two local newspapers and the one radio station, getting me much-needed publicity.

I literally campaigned eighteen or twenty hours a day and in the closing days of the campaign, I was certain that the race would be close. I was right. Now with the polls closed and seventy thousand votes cast, it appeared that I had lost by about three hundred votes.

~

Between 9:30 and 10 p.m. there had been a lot of cheering at the office as Frank McGowan called in to say that we had won the town of Haverstraw by over 1,400 votes. This was followed almost immediately by a call from my cousin, Vince Brophy, reporting a four-hundred-vote victory in Stony Point. But as my family and friends cheered, I whispered to my brother Tom, "I love those people up there, but 1,800 votes just isn't enough from North Rockland."

At ten o'clock, there were groans when a loss of over 1,500 votes was posted from the Republican bastion of Orangetown. But I was somewhat cheered by this news. By that time I knew the numbers better than my friends. A three to six thousand-vote loss by a Democrat in Orangetown was not unusual.

Then came to me what was the crusher. We were losing Clarkstown, with the county seat of New City, by over one thousand votes. I was sure that we couldn't possibly afford more than a five-hundred-vote loss in Clarkstown.

Now it all hinged on the town of Ramapo, which takes in the villages of Suffern and Spring Valley. Stolarik and I were both local boys, and I knew it would be close. I didn't see how I could make up the seven hundred votes I needed. Early returns had me winning Ramapo by four hundred votes. Not enough. Nancy, along with my mother and nine-year-old Patty, the oldest of my five children and the only one with us that night, all looked pretty sad as I said to Tom, "I think we had better go into my private office and write a short concession speech."

I was pleased with myself that I was taking it so well, but when I talked of concession, Johnny Greco piped up and said, "The hell you are, this race is far from over. We are going to win yet!"

It was strange, but Johnny Greco, who is six years older than I and was my first sports idol as he tore up the football field for old Suffern High a quarter of a century before, had not been a part of the long, arduous campaign. Suddenly on this night he was not only there but he was the chief score keeper and certainly the head cheerleader of the small band of "Meehan for DA" supporters.

Johnny kept pointing to our strong North Rockland returns, but I looked at the bad returns from the big housing development in central Clarkstown and kept saying, "We'll never overcome these!"

About twenty minutes later, Tom and I had finished a concession speech of about three hundred words that was a glowing tribute to Bob Stolarik. It wasn't as hard to write as you might think. It had been a bitter, hard-fought campaign, but I knew Bob from my boyhood days in Suffern and he married a high school classmate of mine. I genuinely respected him and after six years as the first assistant district attorney, I was sure he was up to doing a good job as DA.

But as we finished, Johnny burst into the inner office and with a mock scowl said, "Goddamn it, if you Meehan boys would stop wasting your time writing obituaries and listen to me, we'll all be better off. I've got you losing by less than one hundred now, give me two hours and I'll have you winning by at least two hundred!"

I smiled, "Johnny, you're something else, but this is one business where you can't juggle the books. Winning by 1,800 in North Rockland is just not enough!"

"Well, Meehan," Johnny yelled back, "I've got you up by more than 2,100 in North Rockland—1,650 in Haverstraw and just about 500 in Stony Point, and my figures are triple checked!"

"Holy mackerel, John. If you're right, we're in a real ball game. Let's go back to the adding machine."

~

It was a crazy thing. Johnny, the noncampaigner, suddenly became the leader of a resurgence of enthusiasm, telling my disappointed workers what they wanted to hear. "I'm no politician, but I know what I've been hearing the last few weeks," Johnny said. "Bob Meehan is going to win. That's all I've been hearing."

As the crowd gathered around my old sports idol and his adding machine while he shouted orders to telephone certain local town head-quarters for a recheck, I was still convinced that we would lose, but deeply touched by his efforts.

So it was now 12:30 a.m. and we had exact figures from four out of five towns in the county and tentative figures from the fifth and last town, Ramapo. They showed me losing countywide by forty-two votes.

I then said to Tom and another good friend, Frank Strauss, "Look, these results now show us winning Ramapo by 640 votes. Take an adding machine, go down to the Ramapo Headquarters in Suffern and double check. We need a plus of 683 votes in Ramapo to win, and with about 20,000 votes cast in the town, there's a lot of room for mistakes. One thing though, your numbers have to be right!"

Just after they left, I got a call from the Democratic County chairman Dick Sullivan, who was at the Tappan Zee Inn. "Look Bob, I've got about 1,500 people over here and right now they've forgotten about everything but the DA's race. You've got to give me some kind of statement."

"Well Dick, if you want an answer right now, you've got it. We lose by forty-two votes. But damn it, give me fifteen minutes!"

The atmosphere was now tense in my office and everyone was crowded around my desk waiting for a callback from Tom on the private phone.

As the minutes went by, I thought of another idea. I reached in my pocket and pulled out a scrap of paper with another telephone number on it. I had made a point of getting that number earlier in the day for an entirely different reason. I dialed and the phone was answered imme-diately. Without identifying myself I said, "What are your latest returns on the DA's race?"

I could feel my heart pounding through my chest as I heard a man on the other end of the line say, "It's not over yet, but right now we have that son-of-a-bitch Meehan winning by just under one hundred votes."

I put the phone down without saying another word and apparently my face was ashen white. Everyone in the room thought I had received the final bad news and there was silence as I said, "That was Republican headquarters. They've got us winning by just under one hundred."

As the room let out an emotional cheer, Nancy leaned over and put her arm around me and whispered, "Bob, what's wrong? You look like you're going to cry."

"I'm alright, I'm alright," was my only response. But I realized I was on the verge of tears. For the first time, it hit me. After all the dreams of glory, I wasn't really prepared to win.

I regained my composure fast and was on my feet yelling to my people, "Goddamn it, we're not taking Republican figures. We need that Ramapo count!" It came less than five minutes later.

When the phone rang I picked it up on the first ring. It was Tom, his voice quiet and measured.

"Look Bob, I'm sorry to keep you waiting. We just went through all these figures for the second time. The first time through I called out the figures with Frank on the adding machine. The second time I was on the adding machine and we came out with the exact same numbers. Bob, we win Ramapo by 831 votes."

The call to Republican headquarters had helped me; I was now more prepared for victory and was totally calm as I said, "OK, Tom, you've double-checked. We win Ramapo by 831 votes. Meehan Headquarters now claims victory in the race for District Attorney of Rockland County by 149 votes."

Now it was a total release of emotion in my office with shouting and cheering and genuine tears of joy.

"Greco, call Democratic Headquarters and tell them we are on our way. Meehan Headquarters claims victory by 149 votes."

∼

I was smiling and happy as we headed for the Tappan Zee Inn in Nyack, where we received the greatest welcome of my public life.

I know that to the more sophisticated reader, winning the race for district attorney of a small county that they never heard of does not seem that momentous. But I was from an old brickyard family and my father hadn't even graduated from high school. Nancy—who that night was five months pregnant with our sixth child—and I had struggled through law school and starting a private law practice. So to my family and I, this was really a dream come true. Looking back, I can say with certainty that the nine years that lay ahead would be even more exciting and interesting then we dreamed of that night.

Chapter 3

"Tex" Brown, the Meanest Gal in Town

I first met Doris "Tex" Brown on the third Monday in March 1966. She had been indicted back in November 1965, two months before I took office as district attorney, for the crime of First-Degree Assault, assault with a deadly weapon with intent to kill. According to the indictment she had not succeeded. There were no open murder indictments in Rockland County when I took office.

The case was coming up for trial and the star witness for the prosecution, the victim of the stabbing, one George Powell, was sitting in the waiting room when I arrived at the DA's Office at about 8:30 that morning. Investigator Ray Lindemann came in and told me that Powell insisted that he must talk to me personally. He wanted to drop the charges against Tex.

I did not want to see him and I certainly did not want to drop the charges against her or anyone else for that matter.

It had been a tough couple of weeks for the DA's Office and for me personally. We had lost three trials in two weeks, two vehicular death cases and one burglary. I had tried one of the auto death cases myself and the judge threw it out at the end of the People's case. That's bad.

The fact that all three indictments were obtained before I took office made no difference. They were my cases and I lost them.

The day before, the *Journal News* had featured a column entitled "Meehan's Kitty Korp Loses Again." After detailing the three cases tried by myself and my young staff, the columnist wrote, "Although Meehan has only been in office for three months, the Republicans are already lining up to run against him in '68. They want the DA's Office back and their prospects seem to get brighter by the day."

∾

The lost cases and the bad press were the least of my problems. Nancy had almost died that week. Our sixth and last child, Bobby, had been born one week before. But after the caesarean birth, Nancy had developed severe internal bleeding. After Tommy's birth by caesarean four years earlier—Nancy's third C-section—the doctor had warned us against further children. Four caesareans, he insisted, were too many. He was right.

My mother, who had been a widow for over twenty years at that time, was the night nursing supervisor at Good Samaritan Hospital in Suffern. She came down to the waiting room, as she had five times before, to tell me that we had a second son, that everything was fine, and I could see Nancy in about two hours.

I was ecstatic. After five children, I finally had a Junior! I had always said I would name my first son after my father, Tom, whom I so dearly loved and who died two days after my fifteenth birthday. Now—along with big sisters Patty, Kathy, Laurie, and Mary—there would be a Tommy and a Bobby in our house as there had been in my house growing up in Suffern.

The joy was short-lived. Less than half an hour later, my mother came back and found me in the hospital coffee shop with my brothers, Tom and Jack. Before she opened her mouth, I knew something was wrong. I was sure it was the baby. It wasn't, it was Nancy. They were preparing her for emergency surgery.

I was allowed to go see her for a minute in a holding room just outside the operating room on the fourth floor. There was a priest with her when I got there, but he stepped out and left us alone.

Poor little Nancy, she is just under five feet tall and, without being pregnant, not one hundred pounds. She looked even smaller lying there in a light green hospital robe. It was a small, stark room and there was an odor of anesthetic. She was very weak, but she smiled and tried to talk. I must have looked grim, although I tried to smile.

She whispered, "I'm OK. Did you see our little boy?"

I said that I had and he looked great. It was a lie, I hadn't.

But as was typical with Nancy, she was worried about me and kept saying, ever so faintly, "Don't worry, I'm all right." I was worried. She was not all right.

By the following week, the crisis was over. Bobby was fine. Nancy had survived and would be all right again.

Veronica Hickey would not.

One of Ann Hickey's pretty eighteen-year-old twin daughters had fallen in a trampoline accident at Tappan Zee High School and had broken her neck. She had been battling death for fifteen days at that point. That fight with death was to go on in earnest for another six weeks before brave little "Ronkie" was declared "out of the woods." But Ronkie would not be all right. She would never walk again and life would never be quite the same for John and Ann Hickey and their five children.

~

I had just called Nyack Hospital to check on Ronkie's condition and was once again told she was "very critical," when Ray Lindemann showed George Powell into my inner office.

George Powell was of average build, about thirty-five years old and a dark-skinned black man. He was very nervous but showed no outward physical signs from his run-in with Tex five months before. He thanked me for seeing him and, stumbling over his words, told me he just wanted to drop the matter and forget the whole thing. I told him I did not want to. I thought it was a good case and I had no desire to look like a weak DA after what had happened the week before.

But Powell persisted, "Mr. Meehan, she only stuck me a little."

"For God's sake, Powell, it was a butcher knife and let me see, the doctor's report here says the wound was better than two and a half inches deep. They thought you were a goner that night."

He insisted, "But, she didn't mean no harm."

"What do you mean, she didn't mean no harm. You're goddamn lucky that I am not sitting here by myself preparing for a murder trial."

There was no stopping Powell. "I didn't say this before, but I did beat up on her a little and I guess I was drunk."

Now I knew we were in trouble. From reading the police reports, I had learned that Powell and Brown had been living together common-law, but when Powell gave a statement after he got out of the hospital, he had said he was through with her. Further he had said that he had come home from work late, hadn't had a drink, and never laid a hand on her.

My star witness was a perjurer and I told him so. "You know, Mr. Powell, you're now telling me you lied to the grand jury. That's what we call perjury. You know you can go to jail for that—what the hell did you lie to the grand jury for?"

"I was scared," he replied in a whisper.

"What were you scared of man? Did someone make you lie?"

"No, I was scared I'd get in trouble."

"Well, you succeeded. You *are* in trouble. I'm taking you down to see the judge. You've got to tell him the story just like you told me, and I hope he throws the book at you. Oh, and by the way, are you living with that dame again?"

Powell answered sheepishly, "Yes."

I knew my case was over. I would move to dismiss. I also knew there would be no perjury case; we had better things to do with our time than go after the frightened George Powells of the world.

I did, however, go down before court opened to talk to Judge John Skahen and fill him in on the Doris Brown case. John Skahen had been district attorney from 1951 to 1960 and was now family court judge, but sitting in criminal court because of the recent death of the wonderful Judge Herbert Henion.

Judge Skahen was perfectly suited to be a family court judge—he was a very compassionate man. Many said of his three terms as district attorney, "He's too nice a guy to be DA." No one ever said that of me.

The judge congratulated me for doing the right thing and I said, "Judge, I hope you'll read the riot act to this guy. We don't want to exactly congratulate him for being a perjurer." Judge Skahen agreed and he later did a beautiful job reaming out Powell in open court, although I will admit that he winked at me when he was through.

I personally handled what we call the "calendar" that day, which is basically the call of cases for arraignments, pretrial motions, or ready for trial. The last case that Court Clerk Sue Van Epps called out that morning was "*People of the State of New York v. Doris Brown*, Indictment Number 65–118."

The public defender, Arnold Becker, stepped forward and said, "Defendant is ready for trial, your honor." Beside him stood a giant of a woman and it was the first time I ever laid eyes on her.

Doris "Tex" Brown was almost as tall as me at six feet, two inches, and she weighed considerably more than my 190 pounds, with apparently not an ounce of fat on her.

She looked intimidating and her exposed arms in a short-sleeve dress had multiple scars. She also had very discernible scars on her left cheek and the left side of her neck. In sum, she looked like she had been through World War II with a fixed bayonet.

After the public defender answered ready, I said, "Your honor, the People have an application to make to the court before we proceed. I have the victim of this assault here in court this morning and I would like him to be heard by the court."

We then went forward with the proceeding, which ended in the formal dismissal of charges. After Judge Skahen admonished Powell, he turned to Tex and spent a few moments discussing with her the inadvisability of settling family arguments with a butcher knife. He ended by making her promise to mend her ways. I always thought John Skahen had a lot of the Irish priest in him. I say that as a compliment.

Tex answered, "Yes, I promise, I promise. I'll be good. I won't be bad no more. I won't come back no more." To my amazement, she sounded like a sweet little girl. The twenty-five-year-old "meanest gal in town" sounded like a young teenager who had just been scolded by her father and wanted badly to get back in his good graces.

~

When I visited Nancy at the hospital the day before, I had read her the "Kitty Korp" story and when I finished I said, "The cases that will make or break me for reelection in '68 haven't even happened yet." The first of those cases occurred two weeks later. The star witness for the prosecution was Doris Brown of Spring Valley, New York.

I was sitting in the office at about 6:15 on the evening of Monday, April 4, 1966, when I received a call from the desk sergeant at the Spring Valley Police Department. "Mr. Meehan, we have a body over by the medical building on Lawrence Street, it looks like a homicide." I responded, "OK, I'm on my way. Tell the chief I'll be over in a few minutes."

It's hard to explain my feelings as I headed at a reasonably high speed for Spring Valley, five miles away. I was definitely not happy that someone had been done in, but there is a sense of excitement, anticipation, and almost euphoria, that a big case is breaking.

I arrived at the Spring Valley Police Department within ten minutes and told the desk sergeant to call Ray Lindemann and have him come over right away. Ray was then my one and only investigator in the DA's Office.

I was taken in a police cruiser to the scene. A crowd had already gathered and there were several uniformed police officers and two radio cars at the scene. The area was just being roped off, but there was no body. Arthur Lucas had been taken to Ramapo General Hospital three miles away in a desperate attempt to save his life. The attempt had failed. Artie Lucas lay dead in the emergency room with eleven stab wounds in his back, chest, and abdomen. The "Kitty Korp" had its first murder case and I stayed with it personally from that moment until the jury gave its verdict just short of six months later.

$$\sim$$

The actual stabbing had occurred along a stream under a roadway bridge less than two hundred feet from the medical center. Lucas had staggered, mortally wounded, up a steep embankment and collapsed as he tried, but failed, to make it to a nearby building. There was a very large pool of blood where he finally fell, and behind him a trail of blood that led back to the blood-soaked rocks under the bridge. The only foreign object and piece of evidence under the bridge was an empty pint bottle of Thunderbird wine, which lay at the water's edge. The wine bottle was to be the center of a legal battle royale a few months later.

By 8 p.m. that evening, two subjects were brought in for questioning to the Spring Valley Police Station. They were Juan Rivera, a twenty-seven-year-old unemployed, soft spoken but sullen, light-skinned Puerto Rican, and Wilson "Tommie" Biggs, who like the victim was a twenty-three-year-old black man of medium complexion. Unlike Rivera, Biggs was outgoing and gregarious and you literally couldn't shut him up. Neither man would go for spit and denied any involvement.

At that point in time, their only known connection to the crime was that they knew Artie Lucas and had been seen walking toward the center of the village with him about three hours before. They denied even that. Biggs said, "We ain't seen Old Art all day." I was hopeful!

Unlike suspects of the generation to follow, Rivera and Biggs could not rely on Ernesto Miranda and his legal difficulties with the state of Arizona. The Supreme Court of the United States was still seventy days short of its landmark decision in *Miranda v. Arizona*.

Thus, the questioning of Biggs and Rivera continued for about three hours. A few minutes before 11 p.m., Biggs cracked. Tommie Biggs said that he had been there under the bridge when Rivera went wild and stabbed Lucas to death. Confronted with this, Rivera continued in his total denial. By 1 a.m. nothing more had changed.

∽

The new DA had a case . . . one dead body, one defendant, one eyewitness to the crime. The problem was that the eyewitness was Tommie Biggs, whose reputation for honesty, integrity, and sobriety left something to be desired. Besides, it was my considered judgment that my newly acquired friend, Tommie, was a goddamn liar.

Lindemann said, "Let's give this bastard Biggs a lie detector."

"Good idea," I responded and we did give him a lie detector test. It was not a good idea. In fact, it damn near cost us the case.

Today, after a decade of bitter experiences, I am totally anti–lie detector. I have seen one man branded as a liar who was later vindicated by incontrovertible evidence. I have personally received reports on subjects who had passed the test and who I am morally certain were guilty. However, the biggest problem is that in better than 60 percent of the subjects I dealt with, the lie detector findings came back as "inconclusive."

My first inconclusive was on the morning of April 5, 1966; the subject was Tommie Biggs.

By 3 a.m. that morning, we had a witness who placed Biggs, Rivera, and Lucas in a liquor store buying that bottle of Thunderbird wine at 4:45 p.m. We also had evidence that the trio were seen walking west together on Lawrence Street toward the bridge at about 5:15 p.m.

By 4 a.m. I reluctantly made the decision. Charge Juan Rivera with Murder One and hold Tommie Biggs as a material witness. I really had very little choice. I couldn't let Rivera go with the evidence we had against him, and I wanted Biggs in custody while we continued the investigation.

Nothing of any real importance happened until two days later when Barbara Van Dunk came to our office just after visiting her boyfriend, Tommie Biggs, in the Rockland County Jail. Barbara said, "Tommie knows where the knife is, he wants to talk to you."

We had scoured the area for the weapon two days before and Biggs had persistently said he didn't know what Rivera did with it. He now led us to a field not more than one thousand feet from the bridge, a shortcut route to his home that he and Rivera had taken immediately after the stabbing. Biggs said, "Juan threw it in the bushes when we were going through the shortcut."

After about three hours, using twenty men and two metal detectors, we found an open jackknife within two feet of the path. The brownish stains on the knife were analyzed by the lab to be "human blood, insufficient amount to type."

All right, we had a case. We would go to the grand jury on Wednesday, April 13th. It was a vicious murder and we had solved it; the killer was in custody and would soon be indicted. I felt better about things. I tried to convince myself that the case was solid.

～

I took that Friday off to bring Nancy home from the hospital. I decided that I would just try to enjoy the weekend home with Nancy and the kids and our new baby who was to become affectionately known as "Best Boy." I loved how all the kids doted on him, especially Laurie and Mary. They were like little mothers. It was a nice weekend.

Monday was different. I arrived at the office just before nine o'clock and Lindy wanted to see me right away. "Boss, I got a broad in the back room who tells me she was drinking a little wine with the boys under the bridge last week, and that Rivera and Biggs both did it. There were two knives."

"Goddamn it, Lindy, where the hell did you dig her up?"

"Bob, the Spring Valley boys got a line on her at a gin mill in town and called me last night."

"Well, what do you think, Lindy?"

"I think she's telling the truth."

"Well, I'm very sorry to hear that. There goes our neat little case. But I guess I better talk to her."

I then went with Ray Lindemann to the squad room at the opposite end of the DA's Office. The door opened, I walked in, and there sat good old Doris "Tex" Brown. I took one look at her and said, "Goddamn it." Before talking to her, I asked Lindy to step outside.

"For Christ's sake, Lindy, do you know who the hell that is? That's our butcher-knife-wielding friend from the Powell case."

"Yes, I know that Bob, and that's not the worst of it. She has ten, count 'em, ten priors; six for prostitution, two for petty larceny, and two for assault. It gets worse. Both assaults were with a knife."

"Good God, Ray, if she's telling the truth, we might as well forget the whole case. We can't put on two prosecution witnesses who dispute each other—against Rivera—and if we charge Biggs, we lose him. He never admitted to anything himself except that he was there, that means the whole case would rest on Tex and we're dead."

"Look, Bob," Lindy said, "you've got a good head on your shoulders, you work hard and you're honest, but I've been in the business for thirty-four years. If a witness is telling the truth, no matter what they've done, the jury will believe them nine times out of ten. That fucking broad is telling the truth."

Four hours later, after a lot of yelling and cajoling by Lindy and me, that little girl voice was still unruffled. "I know what I seen, they both did it and Tommie started it and I don't care what mean things you say to me."

I now believed her and as I told the jury months later, "I can't pick the caliber of people who choose to sip their Thunderbird wine under the Lawrence Street Bridge on an early spring afternoon. I wish it was the president of the Rockland National Bank or a rabbi or a priest that I was asking you to believe, but Tex Brown was there and saw it all and she is the one who can tell us what, in fact, happened under that bridge."

Two days later, Tex testified before the Rockland County Grand Jury. The following day Juan Rivera and Wilson Tommie Biggs were indicted for First-Degree Murder. The wheels of justice moved forward.

~

The cast of characters who would meet in county court the Wednesday after Labor Day would now begin to assemble. This was the first major case for newly elected county judge Morton B. Silberman. He had been District Attorney of Rockland County for six years and an assistant district attorney for six years preceding that. He was elected county judge the same day I beat his first assistant in the DA's race.

He had been a very good district attorney who had the total confidence of the people of the county, which is vital, and his judgment was good. I just didn't know what type of judge Mort Silberman would be. In the years that followed, I learned; he was and is one of the most outstanding judges I have ever met.

Judge Silberman was very anxious to move the case for trial. Two court-appointed lawyers were assigned to each defendant and the judge told them to make all pretrial motions as expeditiously as possible. He set the trial for Monday, July 25, 1966. I was surprised; it meant no summer vacation, but that was okay with me. This was my first murder case and I was anxious to get going.

I had said to Nancy in the early morning hours following my election, "You know what this means. I'll be trying all kinds of cases, including murders. For a guy who loves criminal law, this is a dream come true."

"Yes, Bob, but won't it be hard to switch from defending them to prosecuting them?"

"Absolutely not. I am a lawyer, I've got a client. My new client is the People of the State of New York and I'll fight for them just like I did for the defendants."

"Well, honey, that's all right with me. But I always said a prayer for you when the jury was out, that your man would be acquitted. I could never pray to God that anyone would be convicted of anything." She never did; she was right.

⁓

But now I was lining up for trial against the heaviest of the local artillery. The defense had four lawyers that appeared for the arraignment on that Monday in mid-April. The first lawyer was David Coral of Suffern, about fifty-five years old, admitted to practice for thirty-four years, former president of the Rockland County Bar Association, former assistant district attorney in the late 1940s, and law clerk to a New York State Supreme Court judge in the 1950s. Not heavy on criminal law since leaving the DA's Office, but a formidable opponent in any trial.

I had known Mr. Coral since the early days of World War II. At age twelve, in slight violation of the New York State Labor Laws, I had gone to work at Paret & Lamouree's Drugstore in Suffern as a stock clerk and soda jerk. Park Avenue in Suffern was then known as "Lawyers Row," and Mr. Coral was one of the young lawyers from the row who came in for coffee in the mornings. I greatly respected Mr. Coral and all the other lawyers. My father had to quit high school to work in the brickyards, so a lawyer was definitely someone to be admired.

Just before the trial of Biggs and Rivera started, we had a pretrial conference in Judge Silberman's chambers. When it was completed, Mr. Coral said, "You know, I've been practicing law for thirty-five years and I guess I'm getting old, but when the District Attorney of Rockland County calls me "Mr. Coral, that's the bitter end. For God's sake, Bob, will you call me Dave?"

"Yes, Dave." It's been so ever since with no lessening of the respect I had for him in 1942.

The second lawyer, who together with Dave Coral, would represent Juan Rivera, was Nicholas Lopes of New City. I had only known Nick for a few years and the year before he made a belated effort to get the Democratic nomination for district attorney away from me when it began to appear that the Democrats had a long shot chance to win. Nick was angry with the party and with me; he felt he was more qualified—he was.

Nick had been a prosecutor of war criminals in Italy with the US Army at the close of World War II. He had also been a lawyer with Senator John McClellan's Racket Busting Committee (formally the United States Senate Select Committee on Improper Activities in Labor and Management) in Washington in the 1950s. By the spring of 1966, however, we were good friends. Nick had been in Italy on a vacation when I was elected in November 1965 and from Rome he sent me one of the nicest letters I have ever received in my life. The friendship got even stronger as the years passed.

The third lawyer was Samuel Miller of Haverstraw. I had no prior dealings with Sam. He was only about fifty-five at the time but had a reputation as an "Old Fox." As I've learned in the years since, particularly that summer and fall of '66, he is an "Old Fox." Personally, I am very partial to Old Foxes.

～

The final lawyer was Gilbert E. McCormack of West Nyack, age forty-two, the former second assistant district attorney. At that time, I thought he was the best criminal lawyer I had ever met. Now, ten years later, after having personally tried many murder cases and other serious crimes, some against heavy hitters from New York City, I believe that the best criminal lawyer I have ever personally met is Gil McCormack.

Gil, without knowing it, is one of those most responsible for me running for district attorney. It was a bitter cold day in January 1965. I had been to see Gil at the DA's Office about a client of mine. Unlike Perry Mason, many of my clients were guilty as sin and I went to McCormack to get the best deal I could for my man. After completing our business, we went across the street to a luncheonette called "The Tor." As we sat there I said to Gil, "This time next year you'll be the district attorney. Looks like Mort will get that new judgeship."

"Hell no, no way, Bob! I've had enough of politics being justice of the peace in Orangetown. No more falling over people and kissing babies for this boy."

My only response was, "I'm surprised." I dropped the subject but it was paramount in my mind as I drove home that evening.

"Nancy, I talked to Gil McCormack today and he said he's not going to run for district attorney in November and I believe him. You know what that means. It means that with Silberman running for judge, Bob Stolarik will be the Republican candidate for district attorney, and he can be beaten."

Nancy frowned, "I hope you're not telling me you want to run?"

"Look, Nance, I never gave it a thought. I assumed McCormack would run and my chances of beating him would be nil, zero, zilch. But Stolarik, that's a different story. It would be damn close, but I could win if things broke right for me."

~

Every case has two distinct times when it is center stage. At the beginning, when the crime is committed, through the preliminary investigation to the grand jury indictment. Then there is a hiatus. Sure, there are pretrial motions and some activity, but basically you move on to other things and it is only the last two to three weeks before a set trial date that the case comes back to being the number one issue on your plate.

And so it was that on July 15, I told Lindy, "Let's get our friend Tex back in here and make sure nothing's changed."

The next morning I got the very bad news from Ray. "Bob, that fucking broad has flown the coop. She moved out about the middle of June and nobody's seen her since. Al Lagatella and his boys are on it but so far all we've got is that she headed south." Al Lagatella was the chief of detectives of the Spring Valley Police Department.

"God, Lindy, you know what this means, no Tex, no case. We ain't got a prayer without her."

So we began the difficult task of finding Doris Brown, with very little to work on. The first thing we did was to ask the Sheriff's Office to put out an information "Want" on her. Then, on my orders, we made up a flyer with the words, "WANTED AS A WITNESS TO MURDER," across the top and a picture of our lovely friend Tex, with a full description of her, especially her size. We used the mug shot from the butcher knife episode with Miller. I was grim but hopeful; after all she did stand out in a crowd.

The "Want" was sent to the usual thirteen-state eastern seaboard list. We also sent one hundred copies to the Texas Rangers Headquarters in Austin, Texas, Tex's hometown. In addition, we gave particular attention to Virginia because six of her prior convictions had been in the Tidewater area of Virginia. No results. We were striking out.

On Thursday, July 21, with the trial set for the following Monday, I went to Judge Silberman with my tale of woe. He was reasonable and understanding. On Monday the 25th, when I most unhappily announced, "The People are not ready for trial," Judge Silberman said, "All right, Mr. Meehan, just as defendants from time to time need a reasonable adjournment, so do the People. I will set this down peremptorily for Wednesday, September 7, 1966. At that time you must proceed to trial or I will entertain motions by the defendants to dismiss the charges."

I knew what peremptorily meant; we must go on that date. But more important, I was beginning to fully realize what the years ahead would prove to me—Judge Silberman meant business. When he said something, he always meant it.

I went up to the DA's Office and sat there with Ray and Ann Hickey and had a cup of coffee. I said, "Look, no vacations, no nothing until old Tex is back in the fold."

~

At about midnight on the evening of August 5, we finally caught a break. I got a call from Chief Adam Krainak of the Spring Valley Police Department. "Bob, Doris Brown was just picked up in Baltimore. They've got her at the West Baltimore precinct house."

I was ecstatic. "That's great, Chief. Let's go get her. I'll go myself. It'll take a lawyer to get her out of Maryland. I'm dying to see her."

The chief said he would go with me and it was agreed we would need a matron to bring her back. I said, "Can you be ready to go with the matron and everything by four o'clock?"

"You're damn right I can. I'll call Baltimore and advise them we are coming."

Twenty minutes later, the chief was back to me by phone. "Bob, bad news, they let her go. They had nothing to hold her on so they got her address and then just let her go."

"Oh, Christ, Adam! We still better head down there. We have to find her."

At about 3:30 a.m., we pulled away from the Spring Valley Police Station in the chief's unmarked radio car and headed for Baltimore. At the wheel was Detective Sergeant Alex Lagatella; beside him in the front seat, Chief Adam Krainak; and in the rear seat with me was our matron, Al Lagatella's wife, Vera.

By this time, I have come to know and like the chief and Al quite well. Chief Krainak was the type of boss who liked to work closely with his men and he never asked them to do anything he wasn't willing to do himself. I liked that.

Al Lagatella was actually a very gentle man who was soft-spoken and very polite with everyone, including criminals. But he could be tough when he had to be. I liked that too. I had never met Vera before, but she proved to be a lovely person. Over the years, Vera and I have become friends. Our main interest in common, outside of police work, was and is trailering and camping. So as we headed south on the New Jersey Turnpike, we spoke of camping and outdoors and children, and it was nice.

We arrived at the West Precinct House in Baltimore at about 7:30 that morning and, with the total assistance of the Baltimore Police Department, we began our day-long search for Doris "Tex" Brown. We had a uniformed police officer assigned to us and we drove around all day in a fully marked police cruiser through the ghetto section of West Baltimore.

First, we went to the given address on Peco Street. There was a 1116 Peco Street, and there was an apartment D, but there was no Tex. A young black couple lived there but they said they didn't know any Doris Brown or Tex or anybody fitting the description.

Despite our frustration we remained determined and proceeded to go from one daytime bar to another, always showing the picture, always with no results. What I remember most about that hot summer day in Baltimore was the looks of hostility on the faces of people on the streets and in the bars. Even the little children playing in the streets looked fearful.

What a shame that somehow the police, who were there to protect them, had become the enemy. I had seen those looks only once before in my life as I walked through the streets of Yokosuka, Japan, in my US Navy uniform not that long after the close of World War II.

By 2 p.m. we had accomplished nothing when the chief said, "Look, that wasn't a phony address she gave. That was an actual apartment. I say that if she was making up an address, it would have probably been bogus all the way. Let's go back over there." We did.

This time only the young woman was there and the chief and Al questioned her saying that Tex had been seen at their apartment. She hadn't, but it worked. "All right, I think I know who you mean, but promise you won't tell anybody I told you." We did. "She lives on top of a delicatessen over on Simpson Street."

The Baltimore officer with us knew the place she was talking about and he also knew the owner of the delicatessen. It was only about six blocks away. We headed right over.

The Baltimore policeman went in alone to the deli and was out in a minute. "Yeah," he said, "she lives up on the fourth floor in the back. She was in the deli about an hour ago and he thinks she went back upstairs."

Chief Krainak, Al Lagatella, and I went directly up to the fourth floor and knocked on the door at the rear. "Come on in, it ain't locked." I would recognize that little girl voice anywhere and I smiled for the first time all day.

I have a sense of humor but I'm not that good at trying to be funny. As I opened the door and saw Tex lying on the bed in just a slip, I did try to be funny. In my best Spencer Tracy, I said, "Doris Brown, I presume." Her completely unrehearsed answer was, "Aw, shit."

Two hours later we were heading at high speed on Maryland's John F. Kennedy Memorial Highway, enroute back to Spring Valley, New York, with Tex sitting between myself and Vera, and the Maryland Court Order safe in my pocket. Two hours and five minutes later, we were stopped on the shoulder of the highway. We were out of gas! I only mentioned this in passing for two reasons. First, that it really happened and second, that those of us in law enforcement are so much more human, and yes, subject to human error. This was in sharp contrast to law officers like Joe Friday and Pete Malloy, embodied by Jack Webb and Martin Milner, in the fictionalized police world.

After being held overnight, the following morning Judge Silberman ordered Doris Brown held without bail in the Rockland County Jail as a material witness to murder. The trial would go forward on September 7.

～

I now had a little less than one month to make final preparations for the important first murder trial of my administration.

To me the primary task was to win the confidence and respect of Tex Brown. The very fact of her flight indicated that she was less than enthusiastic about testifying. Further, testifying in open court, looking into the faces of friends, Rivera and Biggs, was a lot different than talking to twenty-three strangers on the grand jury.

I started by personally visiting the matrons in the women's quarters of the Rockland County Jail the next afternoon. The women's quarters, unlike the male sections, are actually quite nice. You enter through two locked and barred jail doors, but once inside, it is reasonably comfortable, with a living room, a modern bathroom, a kitchen, a small dining area, and eight small but neat bedrooms. It even included a fairly large TV. If not for the barred windows and jail-type barred doors, it would resemble a middle-class apartment.

I joined the two matrons and Tex in the living room for a cup of coffee as I explained the situation. "Now, Doris here is not a prisoner. She has done nothing wrong whatsoever. In fact, she is helping us a great deal and we certainly will appreciate it if you take good care of her and make her stay pleasant."

The matrons, who are deputy sheriffs, of course agreed and all in all it was a pleasant little afternoon get-together with everyone, including Tex exuding goodwill.

After that I made a point of having Tex brought over to my office two or three times a week, not so much to talk about the case but to give her a chance to get out of her closed-in apartment and walk around a bit.

It was apparent that she enjoyed these afternoon visits to the District Attorney's Office. Ann Hickey, without me telling her so, could see what I was driving at and always made a fuss over Doris. They were soon on a first-name basis and Ann would make a point of having something special like homemade cake or donuts to serve when Tex came in.

By Labor Day, Doris Brown was convinced that we were her friends. She was right, we had all come to like her very much, but more important, she was also convinced that she was a defender of good and right against the evils of the world. In this, I was not quite sure she was right, but by then any lingering doubt as to the truth of her story was gone. Doris "Tex" Brown was telling the truth.

~

Despite all the legal maneuvering and battling back and forth, when the trial began on September 7, it still all boiled down to Tex.

Early in the trial we did have a daylong battle over the admissibility of that empty bottle of Thunderbird wine. It seems that pictures of the crime scene under the bridge had been taken by both the Spring Valley Police Department photographer and by the men of the Bureau of Criminal Investigation of the Rockland County Sheriff's Office. The bottle of wine showed exactly at the water's edge in the Spring Valley pictures . . . and six inches from the water in the BCI pictures.

The defense argued that the scene had been tampered with, that the empty bottle and yes, all of the photographs should be excluded from evidence. We won, but not before some tense moments and a good lesson learned. In the years that followed, there were to be no more "scene tampering" charges or the necessity for them.

Late in the second week of the trial, at about 2:30 in the afternoon, I announced, "The People call Doris Brown," and so began the heart of the trial.

What was most amazing to us was the way Tex looked when she took the stand. She looked softer and better looking and nowhere near as fearsome as I thought she had when I first saw her standing with the public defender seven months earlier. True, she wore a rather attractive blue dress and the regular life in jail agreed with her; she had lost about thirty pounds. But it was more than that. She was no longer a sinister-looking, knife-wielding defendant. She was my friend and, throughout my entire life, people I've come to like and admire have always looked so much better in my eyes. Tex was no exception. I wondered what the jury thought.

I spent the first forty minutes with Tex, cataloging everything she had ever done wrong in her life. We went through each of her arrests and convictions in detail. In particular, we went over all the facts concerning the butcher knife episode with Powell and why those charges were dismissed two weeks before Artie Lucas was murdered. I was bound and determined to leave nothing left for the defense attorneys to crack her credibility on and I believe that we succeeded.

Even before we got to the testimony concerning the day and crime in question, I could sense that the jury of ten men and two women were warming up to her. I think they were taken with this big tough-looking woman with a little-girl voice, confessing to all the sins of her past life.

She then testified to the events of April 4, 1966. She had had quite a bit to drink the night before and slept until about two in the afternoon. She made herself a peanut butter and jelly sandwich for lunch and then went out and started walking downtown. "Where were you heading, Tex?" "No place." "What did you have in mind to do?" "Nothing." And so it went. "I just hoped I might see some friends."

She stopped to see a girlfriend on Second Avenue and she played with the friend's children for a time and then headed down Lawrence Street. As she was passing over the bridge, she could hear some loud voices talking down below and she thought she recognized the voice of a friend, Tommie Biggs. "That you down there, Tommie?"

A moment later, Tommie Biggs poked his head out from under the bridge and, smiling, said, "Hi, Tex. Come on down and have a little sip with us." She said she didn't want to at first but he insisted. "So down I went and there was Tommie with Juan and Old Artie Lucas." I then had her formally point to both Biggs and Rivera and identify them in open court.

"Tex, what happened when you first went under the bridge?" "Nothing." Not exactly the answer I was looking for. But after further questioning it developed that all three were in good spirits, none seemed drunk, and they were all drinking out of a pint bottle of wine. Tex said, "I had one sip, maybe two but that's all."

"What happened then, Tex?"

"Well, everything was nice and sunny and friendly-like and then, I don't know why, but Tommie and Juan started getting mad at Artie and before I knew it, they both had knives in their hands."

"Tex, who had knives in their hands?"

"Tommie and Juan."

"Did Artie Lucas have a knife in his hand?"

"No, sir."

"Did he have any type of weapon in his hand?"

"No, no."

"Now, Tex, listen carefully, did you have any knife or weapon on you or in your hand at any time that day under the bridge?"

"Oh no, Mr. Meehan. I never did nothing. I didn't stick anybody that day, honest to God, I didn't."

"Well, we believe you, Tex."

"Objection."

"Objection by Mr. McCormack sustained. Mr. Meehan, you know better than that. I direct the jury to disregard the prosecutor's statement. The question of who is to be believed is for you, the jury, and you alone to decide." Of course, Judge Silberman was correct.

"Tell us what happened after they took out the knives."

"They stuck Artie and kept sticking him and I told them to stop and they wouldn't listen."

"Who was the first to stick him?"

"It was Tommie, but Juan did it too."

"How many times did they stab him?"

"I don't know, but it was too many. They just kept at it. I got scared and got out of there fast."

And so Doris Brown had told her story. The remainder of the direct examination was devoted to why Tex didn't come forward sooner to report what she had seen. All of the answers to this question on direct cross boiled down to "I was scared."

⁓

At about 4:15, I turned it to the defense table and said, "Your witness." Thus began what I knew would be the making or breaking of the case, the cross-examination of Doris "Tex" Brown by the "Old Fox," Sam Miller. If Ray Lindemann was right about the truth winning out that day back in April, we would be all right, if not our case would collapse. Lindy was right.

The more that Miller pounded away, the stronger Tex got. Although he occasionally raised his voice, she never did. "I only know what I seen and Tommie and Juan did it." At about 5:30, Judge Silberman adjourned court for the day when Miller said, "I'll need a great deal more time; I've just begun my cross-examination."

We couldn't see or talk to Tex that night since she was in the middle of cross-examination, but in the DA's Office Lindy and young Jim Freeman, the assistant district attorney who worked with me on the case, and I were all very hopeful. If Tex could hold up in the morning, a conviction was possible.

For three hours more that next morning, Sam Miller hammered away but I was now learning firsthand what Lindy had told me months before. You couldn't shake the truth, especially from a witness who wasn't bright enough to try to spar with a seasoned lawyer on his own ground.

Tex left the witness stand just before noon that second day. I could tell from the faces of the jurors and from the look of concern at the defense table that we had won that battle. The outcome of the war, however, was still far from certain.

The defense had a star witness, Carlton P. Jones of Mahwah, New Jersey. The rule of law is that the prosecutor must advise the defense of important witnesses before hand. The defense has no such obligation except to give notice of alibi witnesses who will place the defendant or defendants somewhere other than the scene of the crime at the time of the crime.

There was no such requirement of notice concerning witnesses like Tex. Carlton Jones was not an alibi witness for Biggs and Rivera. He was there to claim that our friend Tex Brown was twelve miles away in Ramsey, New Jersey, throughout the entire afternoon and evening of Monday, April 4, 1966.

As I listened to the light-skinned, soft-spoken black man relate his story of a beer party in Ramsey with big Tex Brown there at all times, I wrote a note on my yellow pad, "Lindy, who the hell is this guy?" and had the court attendant hand it to Ray, who was sitting in the back of the courtroom.

Lindy sent back a response immediately. "Don't you know? He's a guest next-door at the jail. He's in on a rape charge." I felt better already.

By the time I commenced cross-examination less than an hour later, I had all the details on his case plus one other significant fact that I would put under the category of "funny coincidence." His cellmate in the Rockland County Jail was one Juan Rivera.

Carlton Jones never wavered from his story about Tex and the beer party in Ramsey, but we also won that battle. Real life, as I have said, is not like the world of Joe Friday, and Perry Mason does not do the questioning for the defense or the prosecution. In my years in the courtroom, I have seen many witnesses discredited, but I have never seen one admit that he or she was a straight-out liar in open court. Carlton Jones was discredited.

Of the twenty or thirty other people at the party, he couldn't remember the name of even one other participant. He had never heard of Rivera and Biggs or this murder until he was arrested in Suffern in June. He had never met Tex Brown before or after the beer party.

"Well, Mr. Jones, how is it you remember the exact date, Monday, April 4, 1966, today almost six months later?"

"Because that's the day it was," was his only response.

"I'm not asking you about yesterday or even last week. How do you recall that it was Monday and that it was April 4? After all this is September now."

He never could give an answer except one that really helped us. "Rivera told me it was April 4 and I remembered right away that that was the same day I saw Tex."

"Isn't it true, Mr. Jones, that Rivera told you the whole story, yes, made up the whole story you're telling today?"

Nick Lopes was on his feet objecting and the objection was sustained, but for the defense, the damage was done. The one person in the world who could discredit the star witness for the prosecution was the cellmate of a defendant—it wouldn't hold water.

The defense was now in trouble and they knew it. Juan Rivera never took the stand but when Gil McCormick rose and said, "The defense calls Tommie Biggs," I wrote two words on my legal pad and shoved it in front of Jim Freeman. "We win."

When we charged Tommie Biggs, we lost him as a witness against Rivera. Now we had him back. Biggs put the whole thing in Rivera's lap. Tex wasn't there, it happened just the way he had told us it happened at the police station that night. "Rivera did it, I didn't even have a knife, I didn't do nothing."

The prosecution was now clearly in the driver's seat—one dead body, one defendant in it all the way. Take your pick: believe Tex or believe Tommie; either way, Rivera is guilty of murder. For that reason, I severely limited my cross-examination of Biggs.

McCormick fought a valiant legal battle to get the results of that "inconclusive" lie detector test before the jury. The basic rulings were against him since lie detector evidence is not admissible in New York, but he won quite a few points talking about "something being wrapped around your arm with the electrical wires attached to it that night." Gil McCormick also stressed our failure to initially charge Biggs, but that was overcome much more easily than the oblique reference to the lie detector. After all, the jury had heard repeated testimony that Tex didn't come forward for a week because "I was scared."

After summations in which both defense counsels, Lopes for Rivera and Miller for Biggs, blamed the other, I gave my defense summation. Yes, in defense of the truthfulness of Doris Brown because "she was there."

Judge Silberman gave his instructions and the case went to the jury for its deliberation at midday on September 29, 1966. The following day at about 2 p.m., the jury came back with its verdict.

"Ladies and gentlemen of the jury, have you reached a verdict?"

The foreman stood and said, "Yes, we have, your honor. As to the defendant Juan Rivera, guilty of Murder in the Second Degree. As to the defendant, Tommie Biggs, guilty of Murder in the Second Degree." Intentional murder but without premeditation, the right verdict. Tex had been believed. We had won; the "Kiddy Korp" had come of age.

~

As the years passed, I came to understand that we hadn't won, we had the better case. Justice was served as I firmly believe it is in better than ninety-five out of one hundred jury trials.

But I did win one thing that month of September 1966; the respect of Judge Silberman and my adversaries for the defense. To me that was worth as much as any case.

Four days later, after processing, Doris "Tex" Brown was released from the Rockland County Jail. I requested that the matrons ask Tex to come over to see me before she left and she did. Tex had been in jail for fifty-six days and at eight dollars per day, which is paid to material witnesses, she had just received $448. By the time I saw her she already spent $183.60; $58.60 for a one-way bus ticket back to Dallas, Texas, and $125 for a purebred Chihuahua puppy that she had arranged to buy through one of the matrons.

She was happy; she had always wanted a Chihuahua but couldn't afford it. She had wanted to go home to Texas, too, but she couldn't afford that either. Now she had both plus over $260 in her pocket, more than she had ever had at one time in her life.

Ann brought in coffee and donuts and I invited her to sit with us and she did. Lindy came in and in his gruff way, he said goodbye to Tex. She left about half an hour later and said that she felt this was the beginning of a new life for her. I hope that it was; I don't know, I was never to see her again.

As I think back now to that spring and summer and early fall of 1966 and my first murder trial, my thought invariably turns to Tex. Bobby is now a healthy ten-year-old and the years have been good to Nancy and all of our family. Ronkie Hickey never did walk again. Sadly, she died in her sleep in the early morning hours of her twenty-fourth birthday in May 1972. So life has gone on with good times and bad.

But I suppose it is the unanswered question of life that we turn to most often. Where is Tex, how is she, did she have a new start in life? I hope that large woman with that small dog did find happiness.

Chapter 4

The Handball Player

Nancy and I were spending a relaxing evening at the Elks Club in Haverstraw with Ed McElroy and his wife, Ruth, on a Saturday night in late August 1967. Ed had come to work on January 1, 1967, as my criminal investigator, replacing Ray Lindemann.

The irrepressible old Ray Lindemann had been elected Sheriff of Rockland County in November 1966. I liked Ray and I was happy for him; his lifetime dream of being sheriff had come true. In one respect he would be missed in the DA's Office, but on the plus side, I was able to pick my own replacement. This would be my man, loyal to me, not a holdover from the Republican years who, consciously or unconsciously, would always be comparing me with Mort Silberman and John Skahen.

My first choice for the job without question was Charles Edward McElroy, former police sergeant in the Village of Haverstraw Police Department. He was "Eddie" or "Mack," but never "Charlie," and I liked and respected him greatly.

I loved Haverstraw. It was the old brick town that had been the settling place of the Meehans, Reillys, and Brophys in the New World when our family came from Ireland during the Great Potato Famine of the mid-nineteenth century. But I was not overly impressed at the time with the local police department; the exception was Sergeant Eddie McElroy, who I felt was the heart and soul of their small local force.

I had known Ed for many years, having first met him on the high school football field a score of years earlier. Coach Joe St. Lawrence had led his Suffern Mounties to a championship season in the fall of 1947 and along the way he had beaten the Haverstraw Red Raiders and Co-captain Ed McElroy 12 to 0. I never let him forget it.

I can truthfully say that football and the years of friendship afterward were irrelevant to Ed being my first choice. During my first year in office, we had three significant cases in Haverstraw: one murder, one manslaughter, and the shooting and wounding of a police officer. McElroy investigated all three and had done an outstanding job, particularly on the manslaughter, where a stepfather threw a twenty-month-old baby against the wall for crying too loud. The child died of a fractured skull. It would have been written off as an accidental death if it hadn't been for Ed McElroy.

Eddie was a rugged guy with a voice about three decibels lower than B-movie actor Aldo Ray. He could surely take care of himself, but he wasn't rough or mean, and no defendant or witness ever had anything to fear physically from McElroy.

~

The four of us were enjoying our dinner at the Elks Club when Ed said, "You know the last time we were here together in the spring, we were called out on a murder." A half-hour later, Police Radio called the club. (For nine years I always left a number where I could be reached.) There was an apparent homicide on First Avenue in Spring Valley. Nancy and Ruth would be left at the club alone again; Ed and I headed for Spring Valley. It was about 10:30 p.m.

It was a brutal murder. At the scene we entered a beat-up old house in the Black Hills section of Spring Valley. A quarter century before it had been a nice one-family house in a fine neighborhood. It was now divided into four dingy, filthy apartments and it was owned by a slumlord.

The two-room apartment was in shambles. There was blood on the walls and floors of both rooms, broken and upset furniture, and a violin smashed into pieces.

Partially on the couch and the floor was the nude and bloodied body of Evelyn Dodd. She was only twenty-five and had been a rather pretty, slender young black woman. Bits of the violin were in her hair and there were severe lacerations on her head and face, along with scratch marks on her neck.

The coroner, Dr. Leonard Benedetto of Sloatsburg, arrived a few minutes after we got there. He could establish that she had probably been dead for more than two hours, but couldn't tell us the cause of death. That would have to wait for the autopsy. At that time we had two elected coroners, Dr. Benedetto and Dr. Leo Weishaar. Both were MDs and good men, but neither was a pathologist. Therefore, by law, the autopsy would have to be conducted by the pathologist who happened to be on duty at the hospital that night.

This was a bad system. Some of the pathologists were experienced, some were not; some were good witnesses, some were very bad. We were still two years away from having our own medical examiner in Rockland County.

The body of Evelyn Dodd was brought to the morgue at Nyack Hospital. The next morning an autopsy was performed by a twenty-six-year-old, newly licensed medical doctor and pathologist. His report to the District Attorney's Office gave the cause of death as "manual strangulation." The pathologist's name was Robert Daut (pronounced like the word "doubt"). I could have cried when I heard his name; what an opening for a defense attorney. Forget the Robert, he would be known as "Dr. Reasonable Doubt." And so it was that the following spring, five weeks of a seven-week murder trial were devoted to contesting the finding of young Dr. Daut.

∾

By 1:30 in the morning, we were back in the squad room of the Spring Valley Police Station when Evelyn's thirty-five-year-old boyfriend, Roger Baker, was brought in for questioning. He was a medium-to-small-built black man and, at about five feet, six inches, he was slightly shorter than his dead girlfriend.

By that time I had learned that it was a bad idea for the district attorney himself to be involved in interrogation of suspects, lest he be called as a defense witness at the trial. However, I did sit down with Ed McElroy and Detective Al Lagatella to go over what we had before they started the questioning of Baker. The age of Miranda—the law that required all arrests to include the statement beginning with "You have the right to remain silent . . ."—was now upon us and we had to be careful to cover all bases as to Mr. Baker's constitutional rights.

Once it became the law of the land in 1966, I had "Miranda" cards printed and distributed to all police officers in the county with the requirement that they be read to suspects in full before questioning began. At

2:10 a.m. Ed McElroy read the card and initialed it. It later became a valuable piece of evidence for the prosecution.

Baker, who was outgoing and talkative anyway, waived his rights immediately and the questioning began. He never admitted that night or anytime there after that he had murdered Evelyn, but in an attempt to clear himself he did make statements that were later to be used against him.

Most important, he placed himself at the scene of the crime. However, he said that when he went there at 8:30 p.m., Evelyn was already dead. What had he done? Why hadn't he reported it? His response was the all-too-familiar "I was scared." But more importantly, he said, "I took one look and got out of there." This was of vital importance.

"Did you touch her, did you go in the bedroom, did you move anything?"

"Hell, no," he said, "I just got the fuck out of there."

We discovered that there were brownish stains on both of his blue ankle socks, there were particles under his fingernails, and there was a bloody blue sports shirt with two buttons torn off found on the floor of Evelyn's bedroom. At the time he was questioned, he was wearing a fresh clean, brown-checkered sport shirt.

The laboratory identified the stains on the sock as "human blood, insufficient amount to type." The fingernail scrapings were pronounced to be "blood, insufficient amount to test as to whether animal or human." These were typical findings. Again we worked in the real world; there was no precise television script to help us.

The bloody shirt was better. By the following day, we had located a key witness, one Madelaine Fox, who lived in the apartment next to Roger Baker on Columbus Avenue in Spring Valley. We were interviewing the neighbors to try and find precisely what time he left his apartment and returned.

Lagatella interviewed Madelaine, who was a heavyset, pleasant woman, about fifty years old. She had not seen Baker at any time after 2 p.m. the previous afternoon, but he had been in her apartment from about 12:30 to 2 that afternoon. It seems that she occasionally ironed his clothes and she recalled that she had ironed a blue sports shirt for him and immediately after she ironed it, he put it on.

Madelaine Fox could testify that at about 2 p.m. Baker left her apartment wearing a blue sports shirt, with no buttons missing. She later positively identified the bloody shirt found in Evelyn's apartment as the shirt she had ironed for Baker. Baker was indicted for Murder One, the intentional premeditated murder of Evelyn Dodd by means of "manual strangulation." Those last two words would be the key to the whole trial.

~

This would be the last time we would ever be faced with trying to prove premeditation. A week later—September 1, 1967—the new penal law became effective in New York State, merging First- and Second-Degree Murder into one crime of Murder with no requirement of premeditation, just an intentional killing.

The problem of proving the cause of death as manual strangulation never crossed my mind; after all, that's what the pathologist said. Months later it was to weigh heavily on my mind.

Madelaine proved to be a good witness for the prosecution and, with the exception of one heart-stopping moment during the trial, her testimony went smoothly.

I was only in my twentieth month as district attorney. In the eight years before I took office there had only been two murder cases in Rockland County. This was my ninth homicide. I was now an old pro, but I still felt an adrenaline rush with each new case. That lasted through all my years in the District Attorney's Office.

Baker was out of work, indigent, and rated the public defender. So when he was arraigned in Spring Valley Criminal Court on murder charges at 6:30 the next morning, he was represented by Public Defender Arnold Becker.

To some degree, I was responsible for Arnold standing there that morning. During my campaign for district attorney, I raised the issue that Rockland County needed a public defender's office to replace our appointed defense lawyer system. As I had hoped, Bob Stolarik took the opposite position.

Stolarik was most helpful to me in that respect. Every position I took, he disagreed with and therefore, issues such as "Should we have a public defender?" "Should we have a consumer fraud bureau?" or "Should we have a narcotics squad?" dominated the campaign. The issue of experience in the job was lost, which was just fine with me. After all, Bob had been first assistant DA for six years; I had no experience as a prosecutor.

Within a month after my election, the old County Board of Supervisors, viewing my upset election as something of a mandate, created the Rockland County Office of Public Defender and appointed Arnold Becker to the job.

I didn't really know Arnold well at the time, but for some reason, I was leery of him. He had run for district attorney in 1962 and lost in a landslide to Mort Silberman, but that was no disgrace; Silberman would have beat me in a landslide, too. I had been at the right place at the right time.

So when I took office on January 1, 1966, I had grave doubts as to how well I would get along with the new public defender, who would obviously be my main constant adversary. Becker was to be the public defender until the end of 1971. By that time, and I don't often use the term in reference to another man, I loved Arnold Becker. He fought me like a tiger at every turn, he used every legal device known to God and man to protect his clients, and a few new ones that even God hadn't considered trying.

He swamped us with work, appealing every case all the way up when there was even the faintest hope of success. When my men would sometimes get angry and say something like "That son of a bitch Becker, he did it again. Look at the size of this brief," I would always take Becker's side. "Look boys, Arnold is down there till all hours of the night thinking this stuff up, and for that he doesn't get a thin dime extra. When they start paying him by the page, I'll start bitching too! When you find a public servant willing to put in a seventy-hour week, I say don't knock it."

Arnold had one flaw as a criminal lawyer. He was not a showman; he had none of the qualities of an F. Lee Bailey. He always stuck to the law and facts of the case at hand, never any smoke screens or shifting to some irrelevant point to get the jury's mind away from any facts that pointed to guilt. I suppose by this I am saying it was a flaw that he was as ethical as any lawyer I ever met.

The one point above all that won my admiration of Becker was that he never took anything personally. After a battle royale in the courtroom, he would be friendly and as even-mannered as if nothing hostile had been said. To me this was always the mark of an outstanding lawyer.

                    ∾

On the morning of April 4, 1968, both sides answered, "Ready for trial." Every conceivable pretrial move to throw out the indictment—the admissions by Baker, the socks, the shirt, the fingernail scrapings—had failed, but only after a maximum effort by Becker.

This was the fourth murder trial I was to try, the second for Becker, and for our newest county judge, John Gallucci, his first.

Gallucci had run for county judge in 1965 and been beaten by Mort Silberman in a reasonably close race. To come as close as he had was a tribute to his professional esteem and personal popularity; after all, we hadn't elected a Democratic county judge since 1938.

In 1966, John got a second chance. Judge Herbert Henion died of cancer in January 1966 and Governor Rockefeller appointed the former Republican county chairman, John Reilly, to fill the vacancy until a special election could be held in November. This time John Gallucci pulled an upset in a very close election by winning in his heavily Republican hometown of Orangetown. Thus John Gallucci joined Mort Silberman as a county judge and was presiding in the case of the People versus Roger Baker.

Jury selection began and proceeded forward that day at a tedious pace. With Becker this was to be expected; there was very little he didn't know about a prospective juror when he finished his questioning. We had twenty peremptory challenges each, so this was going to take time. Judge Gallucci, knowing of Becker's thoroughness, had the courtroom filled with about 150 prospective jurors.

The next morning our first big dispute arose. Becker wanted to make a motion on the record before the prospective jurors were brought into the courtroom.

Becker rose and began, "Your honor, in light of the tragic death of the Reverend Martin Luther King last night in Memphis and the racial tensions it has engendered, I move that all prospective jurors be polled as to whether they can fairly sit and decide the fate of this Negro defendant." He went on at much greater length but that was the substance of his motion.

I opposed the motion. "Your honor, I'm sure that all America grieves for Dr. King and is appalled by the events of last evening in Tennessee. But this is not a racial trial. The defendant is black, the victim was black, all of the witnesses other than medical professionals and those involved in law enforcement are black. How can the defendant be prejudiced?"

Judge Gallucci then said, "Mr. Meehan, how can the People be prejudiced? He hasn't asked for a mistrial or dismissal. The request for the polling of the jury is reasonable. Motion granted."

Arnold Becker and Judge Gallucci were right. When the jury was brought in, Judge Gallucci put the question to them in much the same manner that Becker had requested. To my utter amazement 86 out of 145 asked to be excused. Becker had made his point.

With a new panel of over one hundred more jurors brought in and with more questions directed to racial prejudice, we finally got our jury by the middle of the next week and the trial went forward.

Everything was going too well. As was his standard procedure, Becker cross-examined each witness interminably as to every minute detail. Questions of time and distance were Becker's specialties, but since I already knew that we were prepared and there were no major problems.

Item after item that had been found in the blood-splattered apartment were introduced into evidence. Before the trial was over, we had 156 People's exhibits marked in evidence, including what Becker termed "the highly inflammatory" pictures of the nude body of Evelyn Dodd, lying amid the ruins of her apartment.

~

The heart-stopping minute with Madelaine Fox came late in the second week of the trial. We had been moving slowly, methodically, toward conviction and everyone in the courtroom knew it. My direct questioning of Madelaine had gone very smoothly; she spoke clearly and came across as very sincere in everything she said, including identifying Baker's bloody shirt.

The trouble came on cross-examination. Becker took her slowly through the entire story once again and then he went after her.

"Mrs. Fox, do you know one Richard J. Van Zandt?"

"No."

"Mrs. Fox, I point to this gentleman seated at the table directly behind the district attorney and ask, have you ever met this man?" He was pointing to Dick Van Zandt, Chief Investigator for the Public Defender, a truly marvelous person and close personal friend of mine, but more about that later.

Madelaine responded, "Well, I think I met him one time. I'm not sure, but he looks familiar."

"Mrs. Fox, didn't Mr. Van Zandt in fact come to your house last September and didn't you give him a written statement?" She didn't remember, but I knew this was trouble.

"Mrs. Fox, I show you a statement dated the 16th day of September 1967 in Spring Valley, New York, and I ask you, is that your signature?" It was and it contradicted the heart of her story.

Briefly, the written statement said Baker had been at her house that day at about noontime, that she had ironed some clothes including a shirt or two for him, but she didn't remember the color of the shirt or shirts and she doesn't remember whether he put one on when he left. It ended by saying, "I don't recall what Roger was wearing when he left."

Madelaine was now visibly upset and Becker had made his point, but he didn't drop it. He kept after her to admit she had lied in open court in her direct testimony. She clung tenaciously to her original identification of the bloody, blue shirt but was giving vague, nonresponsive answers as to the prior written statement.

Finally, under Becker's continued pressing, she pointed right at me and blurted out loudly, "He made me do it, he made me say it!"

I hadn't, but that made no difference. I thought, "There goes the case and *my reputation.*"

Becker, sensing the kill, said, "Let the record reflect that the witness pointed at Mr. Meehan and that the 'he' she speaks of is Mr. Meehan."

Oh God, I couldn't even object, but then I didn't have to.

Madelaine interrupted and yelled out, "No, not Mr. Meehan, that tall young fellow sitting behind him."

Keeping my wits about me, just barely, I was on my feet and turned and pointed directly at Dick Van Zandt.

"You mean *him?*"

"That's right, the fellow who came to my house."

"Your honor," I said somewhat incredulously, "this time let the record *correctly* reflect that the witness is pointing at Richard J. Van Zandt, Chief Investigator for the Public Defender." This time a stunned Arnold Becker could not object. The damage had been done—to the defense.

Becker immediately called for a recess and got it. After the jury filed out of the courtroom, Becker demanded a hearing forthwith, out of the presence of the jury, to clear Mr. Van Zandt of these "baseless" accusations. I opposed and, of course, I won. There was no basis in fact or law for such a hearing.

When the jury was brought back in, Becker tried vainly to shake her accusations against Van Zandt, but failed. I asked a few more questions on redirect, but I never mentioned the statement or her allegations against Van Zandt. I was quitting while I was ahead and I also did not believe that Dick Van Zandt had done anything intentionally wrong.

When a witness is not overly bright, as was the case with Madelaine, they are easily susceptible to honest suggestion and want to agree with their interviewer. This is a problem that all investigators, particularly police and district attorney's investigators, must constantly guard against. It's one thing to be *clearing* a man on "friendly testimony"; it's another to *convict* him on it. In her attempt to be nice to this friendly young man, she had hurt him and I genuinely felt sorry for Dick.

As any lawyer does, I want to win my case, but not at the expense of a friend, and Dick Van Zandt was a true friend, probably as close a personal friend as any one of my own people in the DA's Office.

$$\sim$$

I had first met Dick during my 1965 election campaign and I must say that although I have met many people in politics whom I admire and respect, few of them ever crossed that invisible line from political to personal friends. Dick and Sheila Van Zandt most certainly had.

They are genuinely nice people and Dick undoubtedly has the quickest wit of anyone I have ever met who was not a professional entertainer. I can remember one time we had lunch together and afterward he almost dragged me to a men's shop next door.

"Bob, you've got to wear something other than those two black suits all the time, after all you weren't elected district undertaker." That was mildly funny and I reluctantly went in with him with no intention of buying anything.

We browsed for a while and then a very officious-acting young man came over and said, in an even more officious tone, "Is there something that I can do for you?" Dick shot back instantaneously in a very stilted voice. "Yes, I demand to see the manager at once. I've been looking over this sport jacket and I just found a pork chop in the pocket."

"A pork chop in the pocket?" the salesman incredulously repeated.

"Yes, young man, a pork chop in the pocket and I demand to see the manager."

As the salesman headed for the back room, I headed for the door.

"For Christ's sake, Dick, let's get the hell out of here, unless you've got a spare pork chop to put in that pocket." He didn't; we left.

More indicative of the kind of people Dick and Sheila are is an incident that occurred two days after I was elected district attorney. Unlike the other elected or reelected officials who took a vacation to Florida or the West Indies to rest up after election, Nancy and I, more within our budget, were going to spend a four-day weekend with my brother, Tom, and his wife, Karen, at their home in Connecticut. Our great friend Lucille Stewart, one of the kindest people I have ever met and a nurse's aide who worked for my mother at the hospital, would take care of the five children and we would have a much-needed rest. On Thursday, Lucille became sick and the trip was off.

That evening, Dick Van Zandt called to invite us to a party the following week and in passing I mentioned our canceled trip. A half-hour later, Dick was back on the phone.

"Look, our house is too small, but if you and Nancy would still like to go to Connecticut, Sheila and I and the kids would be glad to move in for the weekend and take care of your kids."

Within a few minutes it was settled and the next day, Dick and Sheila and their children, Christine, Eric, and Erin, arrived ready to take over. Our oldest, Patty, was then nine and Chris was seven. While we relaxed, the eight children had the time of their lives. My kids have loved the Van Zandts ever since.

Our hearts broke for them the following May 1966 when Chris was run over by a car and killed. I have only openly cried twice since my father's funeral in 1945. First, in the fall of 1963 when they played "Hail to the Chief" in three-quarter time as the body of John Kennedy was borne up the steps of the Capitol. Second, in the spring of 1966 at St. Margaret's Church in Pearl River when Dick Van Zandt, himself, gave the eulogy to his lost little girl.

So you can see that there was little elation for me that night in the DA's Office as we went over the obviously good day for the prosecution in the courtroom. When one of the investigators made a joke at Van Zandt's expense, it didn't go over well with me.

"Damn it, just remember that could've been you. He's on the other side, but he's in the same business we are."

I think Ann Hickey, who was there that night, was glad that I had come to Dick's defense. She had also been there that night in May 1966 keeping vigil over her daughter, Ronkie, at Nyack Hospital when Chris was brought in dying. She saw the anguish of this wonderful family and would never forget it.

$\sim$

But life and the business at hand would go forward and for us that meant the People versus Roger Baker.

"Do you suppose that was all Becker had? Hell the trial's almost over, but I still sense he's got something up his sleeve." I was thinking out loud.

Ed McElroy said, "When do you think you'll finish, Boss?"

"I figure the medical for half a day and that's about it for our case. I have a hunch Baker won't take the stand and this thing can wind up by Friday."

How wrong I was. Baker never did take the stand, but the trial didn't end until three weeks from that Friday. Becker was loaded for bear on the medical.

The next morning, Dr. Robert Daut of Nyack Hospital took the stand. I knew he had just been licensed to practice medicine and had conducted less than a dozen autopsies on his own, so I stressed his training.

"Dr. Daut, how many autopsies have you participated in or witnessed?"

"Several hundred."

"How many involving strangulation."

I had to ask the question because I knew that Becker would; however, I had been careful to say "strangulation." I knew that this was his first autopsy involving "manual strangulation." I just hoped Becker wouldn't pick up on that. He didn't.

Although the movies and television would have you believe otherwise, most people die in bed and of natural causes. Of those unfortunates who die in murderous fashion, it is usually with a knife or a gun. Therefore, medical students and interns have very little experience with strangulation victims.

Dr. Daut was actually a good witness. A handsome young man who spoke well and already seemed to be acquiring an important attribute of a good expert witness, the ability to translate technical information into layman's terms.

To my surprise, Becker was not overly long or hard on the doctor. As I expected, Dr. Daut stuck to the strictly technical language and went through his medical findings, which led to his professional opinion that the cause of death was "manual strangulation." He talked about the petechial hemorrhages of the eyes, and so forth, and so on. Actually, although rare, strangulation has classic signs that are relatively easy to detect.

Becker then ended up with a few seemingly minor negative points.

"Was the hyoid bone fractured?"

"No."

"Was the cricoid bone fractured?"

"No."

"Are you positive of that?"

"Yes."

"All right, the defense has no further questions." Becker sat down and Dr. Daut stepped down. That afternoon, I announced, "The People rest." Now it was Becker's turn.

～

Becker made the usual motions to dismiss at the end of the People's case. Judge Gallucci quickly said, "Denied in all respects." After all, although murder is the most serious of charges, the elements of proof in the indictment are not that complicated. We had to present proof that "Roger Baker on or about the 26th day of August, 1967, in the village of Spring Valley in the county of Rockland and the state of New York, with malice aforethought and premeditated design, did knowingly and intentionally murder and cause the death of one Evelyn Dodd by means of manual strangulation."

I was confident that we had presented strong proof on all points, particularly that Baker had done it. It was obviously a "knowing and intentional" killing. The question of "malice aforethought and premeditated design" was always tough and would be a question for the jury. We hadn't presented any evidence of motive, nor was it a necessary element. Murder is often the end result of a lovers' quarrel. I wasn't worried if they didn't buy premeditation. We still had a conviction for Second Degree Murder. In a nutshell, we had proved that he intentionally murdered her by manual strangulation. Or had we?

Arnold Becker asked for a recess until the next morning, which was granted. Significantly he advised Judge Gallucci, "Your honor, the defense anticipates calling only ONE witness." So that evening in the DA's Office was solely devoted to guessing whom Becker would call. He had never at any time tipped his hand, even during jury selection, as to whether he would put the defendant on the stand, but I continued to believe that he wouldn't. It couldn't be an alibi witness; we had served what is known as an "alibi notice," which meant Becker had to advise eight days in advance of trial of the "name and address of any witnesses who would place the defendant elsewhere at the approximate time of the crime."

I was thinking out loud when I said, "The crazy thing about this business is that it can't be an alibi witness, but it could be a witness who placed someone else entering and leaving her apartment that night. But, God, if he has something like that, I can't believe we wouldn't have something on it by now."

It never entered the discussion that night, and never even crossed my mind that we were in for trouble on the medical issue of "cause of death." In our indictment we had alleged "manual strangulation," and if it wasn't proven beyond a reasonable doubt that Evelyn Dodd died from "manual strangulation," we had no case—not Murder One, not Murder Two, not even Manslaughter. What we would face would be an acquittal.

The next morning, Arnold Becker rose to his feet and said, "The defense calls Dr. Edwin Harbison." I had never heard of him and looked at my assistants and just shrugged my shoulders.

From the time he opened his mouth, it was obvious that he was British. In fact, he looked and spoke a lot like an English aristocrat; in sum, a very impressive witness.

Becker went into a very long litany of Harbison's background and achievements. They were as impressive as he was. He had obtained his undergraduate degree from Oxford and had attended and graduated from the Royal Academy of Medicine in London. Then "after a spell in the North Atlantic with the Royal Navy," he had commenced his career as a pathologist in 1946. I won't take the time to catalog all of his graduate degrees and honors, but Becker most certainly did.

He had come to the United States in 1952 and was a fellow of the American College of Pathologists. He had been in attendance at thousands of autopsies but basically his career in medicine and pathology was in university medical schools. Further he was a consultant on pathology for several hospitals in upstate New York.

"I am called upon by many of my colleagues to review their findings in the more difficult cases," he told the court.

The introduction of Dr. Harbison didn't end there. Becker and Harbison went on in question-and-answer form with almost a history of the medical science of pathology. He had been on the witness stand for better than an hour and a half and still there had been no mention of the death of Evelyn Dodd, but I was getting more apprehensive by the minute.

Then they let us have it.

"Doctor, I show you People's Exhibit 152, the complete autopsy report of Dr. Robert Daut concerning the death of Evelyn Dodd, and I ask you, have you had the chance to review it?"

"Yes, I have thoroughly reviewed it in the same manner that I review autopsy findings of colleagues who called me in for consultations."

"Doctor, what is your opinion as to the physical findings?"

"Sir, I have no opinion. As a consultant, I must rely on the attending pathologist report as to his findings; these are facts, not opinions."

"Well then, Doctor, what is your opinion of Dr. Daut's conclusion as to the matter of the cause of death?"

"Sir, after reviewing his findings, and relying on their accuracy, it is my professional opinion that the stated cause of death, namely manual strangulation, is incorrect."

"Doctor, in your opinion, what was the cause of death?"

"I cannot tell from Dr. Daut's report, but I know that in no circumstances could it have been manual strangulation."

"Upon what do you base your conclusion, Doctor?"

"Unlike ligature strangulation, for manual strangulation, there must be extreme pressure brought to bear on the throat by the hands and this always results in fracture of the hyoid and cricoid bones of the neck."

"Doctor, according to Dr. Daut's report, were the hyoid and cricoid bones of Evelyn Dodd fractured?"

I knew the answer; they obviously were not—Dr. Daut had so testified. We were in trouble, serious trouble, and I knew it.

As Dr. Harbison went on carefully sinking our case, I scribbled a note on my yellow legal pad.

"Mack, go up and tell Ann to get Dr. Helpern on the phone right away. If he's not at the Medical Examiner's Office in New York, find out where he is. It's vital. I want to talk to him within the hour."

I then turned my full attention back to Dr. Harbison. The hyoid and cricoid bones had never meant a thing to me before. This was my first strangulation case of any kind, but Dr. Harbison certainly sounded like he knew what he was talking about.

Becker finished his direct examination of Dr. Harbison at about 11:30 with the usual "Your witness." I rose and said, "Your honor, I realize it's early, but I believe the cross-examination could be rather lengthy and I, therefore, request that we break for lunch now and go directly through with cross this afternoon."

Judge Gallucci was not sympathetic. "Mr. Meehan, we work full days in my courtroom. We will take a ten-minute recess and then commence cross-examination."

"Yes, your honor."

~

I literally ran up the flight of stairs to the DA's Office.

"Annie, break off everything else. Do you have Helpern lined up yet?"

"Yes, I'll get him back on the private line right away."

Within two minutes I was talking to Dr. Milton Helpern, Chief Medical Examiner of the City of New York and one of the foremost forensic pathologists in the world.

Although I was at the time only in my third year as district attorney, I had already established a good relationship with Dr. Helpern. We had hit it off well from the start. I had such great admiration for this salty, old character and he seemed genuinely fond of me. I think the thing that won him over was my candidness about knowing next to nothing about forensic pathology and relying on him so heavily. He hadn't testified on a trial for me yet, but had testified in the Rockland County Grand Jury on another case that would become a local cause célèbre when it later went to trial.

When I got him on the phone I had no time for amenities but got right to the point.

"Doc, we are on a manual strangulation trial up here and it looks like we are in deep trouble. A young pathologist from Nyack Hospital did the autopsy and came back with 'manual strangulation.' Everything went well on our direct case and it looked like we were home free until this morning. The defense just put on a guy, I don't know if you know him, but his name is Dr. Edward Harbison. He said that he didn't know what the cause of death was, but it couldn't be manual strangulation because the hyoid and cricoid bones were not fractured. The fact is they weren't fractured and he says they are fractured in EVERY manual strangulation case. Is that true, doc?"

"Bob, for Christ's sake, he's a handball player. It depends on a lot of things but we have plenty of manual strangulations without the hyoid and cricoid being fractured."

I felt better already, but I pursued it. I already knew what he meant by a handball player—an expert witness who will bat back the opposite opinion of anything you say.

"Well, Doc, what are some of the things that cause them to be fractured or not fractured?"

"Hell, the most important thing is whether the victim was strangled from the front or behind. On a frontal, the thumb pressure will usually fracture both hyoid and cricoid; from the rear, the finger pressure, as often as not, does not cause fractures. Do you know whether it was front or rear?"

"No, we don't. We have no eyewitnesses and the defendant won't go for anything."

"Are there any scratch marks on the neck?"

"Yes, on the sides toward the front."

"Well, for God's sake, that's easy enough. The fingers usually cause the scratch marks, not the thumbs. It must've been from behind. I think you're in good shape."

"Doctor, would you have any percentage of known manual strangulation cases where the hyoid and cricoid were *not* fractured?"

"I'd have to check it out, but as a ballpark figure, I'd say about 25 percent, and a lot higher on cases of manual from the rear."

I was of course thrilled to hear this, but I thought to myself, "Meehan, you damned fool! You are four weeks into a manual strangulation murder case, and you don't even know the basic elements of what you are talking about." That would never happen again during my years in the District Attorney's Office.

"Doc, now the important thing, would you be willing to come up here and testify on rebuttal for us?"

"Sure Bob, just give me a call. In the meantime, I'll have the statistics checked out—I think I'm going to enjoy this one!"

"One last question, Doc, about how many strangulation cases have you handled during your career?"

"Hell, I say well over two thousand strangulations, maybe four to five hundred were manual."

〰

I was a new man as I walked into the courtroom fifteen minutes later. I was now looking forward to the cross of Dr. Harbison. I could even ask him how many cases of this type he had handled. No matter what the answer, it couldn't possibly approach Helpern's experience.

I remember saying to Ed McElroy on the way back to court, "I'll bet you a steak dinner he hasn't done twenty manual strangulations."

Ed boomed back, "Hell, the son of a bitch probably hasn't done ten!"

"Come on, Ed, that would be too much to hope for."

I started my cross-examination of Dr. Edwin Harbison by briefly going over his direct testimony, basically to lock him in tight on the point that these small bones MUST be fractured to find manual strangulation. Next, I asked the questions I would have asked with or without talking to Dr. Helpern.

"Dr. Harbison, have you ever met or spoken in your entire life to one Dr. Robert Daut?"

"No, sir."

"Doctor, were you in attendance at the autopsy of Evelyn Dodd at Nyack Hospital on the 27th day of August, 1967?"

"No, sir."

"Dr. Harbison, at any time since the 27th day of August, 1967, have you actually seen the body of Evelyn Dodd?"

"No, sir."

"Would it be fair to say then, Doctor, that your opinion is based solely upon reading the autopsy report of Dr. Daut?"

"Yes, basically that is correct. However, I did look at the photographs."

"Did you learn anything of significance as to the cause of death from looking at the pictures?"

"In substance, I would say no."

Now I went forward with questions that could only be asked after my brief but enlightening lecture on forensic pathology by Dr. Helpern. I didn't want to overplay my hand though. I had no interest in breaking Dr. Harbison; on the contrary, I wanted to leave his incorrect opinion intact. I was in the same position Becker had been in with Dr. Daut: lock him into statements that could later be refuted by a more experienced witness—a more experienced witness that he was not aware of!

"Doctor, as an expert, *hypothetically* assuming that the hyoid and cricoid bones had been fractured, were all of the other findings by Dr. Daut consistent with death by strangulation?"

"Yes, I would say so."

"Further, again the same hypothetical, the hyoid and cricoid fractured, were all of the other findings consistent with death by *manual* strangulation?"

He wasn't as fast with the answer this time and for the first time he seemed to try to avoid the very specific type of answers he had given on both direct and cross. I persisted and finally he did say, "Yes, I suppose they were."

I then went further. "Doctor, my same hypothetical, hyoid and cricoid fractured, all other findings the same, from the records and from the pictures would there be any way of telling whether the victim was strangled from the front or the rear?"

Becker was becoming increasingly nervous and this time he objected. "Your honor, the question is too hypothetical. There has been no evidence before this court and jury as to whether there was a front or rear attack. In fact, this witness is testifying that there was no such attack!"

"Your honor, there is such evidence. I just want to bring it to the attention of the court and jury."

"All right, Mr. Meehan. I will allow it, subject to connection."

So Dr. Harbison was required to answer. "I can recall nothing that would give such an indication, but then again there was no reason to look into whether it was front or rear when I was faced with conclusive evidence that it was not manual strangulation."

Becker smiled. I tried to look pained; on the surface it was a very bad answer for the prosecution.

"Dr. Harbison, didn't you see any scratch marks on her neck in the pictures or read about them in the report?"

"I don't recall." Good, the expert was faltering!

"Well, Doctor, I have the pictures right here and referring to page 6 of the autopsy report, isn't there a reference to scratch marks on the front sides of the neck?" He had to admit that there was such evidence of scratch marks.

"Now, Dr. Harbison, isn't it a fact that in cases of manual strangulation, if there are scratch marks, they are usually made by the fingernails of the four fingers as opposed to the thumbs, which are flat and applying heavy pressure?"

He equivocated and that was fine with me. He began to appear not quite as sure of himself and not quite as much of an expert as he had presented himself through the morning. I dropped the line of questioning while I was ahead.

I then asked my last question of Dr. Harbison. "Dr. Harbison, you have testified here today about your broad pathological experience in both England and the United States. I now ask you, how many autopsies have you personally conducted where you were the pathologist in charge and where the finding as to cause of death was manual strangulation?" I had carefully worded my question to exclude medical school and intern experience where he would only have been an observer.

Dr. Harbison then, in almost a whisper, answered, "Well, I personally have done none."

I could've kissed him. I couldn't believe it. I turned and walked slowly away from the witness stand toward the back of the courtroom. I caught Ed McElroy's eye and winked as he gave me just the slightest smile. I then turned and walked just as slowly back to the witness stand—I wanted time for that answer to sink in. "Did you just say 'none'?"

His barely audible response, "Yes." There was no "sir" this time.

Again I turned and walked and waited in the silent courtroom, but finally I turned and said, "You mean never?" The same response.

The third time I turned away from the witness stand, Becker was on his feet objecting.

"But your honor, what's Mr. Becker objecting to? I haven't asked a new question."

Judge Gallucci admonished, "Mr. Meehan, will you please get on with the questioning? You've made your point." I knew I had.

"Now, Dr. Harbison, since you have testified that you have never personally conducted an autopsy involving manual strangulation, would it be fair to say then when it comes to the subject of manual strangulation, you, sir, are nothing more than a book doctor?"

Becker sprung to his feet to object. As I knew it would be, the objection was sustained. I then turned to Judge Gallucci and said, "Your honor, I have no further questions of the witness. I thought I was questioning an expert!"

Becker was furious. He not only objected and demanded that my remarks be stricken from the record, but asked that the judge censure me.

"Mr. Meehan, you know better than that. The jury is instructed to disregard Mr. Meehan's final remarks." I didn't mind at all.

~

The defense immediately requested a brief recess and got it. Becker, Van Zandt, and Dr. Harbison huddled together in the passageway outside the courtroom. Five minutes later, we were back in the courtroom and Arnold Becker announced, "I have no redirect examination of this witness. The witness is excused."

I was even more surprised. Dr. Harbison obviously had no significant experience with manual strangulation at any time in his career or Becker would have questioned him on it. But after all, Becker too had decided to quit while he was ahead. Whether or not Dr. Harbison had actual experience, still, he was a learned doctor and professor and I had in no way shaken his professional opinion that this case could not have been manual strangulation. Becker didn't know that for the prosecution, Dr. Harbison was only being set up to be shot down by Dr. Helpern.

Six days later, Dr. Milton Helpern took the stand as a rebuttal witness for the prosecution. To introduce him, I not only went through his forty-two years as a clinical and forensic pathologist but asked, "Dr. Helpern, how many autopsies have you personally conducted where the cause of death was strangulation?"

"Over two thousand."

"Dr. Helpern, how many of those cases involved manual strangulation?"

"Well, I'd say between four and five hundred."

I, of course, had gone through all of his clinical and academic experience and reviewed the list of books he had written on the subject, but my main thrust was that he was not just a "book doctor," that he had been there and knew what he was talking about from hard experience.

His testimony was strong for the prosecution. "Of course there could be manual strangulation without fractures of the hyoid and cricoid"—"If the attack was from the rear the chances of fractures of hyoid and cricoid are only slightly better than fifty-fifty."

Dr. Helpern, in his usual thorough preparation, had gone through the records of one hundred random manual strangulation cases in the files of the New York City Medical Examiner's Office for a period of ten years and was able to state, in seventy-three of the cases, the hyoid and cricoid were fractured, and twenty-seven they were not.

Dr. Helpern was a marvelous witness, highly expert, but still humble; highly technical, but still easy to understand. With all of this, Becker was still not awed and he went after Helpern with a vengeance on cross-examination, but to no avail. The doctor had the statistical facts to support his opinion and Becker didn't have the "experience" ammunition to use it as I had with Dr. Harbison. We clearly won the day—but Becker wasn't going down without a fight.

~

After Helpern's testimony we again rested the People's case. The next afternoon Arnold reopened for the defense by calling Dr. Morris Rosen, chief medical examiner of a county in upstate New York. Here we go again, another expert, but this time one with actual experience in manual strangulation cases. He had been a county medical examiner for six years. Prior to that he had worked and studied under Dr. Milton Helpern at the New York City Medical Examiner's Office.

Dr. Rosen was about forty years old, scholarly, but also easy to understand. As Becker questioned him, he hit back at us hard. "Now, Dr. Rosen, how many cases of manual strangulation has your office handled in the six years that you have been medical examiner?"

"Five, sir."

"All right, and how many of those five cases were the hyoid and cricoid fractured?"

"All five. I have never seen the reverse in a manual strangulation case."

Before direct examination was completed, Dr. Rosen had told of personally conducting ten or fifteen manual strangulation autopsies while working for Dr. Helpern. The same answer, "In all cases, the hyoid and cricoid were fractured."

Luckily for us we were approaching the end of the day when Dr. Rosen's direct testimony ended. I wanted to adjourn to the next morning for cross, but Becker and Rosen fought it, especially since Rosen was over one hundred miles from home and had to be in his office the next morning. Finally, a deal was struck in the judge's chambers. I would only ask Dr. Rosen two questions on cross-examination and he would be excused—*subject to recall*—but only if the prosecution in good faith had evidence to rebut his testimony.

At that point I really didn't expect to recall Dr. Rosen. Sure, he had hurt us somewhat, but our expert was more experienced and just as important; Rosen had also never seen the body of Evelyn Dodd. The only questions I asked were: "Dr. Rosen, have you ever seen the body of Evelyn Dodd in your entire life?"

"No, sir."

"Dr. Rosen, have you ever at any time in your life met or spoken or in any way communicated with the doctor by the name of Robert Daut?"

"No, sir."

"The People have no further questions, your honor."

Dr. Rosen stepped down and as he walked out of the courtroom, I assumed that I was through with him. Again, I was wrong.

◇

Now it was back up to the DA's Office. "OK, Annie, here we go again. Get me Helpern on the phone." Within ten minutes I was listening to Dr. Helpern say to me, "Bob, Dr. Rosen is a gentleman, a scholar, and a fine pathologist. But Robert, my lad, he too is a 'Handball Player.' "

Before the telephone conversation ended, it was agreed that we would meet Dr. Helpern later that evening at the Medical Examiner's Office in New York City. "Bob," the Doc said, "maybe we could have some fun reviewing Rosen's old files."

As Eric Vrhel and I drove to New York City that evening, I was hopeful. After three hours of reviewing records dating between 1956 and 1962, I was more than hopeful. We found eleven autopsies signed by Dr. Rosen in which he listed the cause of death as "manual strangulation." In three of them the hyoid and cricoid were *not* fractured.

By 11:30 that evening, I was on the phone calling the home of Judge John Gallucci. "Judge, we have hard evidence to rebut Rosen and we want him back." After I told the judge exactly what we had, he agreed we had a right of recall and the judge told me to contact Rosen and have him in court the next morning.

As a courtesy, I called Becker first and although he was not too happy to learn of this latest turn of events, he took it well and said he would call Rosen and arrange to have him come in. I told Becker where

I was and it was agreed that he would only call me back in New York City if there was a problem. Arnold did not call back, but I did receive one of the strangest and certainly the most hostile call I had ever had.

Eric and I were sitting with Dr. Helpern in his office having a cup of coffee when an attendant came in and said, "Mr. Meehan, I have a call for you from a Dr. Morris Rosen." Dr. Helpern smiled and said that I could take the call at his desk.

"Hello, Dr. Rosen, this is Mr. Meehan."

"Mr. Meehan, I just talked to Mr. Becker and he told me that you were going through my old cases in the ME's Office, is that true?"

I could tell from the edge in his voice that he was angry, but I tried not to notice it and answered casually, "Yes, as a matter of fact I'm sitting having coffee with your old boss, Dr. Helpern."

"Well, I just called to let you know, Mr. Meehan, that it's people like you who are ruining the respect in this country for law and order. You just want to convict that poor man because he is black!"

"Hey now, hold the phone a minute, Doc. I've got a job to do and . . ."

But before I could finish, he interrupted. Now almost shouting, Rosen continued, "I know your kind, Hitler's storm troopers were made up of the Meehans of the world, and you're out to get me and make me look like a fool because I am a Jew!"

All right, he had gotten to me and I came back hard and mad. "Listen and listen hard, I'll go after murderers whether they're black, white, or green, and as for you, it never even crossed my mind that you were a Jew and I couldn't give a damn whether you are or aren't. But one thing I do know is this, you're a goddamn liar and I'm looking forward to making you look like the horse's ass you are in court tomorrow!" I then slammed down the phone.

Helpern was visibly shocked after hearing just my end of the conversation; Eric was not. He well knew about my infrequent but strong Irish temper.

I never saw or spoke to Dr. Rosen again. He did not appear in court the following morning, but of course Arnold Becker did. In the judge's chambers before the opening of court, it was put on the record by Mr. Becker, "Dr. Morris Rosen refuses to return to testify further. He not only is too busy, but he refuses to return to the same courtroom with Mr. Robert Meehan, District Attorney of Rockland County, who last night in a telephone conversation, referred to Dr. Rosen as a 'horse's ass.'"

Judge Gallucci turned to me for a response and I said, "Your honor, I must most reluctantly admit that last evening on the telephone I did have occasion to call the distinguished medical examiner a 'horse's ass,' but I would like to point out a few things. First, he called me; I didn't call him. Second, he accused me of being anti-black and anti-Semitic. And lastly, he likened me—and apparently my whole family—to Hitler's storm troopers. Your honor, it was only after these false and untrue statements that I reverted to the language of my forefathers in the brickyards."

I think John Gallucci was amused, but he wasn't about to show it and he went forward as the judge that he was. "Gentlemen, what Mr. Meehan and Dr. Rosen said to each other is irrelevant. We have a case to finish and let's get on with it."

After over an hour of haggling, I backed down. Dr. Rosen would not be recalled. I made the tough decision that we already had enough to win, and that a fight in open court in front of the jury could help the defense on an appeal. And so the Doctor Rosen incident ended and two days later the case went to the jury.

Arnold Becker's summation took six hours, most of it going over medical testimony. Mine took fifty minutes; that was all I felt I needed and, besides, by that time the jury was sure tired of listening to speeches. After Judge Gallucci gave his charge, the jury got the case at about noon on a Friday in mid-May. They were back with the verdict at about ten o'clock that night, the only murder case I ever tried without overnight deliberations.

"We, the jury, find the defendant, Roger Baker, guilty of Murder in the Second Degree."

We later learned two significant facts from talking to a juror afterward, which is legally permissible in New York State. First, the last five hours of deliberation were in an argument over whether it should be Murder One or Murder Two. Second, and most significant, the important issue to the jury was "Did he do it?" not "How did he do it?" Our medical dogfight had been mostly for nothing.

≈

Arnold Becker and Dick Van Zandt came up to the DA's Office about half an hour after the verdict to congratulate me. Defense tiger that he was, Arnold was a gentleman and lawyer through and through and, therefore, for him, shaking my hand was not difficult. For Dick, it was. He had worked hard for Baker and it was hard to lose and harder still not to take it personally.

When Arnold and Dick left I said to the crew in my office, "I sense that my buddy, Dick, is still mad at me. I hope I haven't won a case and lost a friend."

I didn't see or hear from Dick again for several days. I had started another murder case that following Monday morning and was quickly becoming enrapt in it, but I must say that it concerned me that Dick hadn't even stopped up for a cup of coffee.

My worry over Dick Van Zandt ended that Thursday. I came up from court at the noon recess and one of the young clerks in my office, Barbara Lichtner, said, "Mr. Meehan, I have a message for you to call back on and the man says it's urgent. I wrote it all down."

"OK, Barbara, let me know what you've got before I return the call."

"Well, Mr. Meehan, a Mr. Horace Sturdley called and said he's got a real problem. The sheriff is at his house now. What happened was this. He ordered a side of beef for his home freezer and it was supposed to cost $142. This morning the delivery came, but they got his order wrong and instead of a side of beef, they delivered a sidecar of beef and they want $22,000. They said if he doesn't pay today the sheriff is going to take all his furniture and foreclose his ranch." Poor dear Barbara was deadly serious as she related this terrible tale.

"Barbara, his *ranch*? Where in God's name is there a ranch in Rockland County? Did he leave his telephone number?"

"Yes, Mr. Meehan, I have the number right here. It's area code 307-555-2187."

"What do you mean 'area code 307'? That's not in Rockland County."

"Oh, yes, Mr. Meehan, he told me his ranch is just outside of Cheyenne, Wyoming."

"For God's sake, Barbara, what is he calling me for?"

"You know I asked him that very question, and he said that he met you once at an Old Fellows barbecue when he was visiting his great aunt in Suffern and you were the only district attorney he knew to call."

"Oh my dear sweet Barbara, don't you know who Mr. Sturdley is?"

"Gee, I never met him, Mr. Meehan."

"Well, Barbara, I'll tell you what I want you to do. Don't call Wyoming. Instead go down to the Public Defender's Office and see Mr. Van

Zandt. Now write this down like you did all the rest. Tell him Mr. Meehan said he should tell his friend Mr. Sturdley to 'Go to hell!'"

That was not the first nor would it be the last absurd complaint call that we would receive from Richard J. Van Zandt, but it is the one I remember best. It meant that Dick was no longer angry with me, that the victory in the court had not in fact lost me my friend.

Chapter 5

Boys' Night Out

When I was growing up in Suffern, my only contact with crime was the radio and the movies. My favorite radio shows were *Gangbusters* and *Mr. District Attorney*, which my brother Tom and I never missed. However it was the movies that made a real impression on me.

The Lafayette Theater in Suffern changed features three times a week, so with rare exceptions, Tom and I went three times a week. It was almost always a double feature and at ten cents admission, both of us saw everything they put on the screen for the hard-to-come-by sum of sixty cents a week. (Between delivering newspapers and working at Paret & Lamouree's Drugstore, we almost always managed to swing it.)

As I look back now at those afternoons and early evenings of the 1930s, I realize that my taste in movies left quite a bit to be desired. I didn't like musicals because dancing and most singing left me cold. I didn't like the Class A comedies of the 1930s because the jokes, frankly, went over my head. Straight romances were just the worst.

We, therefore, headed off to the movies with me saying something like, "Tommy, it's a lousy movie called *The Gay Divorcee* with Fred Astaire and Ginger Rogers, but don't worry there's a *Boston Blackie* with it." It was obvious I loved crime movies, *any* crime movie.

In defense of myself, I will say that Cagney and Bogart and Edward G. Robinson and John Garfield were my favorites. Even then I questioned George Raft's acting credentials. I must add, however, that my taste in later life has evolved. I now will stay up half the night to watch *Shall We Dance* or *It Happened One Night* on the small television in my bedroom.

Crime movies never scared me, so when Robinson and Cagney were wiping out half the male population of New York City in *Little Caesar* and *The Public Enemy*, I enjoyed it immensely. It never occurred to me to be scared; something like that could never happen in Suffern.

I was frightened of one thing though, and that was a prison break. In so many movies, Pat O'Brien played the warden, the chaplain, or a priest on the outside who was a childhood friend of at least one of the inmates. I, of course, liked him; what worried me was George Raft and John Garfield going over the wall and taking some local hostages. Growing up, I wanted to know, how far was the nearest prison from Suffern?

"Bobby, don't you know," my brother Tom would say very seriously. "When we go to visit Aunt Julie or Aunt Kate over in Haverstraw, you can look right across the river at Sing Sing."

"Oh my God, Tommy, you mean if they just swim across the river, they can get us?"

"That's right, Bobby, and remember, it would be easy to steal a car and get right over to Suffern, too!"

Tom was only fifteen months older than I, but he was smarter and much more mature. And he enjoyed pulling my leg. Well, it worked. I generally thought of escaped convicts as a real threat to the Meehans. After all, I had seen enough of them in the movies, swimming away from Alcatraz and Rikers Island. I could easily imagine dangerous convicts breaking out of Sing Sing and swimming across the Hudson. Thank God the Tappan Zee Bridge was still twenty years away.

∽

A little more than a quarter of a century later, I moved into the District Attorney's Office, put up my pictures of John Kennedy, Jim Farley, Nancy, and the kids, and then looked out my window at the beautiful view of the Rockland County Jail. I now worked about five hundred feet away from petty larcenists, drunks, and occasional murderers awaiting trial or sentencing. Happily, the years had somewhat dulled the sharp edge of my fear of prison breaks.

∽

By the spring of 1972 the fear had just about evaporated. After all, I had put almost all the guests in Sheriff Lindemann's hotel. I knew them, and I certainly didn't fear them. The only exception was one particularly notorious convict, but he had long since gone off to state prison to serve a life sentence.

Therefore, when I was called by Police Radio at six o'clock one morning in late June 1972, I took it rather well when I was informed that the morning roll call at the County Jail had come up three short: two bogus check writers and one burglar. I knew all three and the thing that surprised me most was that they would have the nerve to pull a break.

They were Donald Jordan, twenty-six; Peter Wasko, twenty-three; and Joseph Donato, twenty-five. Both Jordan and Wasko were pending trial on Second Degree Forgery. Donato was pending trial on First Degree Burglary, with a detainer lodged by Ohio authorities for Grand Larceny, Auto.

They weren't exactly your desperate criminals in the mold of Bogart's "Duke Mantee" in *The Petrified Forest*, but nevertheless, Lindy and I were anxious to have them back. They also were not exactly jail breakers since they went out the storeroom delivery door in the basement by using the key to the door that they had somehow obtained. Sure enough, the large key was missing from the guardroom, but there had been no violence and no one had the foggiest idea how they got ahold of the key.

All we knew that morning and for two months to follow was that the key was, in fact, missing; the door was, in fact, unlocked; and the boys were certainly missing.

~

The break made big news locally and the press was especially critical of Sheriff Ray Lindemann. I felt bad about that because by 1972, Lindy and I had formed a genuine bond. More than six years of working together had made us good friends.

I suppose it was an unlikely friendship. Lindy is twenty-six years older than me and our basic nature is quite different, if not totally opposite. Ray is very outgoing and regularly—in the company of men and women—uses language that would make a sailor blush. On the other hand, I am generally reserved and never use bad language around women or children. In fact I only really swear in the company of men when I am mad.

It's not that I am a prude, it's just one of the many good lessons my father taught me. My father was a tough guy. He started working in the brickyards on the Hudson when he was twelve years old and at seventeen, he was off to join the infantry at the outbreak of World War I. He worked in the Newburgh Shipyard after the war and was a machinist and welder by the start of World War II. There was no bad language that had not been heard by my father. However I never heard my father say anything worse than "hell" or "damn" in our house and I know that my kids can say the same of me. To put it simply, my father said to Tom and me when we were very young, "If you need to swear to prove you're a man, then you're not really a man!" I never forgot that.

It's strange with that background that Lindy's language never bothered me. He had a disarming way about him that just seemed to make it all right. The fact is that I kind of thought it was amusing. It was not unusual to hear Lindy on a live local radio show, saying something like "Well if that's the case, tell the bastard to go screw himself!" or "Look, I'm the sheriff of this county and no son of a bitch from Albany is going to tell me what to do!" Lindy was colorful, popular, and had a well-deserved reputation for "telling it like it is."

Lindemann's only Achilles heel was the jail. It just seemed that there was one foul-up after another. One serious incident occurred in 1969. A prisoner had been in jail for two days when he died of an overdose of narcotics. The medical examiner ruled that the heroin was injected into his system no more than twelve hours before his death. There was a public outcry with Ray right in the middle of it. How in God's name did the prisoner get the heroin in the jail? Our grand jury investigation never really answered the question.

Then there was a tear gas incident in the summer of 1970. On a hot Sunday afternoon in July, the prisoners became unruly up on the third tier. The guards called in the Sheriff's Road Patrol, but Lindy wasn't home and they couldn't locate him. The long and short of it was that they tear-gassed the prisoners to prevent a possible riot. Well they prevented the riot all right, but boy did they cause trouble!

It seemed that none of them had any experience with tear gas, but a couple of the guards remembered seeing some tear gas canisters on a shelf in the closet of the guard room. So they got them out and let go of the tear gas. One thing they did not do was stop to read the label on the canisters. Like film for a camera, there's an expiration date on the use of tear gas. In the case of the tear gas used in the summer of 1970, the labels read, "Do *Not* Use after October 1, 1953." Further there was a warning, "For External Use Only." And so that afternoon, the tear gas canisters that were at least seventeen years past their expiration dates were fired off *inside* the jail!

The third tier near-riot was quelled and the tier had to be evacuated. So did the second tier and the first tier and the women's quarters and the Guard Room. The whole damned place was unlivable and it wasn't usable again for almost two weeks, and then only after the floors, walls, and ceilings had all been scrubbed down by men wearing gas masks.

We had about eighty prisoners at the time and they ended up being sent to Sing Sing and the Westchester pen at considerable expense to the county. The renewed storm of protest caused another grand jury investigation, which was not to be our last. No one was indicted: we don't have a crime in New York called "Criminal Stupidity." Year after year, the grand jury would hand up what was called a presentment, critical of "the deplorable conditions in our jail." The only extra point added by that grand jury in the fall of 1970 was in essence, "Boys, please, next time read the label!"

~

I'll get back to our "Big Break of '72" in a moment, but I should mention that in the spring of 1973, the prisoners basically won the battle; they set the place on fire and the jail was out of commission for well over a year.

The burning was more than a blessing in disguise. Lindemann finally got the Rockland County Legislature to vote for funds to modernize our 1927 jailhouse. From the day he took office, Lindy had sincerely tried to upgrade the jail with more and better quality jailers, modern equipment, and either a completely new jail or at least a total modernization of the old one. He got slapped down every time, either by the old County Board of Supervisors in the 1960s or the new County Legislature in the early 1970s. After the public outcry died down, all his requests were "tabled" until 1973.

Lindemann was a Republican and so my Democratic friends were, sad to say, somewhat jubilant over his misfortunes. They really thought that their Democratic district attorney should do him in. I wasn't about to. I knew the facts and I was convinced that it was up to the electorate to decide whether we needed a new sheriff.

My public support of Lindemann was a thorn in the side of many of my Democratic supporters who became *former* supporters over the jail issue. They said I was only protecting my "buddy" Lindemann. They were wrong. I thought Lindemann was a good and decent sheriff.

My criteria for public officials are divided into three main points, *and* in this order: first, the official must be honest; second, the official must work hard; and third, and definitely last, he or she must be professionally competent. Think about it for a minute. If a person is highly competent but is lazy, he will probably do a second rate job. If he is highly competent, works hard, but is dishonest, all is lost for the public. On the other hand, if he's totally honest and works very hard at his job, he will probably develop professional competence, if in no other way than through on-the-job training.

Ray Lindemann is honest, works very hard, and was a totally competent investigator and police officer. If his competence as a prison administrator left something to be desired, let the public make the judgment in a voting booth, not the DA in a Grand Jury Room. As it is well known in Rockland County, I went after public officials I deemed to be corrupt in my years as a district attorney, both Democrats and Republicans. Although every DA is accused of it, it was never political; it never had anything to do with their competence or their work habits. I only asked one question, "Were they dishonest and violators of the public trust?"

∿

So in that early summer of 1972 before I left on vacation, I sat down and had a long talk with Lindy. He was feeling pretty low and was uncharacteristically subdued. It ended up with me trying to cheer him up, but it was difficult. He even got to talking about the nine-year-old son he had lost in a drowning accident more than a third of a century before and how as a young police officer, he had been called to respond to the tragedy in Nanuet.

I suppose the story of the loss of the boy, which I already knew about but had never discussed personally with Lindy, made me feel closer to him. Thank God I have never suffered such a loss, but this worst of tragedies has been around me all of my life. Starting with the sudden death of my cousin, Joey Blaney, when I was nine and he was twelve, I have known so many close friends that suffered through such a loss that I consider it a real fear.

But the substance of our talk that day was the return of the prisoners, which was our top priority. "Don't worry," I said to Ray, "we'll get them back sooner or later."

"Yeah, Bob, we'll catch them. But the thing that burns me is that I treated those bastards like gentlemen, and then they go and fuck us up like this."

It was true, Lindemann did treat them like gentleman; he did the same for all his prisoners. However, at the same time he was being nice to the prisoners, he was likely to tell the chairman of the county legislature or the state commissioner of corrections, "Go fuck yourself!" But that was Lindemann through and through.

~

In mid-July, Nancy and I and our six kids left for a once-in-a lifetime cross-country vacation with our trailer. It was the time to go. Patty was sixteen and young enough to still want to go and Bobby was six and old enough to remember the trip all his life.

When I left the DA's Office for the trip with my new chief assistant, Herman Van der Linde, in charge, there were of course some loose ends—including three loose prisoners.

It was a wonderful trip, one of those very rare vacations that was even better than you thought it would be. My only contact with the District Attorney's Office was a daily telephone call to Herman or Ann Hickey. I had full faith in both of them, but I just had to know how things were going. The DA's Office was a lot more than a job; it was a way of life.

So as we crossed the Northern Great Plains with a stop in Rochester, Minnesota, to see our former Cherry Lane neighbors, the Wassinks, I faithfully made the daily calls and always asked for our missing friends, but there was no news to report. Over the Rockies, over the Cascades to the Pacific, and a visit to Nancy's brother, Alan, in Cathlamet, Washington, still nothing. South 1,300 miles to San Diego and the United States Navy chapel where Nancy and I were married, then turning east to visit the Grand Canyon, across the Great Southwest and on to visit my sister, Marilyn, and her family in Memphis, Tennessee; still no news of Jordan, Wasko, and Donato.

Three days from home and camped twenty-five miles south of Louisville, Kentucky, I made my usual call to the office.

"Boss," Annie began, "I've got good news and bad news to report on our desperados. Good news, all three were picked up in Columbus, Ohio; bad news, they let Donato go and he's back among the missing."

I later learned that the three had been riding in the back of a pickup truck when the driver was stopped by the Columbus police for drunken driving. Jordan and Wasko refused to even give their names to the police and so they were taken in with the drunken truck driver. Donato, on the other hand, was polite, courteous, and gave his correct name so they let him go.

The crazy thing is that when they got back to the police station and finally learned Jordan and Wasko's names, they found that not only were all three wanted in Rockland County, New York, on escape charges but that there was a warrant on Donato for auto theft charges out of Columbus, Ohio—their own warrant! It was embarrassing for them, but not nearly as embarrassing as the case would prove to be to Rockland County.

~

When I got back to the office the following Monday, Ed McElroy related the bizarre tale to me that had been told to him by a Columbus detective. Based on that, I told Ed that I wanted to see Jordan and Wasko as soon as they were returned to Rockland County.

Two days later, Jordan and Wasko were sitting in my office with Arnold Becker, who had been Jordan's lawyer on the forgery case. Jordan spoke for the pair and told their story after Becker had obtained certain legal concessions from me.

When the pair were first arrested and jailed in May, one of the first inmates they got to know was Joe Donato. Joe told him that he was friendly with a guard by the name of John Cruz. They both met Cruz and he seemed friendly and would get cigarettes and candy for them, sometimes with his own money. They were impressed that Cruz seemed to genuinely like the prisoners. This was nice but nothing really out of the ordinary, and nothing important happened until they had been in jail about a week.

Then Jordan reported that one night Donato came to them and said, "How would you guys like to go out for a few beers?" They thought he was kidding and joked about it, but Donato said he was serious. "Look, I go out at least once a week for a few cold ones. My buddy, John Cruz, will let us out."

Still unbelieving, Jordan and Wasko headed down to the basement kitchen with Donato for cleanup detail that evening. An hour later they were sitting in the New City Pub, sipping beer, eating pretzels, and generally passing an early summer's evening.

They reported that John Cruz had given them the large key to the storeroom door with instructions to lock the door behind them and to be back by midnight. Cinderella was alive and well in Rockland County.

Jordan went on to say that this procedure had repeated itself on two or three more occasions before the night of the "Great Escape." They explained that they wore their prison dungarees and casual shirts that Cruz lent them and walked about three hundred yards from the jail to the back door of the New City Pub.

The pub has a back entrance from the parking lot and we were able to later verify that the three were getting to be "regulars" at the pub. We also had no reason to doubt the bartender who was surprised to learn that his reasonably well-mannered new clientele were, in fact, on a "Boys' Night Out" from the Rockland County Jail.

Now to the night in question. Like many a bar patron before them who was supposed to be home by a certain witching hour, they had had a few too many. Twelve o'clock came and went and they would just have one more for the road. By 2 a.m. Jordan and Wasko said they were really urging Donato to go back, but he decided to telephone his girlfriend in West Nyack instead. The long and short of it was that they would all go to visit her but they must have a car to get there. Donato finally cajoled Wasko into calling his mother in Stony Point to see whether they could borrow her car.

As it was related to me, both that morning and two days later by Mrs. Wasko, Pete Wasko did in fact call his mother. She did not initially believe his story, "Don't kid me, Sonny" (she always called him "Sonny"). "You're calling from the jail."

"No, Ma, honest. I'm in the pub. Come on down." And so dear Mrs. Wasko got dressed and drove down to the New City Pub, arriving just before three o'clock in the morning.

As she told it, "I pulled into the parking lot and I couldn't believe my eyes. There was Sonny with two of his friends. I said, 'Sonny, you get right back in that jail or I'll tell the sheriff on you.'"

I was very hard-pressed to keep a straight face as this kind, plumpish, motherly figure told me the story of her disobedient little boy.

The three escaped cons would now have no part of going back to the jail. "It's too late, we'll get in trouble." Mrs. Wasko refused to drive them to West Nyack, but she did allow them to drive her back to Stony Point and then take the car. She said goodbye to Sonny and the others as they drove off from Stony Point, leaving her with no car, but a memento of the evening, the key to the storage room door of the Rockland County Jail. Her instructions were to give it back to John Cruz the next day, "so he won't get in trouble."

Fearing that she would get in trouble herself, Mrs. Wasko did not follow through with Sonny's request to return the key. Instead, the next morning she walked down by the Penny Bridge in Stony Point that crosses an inlet of the Hudson River, and threw the large key right into the river. The morning we first questioned Mrs. Wasko about what she did with the key we contacted the Piermont Underwater Rescue team headed by Sergeant Joe Mercurio of the Clarkstown Police Department. I told Joe the basic story and arranged to have Ed McElroy take Mrs. Wasko to meet him and his men at the Penny Bridge that afternoon. Joe had told me he'd make a try but, "Hey Bob, that's a pretty muddy bottom. I don't care how big the goddamn key is, finding it will be a long shot."

About 4:30 that afternoon Joe Mercurio walked into my office with a big grin on his face, holding the large key in his hand. Mrs. Wasko had pointed to the approximate spot where she threw the key in the water. Joe, himself, dove in with his scuba diving gear and on his very first pass came up with the key. Our luck was running well.

I was particularly happy that Joe was able to help us because along with being a police officer I admired and respected, he is Ann Hickey's brother and a personal friend of mine. "Joe, I don't know what it is with you Mercurios, but any time I need help, you're always there!" How true it was; Ann, her two sisters, and her three brothers would always do you a favor, but most important, they wanted absolutely nothing in return.

Jordan and Wasko completed their story, telling of leaving the car in New York City, taking a bus to Ohio with Donato, and bumming around at different odd jobs until the night they had the misfortune of hitching a ride with a drunken truck driver.

~

I now had a difficult legal decision to make. Could we prove a crime against the jailer, John Cruz? Jordan and Wasko had told what we believed to be a truthful story. It was just too absurd to have been manufactured. Plus the totally believable Mrs. Wasko supported the story right down the line and we did find the key exactly where she said we would. Most important, Donato, Jordan, and Wasko did somehow get out of jail.

What was the difficult decision then? It seemed on the surface to be airtight. It wasn't. First, what specific crime did John Cruz commit? It couldn't be aiding or abetting an escape and he couldn't be an accessory before the fact; there are no such crimes in the state of New York. In New York, everyone charged is a principal. For instance, five men are in on a bank robbery; one plans the job, a second drives the getaway car, a third sits in a lookout car, and the fourth and fifth are the only ones who actually enter the bank—all are charged with "acting in concert to commit the crime of Robbery in the First Degree."

Therefore, although John Cruz was not even a prisoner, he would need to be charged with the crime of Escape in the First Degree. Second, and far more legally critical, was the damnable New York criminal law rule on "Corroboration of Accomplice." Many think of this as a technical legal point to be discussed among legal scholars in law schools, but to me it was a bread and butter issue.

When I was president of the New York State District Attorneys Association in 1970 and 1971, my two top priorities were to have the New York State Legislature abolish the rule of corroboration in rape cases and corroboration of accomplices. Both were artificial rules that said, in effect, the jury as a matter of law was not allowed to believe certain types of witnesses—worst of all women who had been defiled.

More about the rape cases later, but I fought in vain to get the accomplice rule changed so that it would be the same as the federal rule in the United States District Courts. Strangely enough, I not only failed to garner much support from even the law and order type legislators, but I also had trouble with my brother district attorneys, who apparently hadn't had the problems with the rule that I had, or at least weren't aware of the problem.

I obviously knew the need for some type of accomplice rule. Otherwise when "thieves fall out" they could easily implicate each other in crimes they had no part of. But in a nutshell, the federal rule said to juries, "Look hard at the testimony of accomplices, consider strongly their motive to lie; does their story make sense? And if, after that, you still believe the accomplice beyond a reasonable doubt, you may convict on the word of the accomplice."

A good rule; without it, many famous cases would not even have resulted in indictments. One that comes to mind is the case in federal court in New Jersey where the former mayor of Newark was convicted of bribery on the word of a host of contractors who gave bribes and the city officials who received the bribes allegedly for the mayor. Everyone involved was an "accomplice" in the eyes of the law.

A bad law, the New York rule: "A defendant may not be convicted of any offense upon the testimony of an accomplice unsupported by corroborative evidence tending to connect the defendant with the commission of such offense." This was a rule that haunted me in my nine years in the District Attorney's Office.

A murderer acquitted after a jury heard an accomplice say that he had personally witnessed the defendant choke the life out of a victim with a stocking. A public official acquitted after a contractor told of four meetings with the official to arrange a $20,000 bribe that was actually paid to an intermediary. And a score of other serious cases that never resulted in indictments because we couldn't get by the archaic New York "accomplice rule."

The morning after the not guilty verdict in the stocking murder case, a juror came to me in tears and said, "But, Mr. Meehan, we had no choice. No one put him at the scene but the accomplice." The juror was right, the verdict was right, the law is wrong.

$\sim$

Now, how did the accomplice rule affect the case of our wayward prisoners? Let's look at the facts against John Cruz. First, Jordan and Wasko obviously put him right in the middle of a crime, but they are accomplices. Secondly, the bartender corroborates that they did in fact frequent the New City Pub, but he himself had no evidence to connect Cruz. Third, Mrs. Wasko certainly corroborates their story about going to the pub and taking off in her car, but again all she could tell of the involvement of Cruz was what "Sonny" and the boys told her. Fourth, the key—Exhibit 1 for the prosecution—but again, how does the key itself involve Cruz without the testimony of Jordan and Wasko? It doesn't.

We, therefore, proceeded as I believe any intellectually honest prosecutor would, given a case where we were morally certain of the accomplice's story. Try to find, without manufacturing it, the necessary corroborative evidence. To do this we tried to establish three things: first, that under no circumstances would Donato, Jordan, and Wasko or any other prisoner have had access to the key cabinet in the guard room. Second, that the key was actually kept in the cabinet at all times when not in use. And third, that John Cruz did have access to the cabinet at the time in question, and by the process of elimination, the other three guards on duty at the time did not in fact surrender the key to anyone.

Again, unlike our friends of the 60- or 120-minute television dramas, this was far from easy to establish. We had a myriad of potential answers.

"Well, the trustees were in and out of there all the time."

"No, I don't remember the last time I saw the storage room key before that night."

"The cabinet was supposed to be locked at all time but sometimes it wasn't."

"Maybe a trustee took it and gave it to Donato."

The only thing certain was that all of the other guards on duty denied giving the key to anyone and all said Cruz was friendly with the prisoners; further, that Cruz was in the guard room alone at times during the shift when the boys took a walk, and that Cruz was in charge of the cleanup crew in the kitchen that evening.

With this thin corroboration, a week later we went to the grand jury and they indicted. A few months later we won a major legal battle. The judge on pretrial motions did not dismiss. In substance, the judge said, "It's a close question of sufficient corroboration, but let the jury decide." We now felt we had a fighting chance with the trial jury.

Don't get me wrong, I had no vendetta against Cruz. On the contrary, I felt kind of sorry for him if, in fact, the boys' story was true. Most modern penologists would say he was ahead of his time. In a business that by its very nature attracts something less than the best of society, it was refreshing to find a man who genuinely cared for the prisoners. I also felt that Cruz must have had a hell of a sense of humor.

It wasn't Cruz, it was the principle of the thing. The law in New York might provide for work release programs, but not for a "Boys' Night Out." And, if we were going to fight the long battle on the corroboration rule, let's do it in a case that wasn't a matter of life or death.

∾

With Donato still missing, we went forward to trial relying heavily on the believability of our boys, Jordan and Wasko. They were both given immunity on the escape charges and reduced one-year sentences after they pled guilty on their forgery cases. All in return for their cooperation and testimony against John Cruz.

The case was a minor sensation in Rockland County. I'll always remember that fall of 1972 when Sheriff Lindemann was running for reelection. His Democratic opponent, Jack Shea, had paid commercials on the local radio station and they always ended with, "Sheriff, it's ten o'clock. Do you know where your prisoners are?" The radio ads were three things: unwarranted—it wasn't Lindy's fault; funny, no question about that; and very effective. Lindemann, a clear favorite, damn near lost the election.

After more legal snags, the case finally went to trial in early May of 1973. The local press loved it and the jury seemed to be genuinely amused. They liked Jordan and Wasko, and they especially liked Wasko's mother.

After Judge Ted Kelly's tough but fair charge on the need for corroboration, the case went to the jury early on a Wednesday afternoon. By 1:30 a.m. when they still hadn't reached a verdict, Judge Kelly locked them up for the night to continue deliberations the next morning.

I didn't personally try the case but I was there until the jury was sent out. I said to the trial assistant DA, Werner Loeb, "Hell, Werner, with this kind of corroboration you've done some kind of job just to get them to deliberate this long." At about 2 a.m., I headed home into the foggy night. For me, the night was to prove far more memorable than the verdict the next day, but more of that later.

The jury was back with a verdict at about one o'clock the next afternoon—"not guilty." There would be no appeal to renew the test of the corroboration rule; an acquittal, of course, cannot be appealed.

~

Like every other prosecutor worth his salt, I don't like to see a man suffer the disgrace of indictment if he is to be ultimately found not guilty by a jury of his peers, but unlike many of my fellow prosecutors, I was not afraid to lose. After all, if a prosecutor only went with sure things, he could win all of his cases and we could forget all about defense attorneys, juries, and trial judges and just say, "If you say so, Mr. Prosecutor, it must be so."

Unfortunately, there are district attorneys who take this view—they want to develop a halo of infallibility. Watch out for them. These prosecutors do not share the strong belief that public confidence will be served by an open trial and a decision by a jury of average citizens. I actually had the district attorney of another New York county say to me back in the 1960s, "Bob, I have a golden rule. Never indict white-collar criminals or politicians. All you can do is buy yourself grief. The public screams for an indictment, expects a conviction, but cheers for an acquittal and blames you." It is my personal belief that the people of his county were not getting their money's worth.

A new district attorney who is looking for only winners is easy to spot. Don't check his win–loss record, he's ensured that it will be in his favor. Simply check one statistic—the total number of indictments in a year. If it's down 20 or 25 percent in a year, there's a problem. He's throwing out every tough case and guilty people are going free to preserve his record. A fighter he is not.

~

I never did win the corroboration fight in my nine years as a district attorney, but I don't regret the fight. However, I'll always consider the change in the rape corroboration rule, which had its first breakthrough in the State Legislature when I was president of the DA's Association, one of the major accomplishments of my years as DA. There was great fanfare by the women's groups in 1974 when the rule was finally abolished altogether in New York. But the lonely battle, before the issue was popular, was won in 1971 when the law was changed so that the testimony of the rape victim alone was sufficient to establish the identity of the perpetrator.

I like to think that a true story that I told two committees of the New York Senate and Assembly in the spring of 1971 started the wheels in motion to change that baseless, unfair rule. A seventeen-year-old girl was hitchhiking and was picked up by a twenty-six-year-old man on a motorcycle. He rode her off the road and into the woods, where he pulled a knife, made her strip, stripped himself, and proceeded in broad daylight to rape and sodomize her for almost five hours. When he left the ravaged girl and rode away on his cycle, she staggered back to the highway and immediately reported her attack to the police. Evidence of recent intercourse and her black and blue body were ample evidence of a vicious attack. She described the perpetrator in minute detail, right down to his appendectomy scar and another large scar on the front of his right thigh. After all they had been naked together in daylight for all those hours.

A man with a sex crime record was picked up in Passaic, New Jersey, and he fit the description right down to the two scars. The victim, without hesitation, picked him out of a carefully prepared and legally correct lineup. The result? Not even an indictment.

There was no choice, the man had to be turned free. Why? Because no one else had seen him come or go that day, the only one who could establish his identity was the victim, and the laws of the state of New York in the summer of 1970 said that as a matter of law the testimony of the victim alone was not enough to prove that the crime of rape had occurred.

So a law devised and theorized by politicians and legal scholars, out of touch with reality, finally bit the dust in June 1971. Common sense prevailed. If a woman was trying to do in her ex-lover with a bogus rape charge, we have to hope that a jury would see through it. But there would be no more artificial rules. Now a woman could report a rape the same way she can report that her purse was snatched, and be believed and not thwarted by the law.

The day, too, will come for the absurd accomplice rule. I hope it doesn't take a multiple murder to prove the point. I hope I am alive to see it.[1]

The DA's Office no longer overlooks the county jail, but I'm glad to report that the renovation work has been completed and it is a better and safer place to house prisoners.

Donato was finally picked up in St. Louis in late 1973 and is doing three to ten in state prison. By the way, he also said Cruz let him out—but just another accomplice.

Lindy is still sheriff. He was reelected in 1975 but only by about six hundred votes. At seventy-one, it looks like the last time around for the fiery old sheriff, but if he does go out in 1978, he can look back at forty-six years in law enforcement with his head held high. He sure as hell did "tell it like it is."

---

1. See the notes section, p. 239.

Chapter 6

A Man's Home Is His Castle

One thing the Meehans always had, in good times and bad, was a dog. Life in the thirties in Suffern was lean, and so too were our dogs. There was never the expense of buying dog food; no dog of ours ever ate dog food. He ate leftovers from our house or the neighbors and they were all marvelously healthy dogs.

If I live to be ninety-five, the dog I will remember most was a mongrel fox terrier by the name of "Fitz." Now that was not his correct name. My dad had insisted that all our dogs be named for members of the Brooklyn Dodgers. In that summer of 1940, it was only appropriate that our new puppy would be named "Fat Freddie Fitzsimmons," after the former Giant, turned Dodger ace pitcher, who that year compiled an enviable 16 to 2 win-loss record. That was the season when our doormat Dodgers finally came alive and made a run at the Cincinnati Reds, only to fade in September.

I broke my leg that summer and spent most of July and August on crutches, but the surging Dodgers were my salvation. We were still a decade away from watching them on television, but Leo Durocher's men—brought to us by the radio voice of Red Barber—were our heart's delight. My favorite was the rookie, Harold "Pee Wee" Reese. I can well remember sitting listening to our Dodgers on a Saturday afternoon in late summer when my father walked in the house and plunked a four-week-old puppy, to be known as "Fitz," on my lap. *That* was my father. Whoever was hurt, whoever needed help, that was the special favorite, and so it was *Bobby* who needed a lift in the summer of 1940, and what greater lift for a ten-year-old than a new dog.

We only had my father for a little more than five years from that day, but "Fitz" was with us for seventeen years. Twice, first in 1943 and then again in 1946, Fitz was hit and hit hard by cars and we thought we had lost him. The first time in 1943, I remember carrying the bloodied Fitzsimmons from school to Suffern's wonderful old veterinarian, Dr. Harold Sherwood.

Dr. Sherwood's office was only a few hundred yards from the school and all of us revered the man. He was probably past sixty by then and to me, an old man; but he was a wonderful old man. Although he could be crusty, he had such a feeling for animals and small children that he truly came across as a saint.

In our little corner of the world, the word *veterinarian* and Dr. Sherwood were synonymous, so it's no wonder that I grew up with an admiration for veterinarians that had no bounds. It is, therefore, ironic that more than a quarter of a century later, my most memorable murder case involved a defendant who was probably the most popular veterinarian in Rockland County.

~

It was mid-May 1967, and Nancy and I were spending our first evening with Ed and Ruth McElroy at the Elks Club in Haverstraw. By 11:30, Ed and I had left the girls behind and were speeding south toward Palisades—Ed heading for his first murder scene as chief investigator for the District Attorney's Office, and I, a seasoned veteran of seventeen months, facing my sixth.

When we pulled into the long two-hundred-yard driveway of Dr. Malcolm Sheffield, it was truly an eerie scene. The victim had already been removed by ambulance to Nyack Hospital with a four-inch hole in the left side of his skull, caused by a shotgun blast. The scene was illuminated by the flashing lights of three Orangetown police cars, as well as fire emergency arc lights.

A Volkswagen Microbus was sitting along the side of a barn with the rear smashed directly into a large dog kennel. The bus was covered with blood both inside and out and the glass in the driver's door window was shattered. In the middle of the stone driveway was a shotgun lying among minute fragments of glass in an area that was only then being roped off under the glare of artificial light.

When Ed and I got out of the car, the first person I spoke to was Detective Sergeant George Barnes of the Orangetown Police Department. Before he opened his mouth, I already felt better. I knew the case was being handled by the best the department had to offer; for that matter, one of the top three or four police officers I've ever known. George was a few years younger than me and actually looks a lot like me, although a little thinner, with an even more hawkish face. He got right to the point.

It seems that the forty-three-year-old Dr. Sheffield was divorced from his wife and had been seeing a thirty-six-year-old woman by the name of Pat Kelly who worked at his animal hospital. About a month earlier, Pat left him and took up with a twenty-one-year-old animal attendant by the name of Peter Hanlon.

Pat and Pete were living together at Pat's apartment, just over two miles from Dr. Sheffield's house. At about eleven o'clock, Dr. Sheffield called and asked Pat to come over for a drink. She refused; he became belligerent. Peter Hanlon then took the phone and had a verbal fight with Dr. Sheffield that ended with Hanlon saying to Sheffield, "All right, you son of a bitch, I'm coming over to kill you." George had learned all of this from the hysterical Pat Kelly.

"OK, George, where is Pat and where's the doctor?"

"She's down at the station, Mr. Meehan. We had to get her out of here. She was throwing handfuls of the goddamn gravel at Sheffield."

"Where's the Doc?"

"He's in the house, but you can't talk to him. He's got his lawyer, Jerry Tobias, with him."

"For Christ's sake, George, how the hell did he get a lawyer here so fast?"

"Mr. Meehan, looks to me like the first person he called was his lawyer."

This was later to prove of some significance. A trained medical man, a mortally wounded subject, and the first person he called was a lawyer!

I went into the house and talked to Jerry Tobias who I knew and liked rather well.

"Bob, my man wants to cooperate all he can. The thing was an accident, pure and simple, but let's wait until he calms down before you question him." I agreed and no formal arrest was made.

Pictures and exact measurements were taken by both the Orangetown Police Department and John Slater's men from the Sheriff's Office.

I, of course, sensed we had a difficult case on our hands and I wanted the scene protected and worked over to the last detail. It was, and those details later became the heart of the case.

~

About an hour later, I left Dr. Sheffield's home and went to Nyack Hospital where I viewed the body of Peter Hanlon. There was a horrible gaping wound on the left side of his skull and the left side of his face was burned black in an upward trajectory from the chin caused by a firing at very close range. The upward trajectory of the shot would also prove of vital importance.

We then proceeded to Orangetown Police headquarters where I first met Pat Kelly in the squad room. She was a very small woman, not much taller than Nancy, and rather attractive, although she was obviously not looking her best with eyes puffy and red from crying.

By the time I got there she was over her hysterics, although she did a lot more crying that night. She was totally cooperative with us, in fact too cooperative. It was obvious she was out to do in Dr. Sheffield.

With her permission, we tape-recorded an interview that lasted about an hour. She freely admitted that she had been Dr. Sheffield's mistress for almost two years and that, although she still worked at his animal hospital, she had broken off with him personally about six weeks before. She also unhesitatingly told us that she was the cause of the breakup of Dr. Sheffield's marriage.

Pat told of meeting Pete Hanlon at the animal hospital and taking him under her wing in a rather motherly fashion. Although she and Pete had been sharing the same apartment for over a month, she flatly denied any sexual relations with him and said that he was like another son to her. Pat had two teenage sons by a marriage that had ended in divorce before she met Dr. Sheffield.

She painted a picture of Dr. Sheffield as a belligerent, mean, antagonistic, and brutal man who had become enraged with jealousy over allegations that she was having an affair with Hanlon. At the same time she depicted Pete Hanlon as a quiet, gentle, loving boy who would never harm anyone. She was sure that vicious Dr. Sheffield had brutally murdered the innocent boy.

There were problems with her story—plenty of them. Besides the obvious hostility toward Dr. Sheffield, we couldn't be the least bit sure that the romance breakup hadn't been the other way around and that she wasn't the classic "woman scorned."

Add to that we were faced with the facts that this "vicious" Dr. Sheffield was forty-three years old; five feet, six inches tall; about 140 pounds; and a professional man who was highly regarded in the community. Further, he had won medals for bravery, serving in the US Air Force during World War II, and had never had any trouble whatsoever with the law.

On the other side of the coin, the "gentle, innocent," twenty-one-year-old Pete Hanlon was six feet, two inches; pushing two hundred pounds; and in and out of trouble with the law since he was sixteen, the most serious case being the sale of narcotics. I was beginning to realize after a year and a half in the District Attorney's Office that teenage peddlers of marijuana were not exactly the black hearts they were depicted to be, but I also was well aware of the public perception of them and I knew it could make things complicated if we were to go forward with a homicide case.

The critical telephone call that set the events in motion was also not helpful. We knew she would be slanting things against Dr. Sheffield and she did talk about him calling her "a fucking little whore" when she refused his invitation to go over to his house. But the long and short of it was, although he used foul language and made disgusting sexual accusations against her, he never threatened her or Pete Hanlon while she was on the phone.

After Pete grabbed the phone, she could, of course, no longer hear Dr. Sheffield's end of the conversation, but she did relate the last thing Pete said: "Why you son of a bitch. I'm coming over there and kill you." Pat then said Pete ran out the door, jumped in her Volkswagen bus, and took off for Sheffield's house at high speed before she could stop him. She did, however, report one more call. Pat said that about five minutes after Pete left, the phone rang; she answered and Dr. Sheffield said, "I just killed your boyfriend." As she started to exclaim that he was only trying to scare her, Dr. Sheffield hung up. When she tried to call him right back, the line was busy and there were no more phone calls.

~

At about two o'clock in the morning after completing our questioning of Pat, we proceeded to interview Dr. Malcolm Sheffield. The ground rules set by his lawyer, Tobias, was that there would be no tape-recording and that he would be present at all times and might direct his client not to answer certain questions.

Present to question the doctor were George Barnes, Ed McElroy, and myself. (I had not yet set my rule of later years to never personally question witnesses, and to leave the job to trained investigators.)

Dr. Sheffield was a nice-looking man, clean-cut, short but in good shape, with particularly rugged looking arms for a man of his size. He was calm, soft-spoken, and rather likable. I was keenly aware that he was the only one alive who had been in the driveway that night. His two sons were with their mother and he was home alone. Therefore, we were now going to get the only first-person account of what happened. I expected a certain story and I was ready to believe it—that was *not* the story he told.

George began, "OK, Doc, tell us what happened, from the top. Begin with where you were and what you were doing before the trouble started last night."

"All right. I was home by myself. I left the animal hospital at about eight o'clock and went directly home. I made dinner for myself, watched TV, and looked at the newspaper. About eleven o'clock, I decided to have a drink so I called Pat to see if she wanted to come over for a drink. Hell, I was nice as pie to her, but right off the bat she was mad. She said I only called her when I wanted a "piece of ass" and stuff like that. I said, 'Forget the whole thing, forget I called,' but she persisted and with her foul little tongue she really went after me. Next thing I know, Pete gets on the phone and starts giving me more lip and ends up telling me he's coming over to kill me."

At this point, George Barnes interrupted to ask a few questions.

"Was Pat your former mistress?"

"Hell, no."

"Well did you ever live together with her or have sexual relations?"

"We never lived together, but she did spend a few nights with me. Hell, it was OK, we're both divorced."

"Did you call her 'a whore' on the phone?"

"I don't know, maybe I did, but she is a little whore."

"OK, Doc, go on. What happened then?"

"It was just a few minutes later, I hear the screeching of tires and here comes Pat's Volks traveling down my driveway. Well, I don't mind telling you, I was scared. I keep a shotgun in the front closet to scare away animals that might come after mine, so I grabbed the gun and picked up two shells, stuck one in the chamber, and went out the front door. The Volks came to a screeching stop at the end of the driveway by my front walk. I went out with a shotgun in my hand and over toward the driver's side of the bus. It was dark in the Volkswagen but I could see Pete Hanlon behind the wheel. I yelled something like, 'Get the hell out of here' but I wasn't pointing the gun at him. He paid no attention, and he flung open the driver's door and started to get out, but the door hit the muzzle of my shotgun and jerked the gun causing it to accidentally go off. It was an accident. I definitely did not mean to pull the trigger. The door hitting it caused it to go off."

"OK, what happened then?"

"I could see he was hit in the head and hurt bad and I immediately tried to stop the bleeding but seeing that it was impossible, I ran into the house and first called the police, then I called Dr. Fletcher, and then I went back out to try to help Pete."

"Doc, did you make any other calls at that time?"

"No."

"Didn't you call Mr. Tobias?"

"No, I didn't call him until about twenty minutes later."

"Didn't you call Pat?"

"No, I don't think I did."

"Well, what happened next?"

"You know the rest of the story. The police were there within a couple of minutes and that's it. An ambulance came in about fifteen minutes and took Pete away and I guess there's nothing more to tell."

"Well didn't the Volks roll back along the side of the barn and into the doghouse?"

"Yes, I guess it did."

"Where was Hanlon when this was happening?"

"He was half in, half hanging out of the Volks."

"Did you get in and back up the Volks yourself?"

"No, absolutely not."

∾

That was the most important answer and the most incriminating of the entire session. A lot more questions and answers were covered before we quit almost two hours later but Sheffield's main contention never varied.

The shotgun blast was an accident, an accident caused not by Sheffield, but by Hanlon throwing open the door. The defense was "accident."

All deaths can be classified as natural, accidental, suicidal, or homicidal. In rare occasions we become interested in accidental deaths caused by "criminal negligence." However, by and large as district attorney I was really only interested in the last type—homicidal.

Within the homicidal category there are still many legitimate defenses, of course, the most common being "self-defense." But this case had another classic defense—I had hoped that Dr. Sheffield's story would be a combination of self-defense and the ancient English common-law theory that "a man's home is his castle."

Ed McElroy, George Barnes, and I then went back to the captain's office to talk over what we had.

"Damn him," I said. "With that fluky accident story, he gives me nothing to hang my hat on. It just makes him sound guilty.

"As God is my witness, if he just said something like 'Look boys, I'm forty-three years old. I weigh 140 pounds soaking wet. This twenty-one-year-old, 200-pound narcotics pusher called me up and said he's coming over to kill me. Sure enough, he comes speeding onto my property in the middle of the night. Hell, I don't know if he's got a gun or blackjack or crowbar in that bus. All I know is that he's half my age and twice my size and coming at me so I defended myself and my property at night. I'm sorry he's dead but it was his own fault.' If Sheffield had said that, he would've been up and out of here an hour ago. Don't you see, it's "A man's home is his castle!""

~

The people of our county had a right to expect their district attorney to give equal justice to all. If I wasn't going to charge a professional man like Dr. Sheffield, I damn well had better have a good reason, but he didn't give me one.

The case of Dr. Sheffield went on for five years with thousands of pages of transcripts in courts at all levels, but there was never a word about a man's home being his castle. When the doctor hired the distinguished criminal lawyer Maurice Edelbaum to defend him three weeks later, I was certain they would switch the theory of defense, but they never did. On the contrary, they hired experts to prove the "accident" theory and locked that in as the centerpiece of their defense. The jury, very correctly, had to be instructed to decide the case on the accident theory.

Now, of course it was not the obligation of the defense to prove that it was an accident. On the contrary, it was our burden to prove beyond a reasonable doubt and to a moral certainty that it was not an accident.

~

On my orders, Dr. Malcolm Sheffield was formally charged with First-Degree Murder at six o'clock that morning. It was my opinion that we could sustain the burden of proof, even without an eyewitness. Without going through thousands of pages, our incontrovertible physical facts were as follows:

First, the Volkswagen, with a standard transmission, must have been in reverse gear at the instant of the shot. This requires the voluntary acts of depressing the clutch and shifting the gear, acts that could not have been voluntarily performed by a man with Hanlon's injury. The unmistakable conclusion—the Volks was *already* in reverse gear and backed up when Hanlon's body went limp and his foot eased off the clutch.

Second, a person wouldn't be getting out of a vehicle on the left side with his left foot depressed on the clutch.

Third, if the driver's door had been open, the door would have been taken off as it rolled backward so close alongside the barn that it scraped the side of the car.

Fourth, all but minute particles of the glass were on the floor *inside* the microbus. If the door had been open, a lot of the shattered glass would have been in the driveway at the point of the shot. As McElroy explained—and later verified by an expert—the minute particles could be caused by "back blast."

Fifth, the largest pool of blood was in the passenger seat beside where the driver would sit, indicating the boy's body had been blasted over in that direction by the force of the almost point-blank shot.

Sixth, the metal strip between the regular door window and the vent had a dent in it to show almost the exact point of entry and the overhead above the driver's seat showed where the mass of the shot came to rest. We knew the victim's head had to be between the two, thus well within the vehicle. (It was more than a year later we thought of another obvious geometric fact that we had overlooked. It was to prove vital to our case.)

Seventh, if you push the muzzle of a rifle or shotgun back toward the man holding it, it wouldn't cause the trigger finger to tighten; on the contrary, it would cause an easing of pressure and we were able to show this was not a *hair* trigger.

In the next year, more time and effort were spent on measurements and diagrams and pictures, including aerial photos of the scene, than on any other case I had ever handled.

Ed McElroy and George Barnes jointly ran the investigation and they were also present, as required by law, when the defense experts spent days testing the shotgun and the Volkswagen Microbus, which had been impounded on orders of Judge Mort Silberman. When the Volks was impounded, it did have the scrapes on the left side and some rear-end damage where it hit the kennel. But it was less than a year old and reasonably valuable. When the order of impounding was finally rescinded in 1972, it was a six-year-old piece of junk, the loser being the bank that financed it for Pat Kelly.

~

There was one terribly significant fact later discovered in reference to the Volkswagen, but unfortunately for us, it was discovered too late and as the case developed we were never able to use it.

When the Volks was first impounded that night and in the days that immediately followed, our men treated it like a piece of fragile crystal. They didn't want to disturb anything in the front seat, or the location of the blood or glass, until we were sure we had all the pictures and tests done that we needed. Therefore although the critical driver's side door was opened and closed on many occasions, and many tests were done inside the Volks, no one had actually gotten into the vehicle, sat in the driver's seat, and closed the door behind them.

About three weeks after the killing in early June, Ed McElroy and George Barnes went down to the garage where the Volkswagen was first impounded. They had already been over the bus time and again, but this time they decide to try to reenact the crime the way Sheffield said it happened.

Ed stood outside the Volks, holding the shotgun the way the doctor said he had. George got in the driver's seat and closed the door. Then with Ed approaching with the gun, George pulled the handle to open the door.

Nothing happened. The door wouldn't open! Mac then opened the door easily by using the outside handle and both tried the inside handle, still nothing; it wouldn't work. They contacted me immediately.

The first thing I said was, "Check with everyone involved. Have they tried the door handle since that night?" The answer was "no." This was too good to be true. If we could prove the inside handle didn't work that night, Sheffield's defense was destroyed. On my recommendation we contacted World Wide Volkswagen, which conveniently had an office in Rockland County. We arranged to have a Volkswagen expert, who was a graduate engineer, come and take the door apart to find out what was wrong.

The next morning, with George and Ed present, the Volkswagen man slowly and carefully took the door apart. You didn't have to be a graduate engineer to see what was wrong. A cotter pin had come out and the arm from the inside handle to the latch was disconnected. If the door was in that condition at approximately 11:25 p.m. on May 12, 1967, it could not possibly have been opened from the inside by Pete Hanlon. But was it? Our evidence only showed that door was in that condition on June 3, 1967—a world of difference.

"Ed, let's get Pat Kelly back in here right away."

So that afternoon, Pat returned to the DA's Office. The three weeks hadn't dulled the sharp edge of her feelings against Dr. Sheffield.

"Oh, Mr. Meehan, that door absolutely didn't work. I had to either slide open the window and reach out to the outside handle or go out the other door."

"Pat, when was the last time that you used the Volks before the night Pete was killed?"

"That same afternoon. I went shopping and to the laundromat, and I can tell you definitely, the door wasn't working."

"How long had it been broken?"

"A month or more. I always meant to take it back to the dealer, but I never got around to it."

"Pat, why didn't you tell us this before?"

"You never asked!"

Her answer was so true; we never did ask her. She had been questioned in detail *before* we talked to Sheffield and when we requestioned her, we limited it to those things that we thought she had knowledge of. She obviously wasn't a witness to the crime, so it never occurred to us to talk to her about that aspect of the case. It was a major error on our part, but as I look back it's one of those things that just never occurs to you. We reviewed our questioning of her that night and there were even questions about the standard transmission and the clutch being in good working condition. We had assumed the door handles worked on an almost new vehicle. We had forgotten the cardinal rule—never assume.

However, with Pat's testimony, we now had the necessary legal connection. The findings of June 3 and June 4 would be admissible to support her statement of the condition as of May 12th. Of course, I knew we were in for a fight on it. It was just *too convenient* of a finding for the prosecution, with not a word about it in the record until three weeks after the fact.

Before this Pat Kelly had been a key witness for only one part of the case—motive. Motive is not an element of the actual crime and juries are instructed that there is no requirement for the prosecution to present evidence of motive, but it sure as hell helps. The jurors are, however, instructed that they may consider motive or lack of motive, particularly in circumstantial evidence cases. To me the love triangle motive was critical to our case. Pat would now be even more of a star witness for the prosecution, or so I thought in June 1967.

∾

The defense hired a ballistics expert named Duncan McGeorge from upstate New York. He was good, in fact more than good, but no one could possibly be as good as he himself thought he was. Since Dr. Milton Helpern was drawn into this case as an expert, I was to hear McGeorge referred to as the now familiar *handball player*, but I must say I personally did respect his ability and, other than his superiority complex, I liked him.

I will, however, say that the feeling was not mutual. He probably spent a lot of time with Dr. Sheffield during the year before the trial and seemed to develop Sheffield's attitude that all of his troubles were caused by "that son of a bitch Meehan." I'm glad to report that Maury Edelbaum was just the opposite. He had a job to do, but there was nothing personal about it.

I had never met Edelbaum before and I never saw him in action but his reputation preceded him. He had been practicing law since 1930 and had handled scores of tough and famous cases in New York City and elsewhere. One of my jobs was to learn as much as I could about him before the trial began. Knowing your opponent is damned important.

The case was to be tried by Judge Morton Silberman and he originally set the trial for the first Monday in January 1968. I remember going down to DA Hogan's office in New York just before Christmas and talking to a friend of mine, ADA Sam Fierro, who had tried two cases against Edelbaum, one win, one loss. There was no transcript available on the one Sam lost; after all, on an acquittal with no appeal there's no reason to type the minutes. But I did get the eight-hundred-page transcript of a conviction based on the holdup of a loan company on the lower eastside of Manhattan.

I took a few days off between Christmas and New Year's that year and sat home reading the transcript. I well remember saying to Nancy, "You know, this guy, Edelbaum, is good but I haven't even gotten to his summation yet and he's called the NYPD the 'Gestapo' five times. I sure wish he would do that out here. How to turn a Rockland County jury off? Call the Orangetown Police the 'Gestapo'! But I assume he'll change his style up here in the country." I was wrong. He used the term "Gestapo" three times during the month-long trial, twice referring to the Orangetown Police and once in reference to my investigators. It was a gift.

I was quite disappointed when the trial was called off in January and put over to April 1st because Edelbaum was going to be engaged on a federal case. It's like a ball player getting ready for a game. You've got to get psyched up for battle. In this case it happened twice. The last week in March, it was again put off, but this time I kept very busy spending April and half of May trying the Baker case. The Monday morning after the guilty verdict on Baker I was back in court picking a jury for the Sheffield murder case.

I'll mention one mistake that Edelbaum made. It's important because he made very few. To assist with jury selection, he very correctly engaged a Rockland County lawyer who would be more familiar with local residents. The mistake was that the local guy was not a criminal lawyer and, in fact, not even a trial lawyer, which gave me a clear edge in this important part of the trial.

For instance, apparently in New York City, it is considered good for the defense to get blacks on the jury because they are thought to be more liberal. This is totally untrue in Rockland County. Our black population in Rockland is not anti-police or "the system." In fact, I thought of them as law and order types, particularly good for the prosecution. Therefore, when the first juror seated, who would be foreman, was a black man from the mountainside community of Hillburn, they thought they had pulled a "coup d'état." They should have checked the records. Little Hillburn is about 60 percent black and the crime rate, particularly crimes of violence, is about zero.

I went to Suffern High School with a lot of black kids from Hillburn. Hell, if everyone in the county were as honest as they were, district attorney would have been a boring job. It wasn't. My only ironclad requirement for every juror in this case had nothing to do with color. My only question was, "Have you ever driven a standard transmission car?" The answer had to be yes or I tried to get them off the jury and succeeded.

~

Jury selection took almost a week and after that the whole trial hinged on the physical facts and geometry of the scene. Unlike my earlier murder cases, there was no need to fight on the cause of death or establish that the defendant did it. Those points were obvious. Time, distance, and angles were the keys.

Time proved to be a significant issue. The fact that a medically trained man calls a lawyer before he calls for medical assistance does not make him guilty of murder, but it sure doesn't help him in the eyes of the jury. You remember that Dr. Sheffield said he called the police and Dr. Fletcher in that order with no other calls until twenty minutes later when he called his lawyer. We were able to establish from the Orangetown Police log that day they had received two calls, one at 11:31 p.m. from Dr. Sheffield and a second one at 11:34 p.m. from Pat Kelly. If Sheffield didn't call Kelly, how did she know to call the police?

However, far more important, Jerry Tobias lived in Spring Valley, which is a toll call from Palisades. We put a telephone company security officer on the stand who reported that the automatic tapes that register tolls from non–pay phones indicate that the call had been placed from Dr. Sheffield's home phone to the home of Jerome Tobias in Spring Valley at 11:26 p.m. and that the call had lasted for four minutes. Without saying it, the jury could surmise that he spent four minutes discussing his legal problems before he called for any help for the mortally wounded boy—a definite plus for our side.

After that there were many more witnesses, but only two that were really interesting—for entirely opposite reasons: the ballistics expert, McGeorge, because he went to the key factual issue of the case and, the girlfriend, Pat Kelly, who would give me a memorable lesson in human nature.

Let's talk about Pat first. When we thought the trial was going to begin in January, we had her in the Friday before to listen to her tape-recording and go over the critical testimony about the inoperable door handle. Everything was fine; nothing had changed, her testimony was as strong as ever. The same thing again in late March as we prepared for the April trial date that never came.

On a Friday evening in mid-May, right after the guilty verdict came in on Baker, I told Ed McElroy to contact Pat and have her in again on Monday to listen to the tape and be prepared to finally testify.

At about noon on Saturday, Ed called me at home and said, "Hey, boss, we got problems. Our little Irish girlfriend doesn't want to talk to us anymore; she says Edelbaum told her she didn't have to."

"Goddamn it, Ed, you know what this means. I'm afraid they've kissed and made up and that means trouble for us!" It did.

Maury Edelbaum, legally and correctly, was supplied with a transcript of the tape recording of Pat's interview and also with copies of McElroy and Barnes's report of their June 4th interview with Pat concerning the door. He knew what he was up against.

When Pat took the stand the second week of the trial, she looked quite pretty and spoke in a very sweet manner, a manner very different than that of a year before or even two months before. In summary, Pat said that Dr. Sheffield was a pretty nice guy, a great veterinarian, and a compassionate man.

As I said to Ed and Eric Vrhel that evening, "It was like listening to her tape, only where the word 'vicious' appeared it was changed to 'gentle' and where the word 'brutal' appeared it changed to 'loving.' "

It was clear Pat was now out to sink us. However, even with her about-face, she still admitted that she had had sexual relations with Dr. Sheffield, and that they had broken off about six weeks before the fateful night "by mutual understanding." She said that Pete Hanlon "was kind of like an adopted son" who was living with her at the time in question.

The only problem was that in the intervening year, Pete was no longer so "sweet and gentle"; he in fact had quite a temper.

Even with all of this, I still expected that Pat couldn't avoid helping us, to a small degree with the phone call from Dr. Sheffield just after the killing and to a large degree with the testimony about the broken door handle. I was wrong.

"Pat, I now call your attention to the time just a few minutes after Pete Hanlon left to go to Dr. Sheffield's house. Did you receive any telephone call or calls?"

"I don't recall."

After trying again to ask the question, in six different ways, I still was stuck with the same answer.

"Well then, Pat, I call your attention to that same time frame, a few minutes after Pete left. Did you make or place any telephone calls?"

"I don't recall" . . . more of the same.

"Well, did you, in fact, go to Dr. Sheffield's home a few minutes later?"

"Yes."

"How did you know to go there?"

"I just don't remember, it was all so confusing."

At this point it became obvious she wasn't going to help us and I moved to have her declared a "hostile witness."

Edelbaum strongly objected. "Your honor, what's hostile about saying 'I don't recall'?" He was right and Judge Silberman agreed, she was my witness and I was stuck with the answers.

All right, no matter what, she had still helped us on the triangle motive. It wasn't nearly as strong as I had hoped, but then again, I hoped the jury would see through her. I had one last point to make with Pat—the door. After going through her purchase and continued ownership of the Volkswagen Microbus since it was new and coming right up to the day in question, I asked:

"Mrs. Kelly, that day when you last used the Volkswagen before the night of Pete's death, was there anything wrong with the vehicle, physically or mechanically?"

"I don't recall."

Again I tried all types of questions but to no avail. In fact I was finally able to ask:

"Pat, wasn't the inside door handle on the driver side broken and not working?"

"I don't recall.

"Didn't you, in fact, have to get in and out the other door or open the window and reach out to the outside handle?"

"I don't recall."

I then tried in vain to get testimony before the jury as to her prior statements about Sheffield in general and the inoperable door handle in particular. This time the law was on the side of the defense.

Prior testimony can only legally be used for two reasons; first, to refresh a witness's memory or, second, to impeach the witness's credibility with an inconsistent or opposite answer.

It is common procedure to ask a witness such as a doctor or a police officer if reading his report made at the time of the incident would "refresh his recollection." The witness routinely answers "yes" and the report or statement is used for that very purpose.

When I asked Pat the same question, her answer was a flat "no." No it would not refresh her recollection and, therefore, I couldn't refer to it. I was also dead on the credibility issue. If Pat Kelly had answered, "The door handle worked perfectly," I would have had the absolute right to introduce her statement of June 1967 that it wasn't working as a "prior inconsistent statement."

I will not now speculate as to why Pat gave those answers that are the best possible for the defense, but all I know was that after two of the most frustrating hours of my courtroom career, Pat left the stand. Edelbaum and the defense had clearly won the day. Not only had she helped us precious little on motive, but we now knew we could never get in the testimony of the broken door handle. I almost think Judge Silberman felt sorry for the prosecution, but he knew the rules of evidence as well as any man I've ever met, and he wasn't about to bend them.

～

If we were going to be successful, we would have to break McGeorge's testimony. No doubt about it, as to the facts of the case, the expert Duncan McGeorge was the most interesting witness of all. What an expert he was!

McGeorge stated as a fact that the door of the car was open twenty-eight and a half degrees at the moment that the gun was accidentally discharged and then it continued to an open position at fifty-nine degrees before stopping. He wasn't even calling these opinions, which an expert has a legal privilege to give; these were *facts*. It was all based on the trajectory through the door window strip and on into the overhead, throwing in Dr. Sheffield's height and a few other factors. Every other expert I've talked to before or since has told me that certainty of that kind does not exist, not even from a television writer's pen.

But now came the clincher for the defense: "high-velocity blood splatters." According to McGeorge, there were high-velocity blood splatters on the outside of the Volks, just to the rear of the door and on the edge of the front bumper, just forward of the door. He said that these "splatters" could only have gotten there at the exact moment of firing because of the "high velocity" with which they hit the Volks. Therefore, Pete Hanlon's head had to be outside the plane of the door and since we know the window was closed, the door had to be open.

On cross I hammered away at his exactitude and things like "Why no glass on the ground if the door was opened?" "How do you get your head out of the door with your foot on the clutch?" His answers were somewhat vague, but on "high-velocity blood splatters," he never wavered. "But, Mr. Meehan, you're forgetting one vital fact. No matter how difficult it was to have his head out the door and no matter how far the glass flew before it fell, we know as a *fact* the door was open at the instant of impact. The high-velocity blood splatters were on the outside of the Volkswagen so the door had to be open!"

McGeorge would have no part of any theory that the blood could have gotten there when the bleeding victim was removed from the car through that door as he was. "Mr. Meehan, you just don't seem to understand 'high-velocity blood splatters.'" It's true. I didn't.

"Where did you first learn about these splatters, Saint George? I mean Mr. McGeorge."

"Objection."

"Sustained."

"Oh, I'm sorry, your honor, he's so infallible, I got to thinking he was the Pope or a saint or something."

"Mr. Meehan, we'll have no more of that in my courtroom."

Sometimes I just can't help myself, but there was no more of it. Pushing Judge Silberman's patience was a large mistake.

It seemed that McGeorge had read a book on forensic pathology that described "high-velocity blood splatters" as a theory, not an exact science. I didn't hit him on the theory versus fact issue. I decided I would leave that for my friend and rebuttal witness who wrote the book, Dr. Milton Helpern.

～

So in the last week of trial, back to the rescue of the "Hayseed DA" came the silver-haired chief medical examiner of the City of New York. I have always admired his humility, but it was a greater asset than ever after following McGeorge to the stand.

Actually the theory that he had developed was very simple. If a drop of blood or any other liquid fell on a flat surface, it would be round; if it had splattered, the drops would be elongated with the larger portion of the blood away from the direction it came from. The higher the speed, the more elongated the drops.

"Dr. Helpern, would there be any way of measuring with any degree of certainty, the speed of the blood before it hits the surface?"

"Oh, no, it's not that exact a science."

"Well, for instance, Doctor, if the blood splattered onto a surface at the instant of a shotgun blast, could you distinguish it from the blood that got on the same surface by me putting my finger into a bowl of blood and then flicking my finger toward the surface?"

"If you flicked your finger with any force it would probably be indistinguishable."

I don't say for a minute that we totally shot down the McGeorge testimony, but at least we got it back into the real world of differing professional opinions, not facts. The jury could make its own decision, one way or the other.

～

I would have to say that summations in this case were more important and more heated than in any case I had ever tried. Having been a defense attorney for the first six years of my career and a prosecutor ever since, I have always felt that the greatest single trial advantage that the prosecutor has is that he sums up *last*. Therefore, you can't really prepare your summation completely in advance. You wait to hear what the defense attorney says and then try to shoot him down, knowing that at least between the lawyers, you will have the last word.

Nevertheless, with summations scheduled to begin at 9:30 a.m., I was sitting in Eric Vrhel's kitchen drinking coffee and going over the facts one last time at four o'clock in the morning. Eric was as tireless as I when it came to preparing cases and as good or better at analyzing facts. It was almost 4:30 a.m. when Eric thought of that obvious geometric fact we had overlooked.

We not only knew the point of entry, the final lodging place of the shot in the overhead, and that the side of his head had to be in that line, but as Eric then pointed out, we knew the *angle* of his head in that line of fire. The burns upward from his chin and cheek past his ear and into his head meant that his head had to be leaning *away* from the door not *toward* the door. Very importantly, this was consistent with the natural instinct to pull your head back and away from the muzzle of a gun, not toward it, and consistent with Hanlon's head falling into the passenger seat where the large pool of blood was found. After this I was more than ready for summation.

Maury Edelbaum gave a great, stirring, and compassionate summation. He was personally critical of me, but in a clever way. After all he had to be careful. He was the big city lawyer and, for good or bad, I was their DA.

Toward the end of his hour-long summation, Maury walked forward right behind me, put his hand on my right shoulder and said, "Now this is a nice young man but I don't know if he's been around long enough to know that he's thwarting justice in this case. I fear that your young district attorney is trying to make a name for himself at the expense of destroying the life of an innocent man. I've been practicing law for almost forty years. Maybe by the time Mr. Meehan has been at it half as long, his sense of justice and fair play will be as strong as I know it is in the hearts of you, the members of the jury." A smart guy this Edelbaum, but then I still had the last word.

～

The heart of my summation was the demonstration of the angle of the head. I knew the judge wouldn't charge the jury until the next morning so I did my demonstration hoping that at least some of the jurors would try getting out of a car that way when they went home in the evening. To start with, I went through all the pictures of the Volkswagen and of the face and head of the deceased, Pete Hanlon. Then I actually sat in a chair, holding the gun with a muzzle pointed at myself as I said, "Get in a car, any car or truck, open the door about twenty-eight degrees or any other degree for that matter. Now try to get out with your left foot on the clutch or where a clutch would be, keeping your head in a position where it is exactly between the approximate point of the door window of the Volks and a point in the overhead above the driver's seat. Now, very important, make sure your head is outside the plane of the door and even more important make sure your chin is in a line nearest to the strip with the top of your head in the line with the spot in the overhead."

Then, in an uncharacteristically loud voice, I said, "Try it, I implore you to try it. It's impossible, absolutely impossible. You don't need an expert, you just need common sense." The courtroom was hushed. I could sense I had made my point. Eric and I had tried it in his neighbor's Volkswagen Microbus at 5:30 in the morning. We knew it was impossible.

Having completed all my important points, I couldn't resist the temptation to let Maury Edelbaum have a little taste of his own medicine. "Ladies and gentlemen of the jury, I realize that my experience is small compared to that of the distinguished Mr. Edelbaum, but if you recall on jury selection, I did ask you to decide this case, *not* on who was the better lawyer, because that way the People would obviously lose, but on the *facts*, and ladies and gentlemen of the jury, the facts point conclusively to guilt. But just as important (and now I again raise my voice) I'll be damned if some smart lawyer from New York City is going to come up here to Rockland County and give us a lecture on justice. Mr. Edelbaum, we've had justice just as long as you, and by the look of things, justice is going to survive in the common sense of us hicks long after the likes of you are gone. Who the *hell* do you think you are to come up here and give the good people of this county a lesson in justice. You are going to see true justice in the verdict of this jury and although you might not like it, the Gods of Justice will."

Edelbaum was on his feet as though I had just stolen his pants. "I demand a mistrial. Mr. Meehan has gone beyond all bounds of fair play." But what he was forgetting was that the prosecution has the right to not only sum up the evidence, but also to respond to the defense's summation. If he could put his hand on my shoulder, I could bash him in the teeth. It may be a shame for defendants to be caught in this legal crossfire, but if the defense attorney starts it, it's a hell of a temptation to the DA to finish it—and so I did. I wish I hadn't. It was more trouble than it was worth.

～

Judge Silberman gave the best charge to a jury that I ever heard. This is a human being sitting up there in his black robes and he obviously has an opinion as to guilt or innocence. But if any of those twelve jurors could detect his leaning in this case, they were more perceptive than Maury Edelbaum or me because we sure as hell couldn't. In politics being "down the middle" is sometimes seen as a sign of weakness—in a courtroom, a judge who was "down the middle" was a giant. Mort Silberman was a giant.

The jury got the case at about one o'clock on a sunny Friday afternoon in mid-June and thus began one of the longest deliberations we ever had in Rockland County. As happens in most cases, but much more so in the Sheffield case, the jury asked a lot of questions and for the reading of much of the critical testimony. To me the most significant thing was that a pattern was being set by the questions. The jury seemed to be moving inevitably toward acquittal. Maury Edelbaum sensed it and I voiced it. I also sensed that Judge Silberman thought there would be an acquittal.

As the hours rolled by in the District Attorney's Office, we got to thinking that the jury may have decided in our favor on the "accident" theory, but the unspoken "man's home is his castle" principle was still going to win the day.

It hadn't been said but it was there; to me it would always be there. Was I wrong to pursue the case in the first place? Should I have just said, "I don't give a damn what defense he uses, 'A man's home is his castle' and that's that!" But I thought otherwise; let an impartial jury decide. If that was their verdict, so be it.

～

By late afternoon of the second day there was an atmosphere of gloom in our office. The jury hadn't asked a question in several hours, but the last question had been "can we have a redefinition of reasonable doubt." Always a bad question for the DA. They aren't hung up on degree of guilt, but are still deliberating as to guilt or innocence. At about six o'clock the jury foreman sent out a note to Judge Silberman that read: "We are hopelessly deadlocked as to degree of guilt or innocence." At this point an interesting thing happened. I had been through three cases that ended in hung juries and two of them were before Judge Silberman. In all of those previous cases, I had been convinced that the jury had been leaning heavily for conviction. I didn't want a hung jury and I made a request to the judge for what is known in the trade as the "Boiler Plate Charge." Each and every time the request was denied, it turned out I was right, the juries had been 11 to 1 for conviction twice and 10 to 2 for conviction the third time. The Boiler Plate Charge might have won those cases for me.

The Boiler Plate Charge, in essence, says, "Members of the jury, you are as good as any twelve people in this county. If you don't reach a verdict, then all of the time and expense of the court, the district attorney, and the defense will have been wasted. If you don't come to a decision, twelve other citizens will have to hear and see all this evidence again and eventually a decision will have to be made. I am convinced that you twelve citizens are capable of making the decision. I, therefore, instruct you to return to the jury room for further deliberations remembering that I don't expect you in any way to compromise your own principles or beliefs, but I do expect that by further proper deliberations, a verdict may be reached."

When the note came out from the jury, Maury Edelbaum and I were called into Judge Silberman's chambers to discuss the possibility of declaring a mistrial on the basis of a hung jury. Immediately after the judge read the note to us, Edelbaum said, "Judge, how about the Boiler Plate Charge?" I smiled because I was sure from my experience that Judge Silberman would have no part of it. To my surprise, after only a slight hesitation, the judge said, "Yes." At first I thought to myself that this sure was a double standard. However, after a few minutes I realized he was right; that's why he was the judge and I wasn't. It's the defendant's constitutional rights we are trying to protect and if he wants the charge and in fact requests it, he can't later say that his right to a fair trial and verdict was violated.

As we went back into the courtroom for Judge Silberman to read the charge, I knew one thing for certain; this crafty old adversary of mine, who had been through the mill on this type of case, was convinced that the jury was close to acquittal. Otherwise he would've gladly settled for a hung jury.

After the jury filed out for what I was now sure would be their final hours of deliberation, I said to Eric, "Well, we've got at least two on our side. They did say *degrees* of guilt, but I don't think we have a chance for them to hang unless there are at least four on our side." By this time,

I had given up all hope for conviction. I was convinced that Edelbaum understood these things far better than I.

At 8:30 that night, word came from the foreman. "We have reached a verdict." Within five minutes, we were all back in a packed courtroom. Court Clerk Sue Van Epps rose and said, "Ladies and gentlemen of the jury, have you reached a verdict and if so who speaks for you and what is that verdict?" The foreman rose and said, very softly, "We, the jury, find the defendant Guilty of Manslaughter in the First Degree." An intentional killing but done in the "heat of passion."

There was stony silence in the courtroom, which apparently held more friends of Dr. Sheffield than I realized. A few seconds later, I heard a scream and as I turned I saw Dr. Sheffield's elderly mother topple over into the aisle. Ed McElroy seemed to be the only one in the courtroom to have the presence of mind to go immediately to her assistance. She came to in a moment and began crying loudly as her ashen-faced son tried now to comfort her.

~

It is always a good feeling to be successful after a long endeavor such as this trial, but there was no joy at the district attorney's table. Seeing human misery on the actual stage of life can never be pleasant. But within moments we were back in the middle of a legal battle that would last for almost four more years.

After having the jury polled, Maury Edelbaum rose and said, "I move to have the verdict set aside based upon all exceptions and objections taken during the trial and further upon the grounds of *juror misconduct*. Your honor is familiar with the misconduct I speak of and I believe it is more than sufficient cause to set aside the verdict."

I was completely in the dark. I had no idea what he was talking about and I was even more stunned that the judge seemed totally aware of some problem. Judge Silberman responded, "I will reserve decision on your motion. Please submit this matter in writing. I will defer setting a sentence date until the motion is decided. You have one week to submit and the district attorney will have three additional days to respond. The jury is excused with the thanks of the court. Court is now adjourned."

~

Within minutes I was in the judge's chambers and learned of the alleged misconduct. While our lives in the courthouse in Rockland County had revolved around the case of the People versus Malcolm Sheffield for the last month, the nation and the world had continued to move forward until one very dark night. During the third week of our trial on the 5th of June, at 12:15 a.m. Pacific Daylight Savings Time, Bobby Kennedy was shot at the Biltmore Hotel in Los Angeles after claiming victory in the California presidential primary. He would die early the following morning on June 6th, 1968.

His death hit me very hard. I found him to be an inspirational leader and he had been kind enough to come to a campaign event for me shortly after he was sworn in as a United States Senator from New York. Less than three months before he died, he sent me a personal telegram informing me of his intention to run for president. This telegram remains one of my most cherished possessions.

Court was adjourned that Thursday and Friday out of respect for our fallen senator, but not before the jury had come to the courthouse that morning of Thursday, June 6th.

Arthur Moskoff, a New City lawyer, had reported to Maury Edelbaum and then to Judge Silberman that he had been present in the Tor Restaurant across the street from the courthouse on the morning of June 6 and he had overheard jurors from our case talking about the death of Senator Kennedy. He further reported hearing one of them say something to the effect, "This violence has got to end. We've got to do our job on this trial to make sure it doesn't happen again, at least in Rockland County." If this allegation was true then at least one juror had allowed the verdict to be influenced by an outside event, the death of Robert Kennedy, and that would be improper.

It turned out that Moskoff hadn't reported the event until eight days later, the day the jury got the case for deliberation, and that's why I hadn't been told. Of course, I felt I should have been told immediately upon the judge learning of it on June 14th, but Judge Silberman thought otherwise. I suppose he reasoned that if there was an acquittal, a juror prejudiced for conviction would become irrelevant and the issue would only have to be aired if there was a conviction. The issue now had to be aired.

The verdict had legally pleased us. The jury system again had reached the proper verdict. They had been instructed to decide on the accidental theory of defense and they had, but they also decided that a man like

Dr. Sheffield wasn't about to blow a young boy's head off with a shotgun, unless it was in the "heat of passion." We also learned from talking to jurors after the verdict that they had been hung up 10 to 2 for some type of conviction at the time they sent out their "hopelessly deadlocked" note. We had all been wrong, especially Edelbaum. He had acted on his wrong judgment; I hadn't.

∾

It was almost a month later when we finally had the hearing. The jurors were all brought into the courtroom individually and questioned. Three admitted to being at the Tor Restaurant that morning and talking about the Kennedy assassination, but all vehemently denied ever in any way mentioning Dr. Sheffield's case or in any way equating Kennedy's violent death with Dr. Sheffield. Moskoff gave his testimony but wasn't sure exactly what was said and, just as important, could not recall which of the three had allegedly said it.

In New York State, a jury verdict is presumed to be good and proper and the defendant has the burden of proving, not beyond a reasonable doubt, but by a preponderance of the evidence, that the jury acted improperly. The defense clearly did not meet this burden. Judge Silberman ruled that the verdict would stand; sentencing was set for mid-September.

On September 14, 1968, Malcolm Sheffield was sentenced to a term of three and a half to ten years in state prison for the manslaughter death of Pete Hanlon. The defense immediately obtained what is known as a Certificate of Reasonable Doubt. It simply means that the defendant would not commence his prison sentence, but would remain out on bail pending appeals. It is a system that I generally find no fault with, *except* that it is another place in our law where wealth—the ability to pay for a large bail bond—means extra privilege. There had been no certificate for the men I convicted of homicide before. They couldn't afford it so they spent every day awaiting trial and every day during the years of appeal in jail.

∾

On March 2, 1972, the Court of Appeals of the State of New York, our highest court, affirmed the conviction. The vote was 6 to 1. The judge who voted against us was Chief Judge Stanley Fuld. His reason: "The prosecutor's summation was inflammatory and contained a personal attack on the defense attorney." By this time I was a little older and hopefully a little wiser. I learned a good lesson about the inadvisability of "getting even" with the defense attorney on summation. Thankfully for me it didn't cost us a case.

So in that month of March 1972, Dr. Sheffield let go his last salvo against me. When he arrived in court on the last Monday in March to be sentenced, he had a new lawyer with him, Arnold Roseman of Westchester County.

Now Arnold Roseman is a nice person and an outstanding lawyer. In fact he was later to be appointed a member of the New York State Commission of Investigations. But I never had any dealings with him before and he just caught me on the wrong day.

Roseman came into my office just before court opened and introduced himself in the most pleasant of manners and in fact was quite complimentary to me saying that he had heard in Westchester that I was a very "fair" DA. By the time he left he must have decided that the reports of my fairness were grossly exaggerated.

He began, "Mr. Meehan, Dr. Sheffield only contacted me on Friday and I want to make an application to the United States District Court in this matter. I therefore would like you to consent to a one-week adjournment before the doctor surrenders."

Now this was not an unreasonable request, especially from a new lawyer on the case, but we were rapidly approaching the fifth anniversary of the death of Pete Hanlon and I had had all the adjournments I could take and I let him know it.

"Look, Roseman, this case is on for 9:30 this morning. If you want an adjournment to a quarter to ten, I'll fight you all the way. I've had it with this case."

Roseman has always disliked me since that day, but I can say in all candor and having dealt with him subsequently, I both respect and personally like him.

A half an hour later, Dr. Malcolm Sheffield presented himself in the courtroom to surrender and begin his sentence. Judge Silberman had moved up to State Supreme Court as I knew he would, so Judge Ted Kelly presided.

This was not a formal sentencing. Hell, he had been sentenced almost four years earlier, and by right he wasn't entitled to make a statement, but through his lawyer, Dr. Sheffield requested to be heard and I consented.

Dr. Sheffield then proceeded to read a five-minute prepared written statement that could be summed up in one short sentence, "Meehan is a son of a bitch." He liberally used terms such as "vindictive, persecutor, tyrant, scourge of the county," and so forth, and so on. When he was through, Judge Kelly turned to me and asked if I wanted to respond. "Judge, my understanding of this proceeding is that you are sending Dr. Sheffield to jail today, not me. If I can be assured that this is the case, then I have nothing to say." Judge Kelly smiled faintly, turned and ordered Dr. Sheffield off to jail.

~

The case against Dr. Sheffield did nothing to dissuade my admiration of veterinarians . . . and dogs. Three years after his conviction, I finally convinced Nancy that it was time to add a dog to our family. I presented my six children with "J. Pinkerton Snoopington," a beagle puppy named for a memorable character in one of my favorite movies, The Bank Dick. My kids christened the puppy "Snoopy," and he certainly lived up to his name. Snoopy was a sweet-tempered scoundrel who laid in wait every time the front door opened, looking for a chance to make a break for it and go off on an adventure. And it was always poor Nancy who paid the consequences.

One evening, after Snoopy had run out several hours earlier, Nancy was preparing the family dinner when the phone rang. It seems that a new family was in the process of moving into a house about a quarter-mile down the road. The wife had prepared their first night's meal in advance and it was wrapped in plastic, sitting on a table in their open garage. Snoopy gladly accepted the invitation and was discovered standing atop the table finishing off the ham and potatoes. Needless to say, the family was not happy. Nancy, without missing a beat, quickly packed up the Shepherd's Pie she had prepared for us to bring to our new neighbors, while instructing our oldest daughter, Patty, to open up a couple cans of Spaghetti-O's for our dinner.

Returning from another adventure some months later, Snoopy bounded into the house as we were all heading out in our Sunday morning finest to go to church and a pancake breakfast political fundraiser.

It quickly became obvious that Snoopy had run afoul of a skunk. I was able to jump out of the way in the nick of time, but Nancy and the kids were not so lucky. At the breakfast a little later, I made apologies for my absent family while Nancy hauled Snoopy into the bathtub and got out the tomato juice.

~

One final note on Dr. Sheffield. Some of the owners of his patient animals had organized a protest parade on a Saturday morning prior to the sentencing. They paraded down Main Street in New City, riding their horses or walking with their dogs and even a few pigs on leashes. They carried placards urging Judge Kelly not to send their wonderful veterinarian away and others aimed in scorn at me.

The parade was well prepared with good advance press and had planned for a large contingent of marchers. It was a total and utter failure. No one in Rockland County cared about Dr. Sheffield that Saturday morning. They were still in shock. At 7:55 a.m. the day before, March 24th, 1972, disaster struck in Rockland County.

Meehan May Be The D.A.

By ANN CRAWFORD
Journal-News Staff Writer

The outcome of the most bitterly contested race in the county — for District Attorney — was still in doubt this morning, and Republicans had asked for a recount.

Unofficial totals had Democrat Robert R. Meehan ahead of Republican Robert J. Stolarik.

The Journal-News "district-by-district totals unofficially gave the race to Meehan by 71 votes, showing 27,887 for him and 27,816 for Stolarik.

OFFICIALS in both party headquarters were frantically rechecking their totals at 3 a.m. when Republican County chairman John J. Reilly declared that he would have the ballots impounded for a recount.

Meehan was cheered by jubilant Democrats as the first Democratic district attorney here in 30 years, and the party faithful at Democratic headquarters in the Tappan Zee Motor Inn plainly counted the courthouse victory as the most important in the county.

They cheered the news of a Democratic sweep in Ramapo and the capture of two Assembly seats, but saved their real salute for Meehan when he was announced as a winner. Most of the 500 committeemen and party workers had left the ballroom by the time the vote challenge was made known.

DISCREPANCIES between the party figures were concentrated in the three large towns —Orangetown, Ramapo and Clarkstown — where differences of as many as 100 votes were recorded.

Republicans gave this tally at 3 a.m.: In Orangetown, Stolarik 7,577, Meehan 8,364; in Clarkstown, Stolarik 8,748, Meehan 7,492; in Ramapo, Stolarik 7577, Meehan 8,364; in Stony Point, Stolarik 1,708, Meehan 2,068; in Haverstraw, Stolarik 1,573, Meehan 3,163.

Democrats, on the other hand, recorded the following totals at about the same time: In Orangetown, Stolarik 8,289, Meehan 6,679; in Clarkstown, Stolarik 8,653, Meehan 7,611; in Ramapo, Stolarik 7,-

(Turn to Page 3, Column 6)

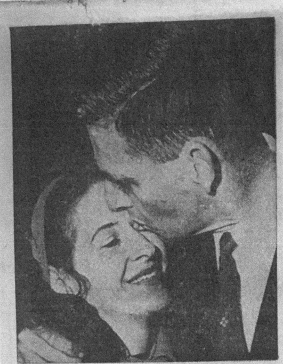

HAPPY ROBERT MEEHAN EMBRACES WIFE
... Strictly unofficially, he beat Stolarik

Staff photo by Art Gunther

(Continued from Page One)

540, Meehan 8,378; in Stony Point, Stolarik 1,700, Meehan 2,085; in Haverstraw, Stolarik 1,582, Meehan 3,160.

The Democrats have regarded a Meehan victory as their first real opportunity to crack the solidly Republican County Courthouse, with its attendant patronage jobs.

This year's close race has no precedent in Rockland district attorney contests. In 1,962, for instance, incumbent Morton B. Silberman beat Democrat Arnold Becker 32,-527 to 18,587.

Robert Meehan celebrates his improbable win as Rockland DA with his wife, Nancy, November 3, 1965. © The Journal-News—USA TODAY NETWORK.

The author, known as Bobby at the time, with his older brother and best friend, Tommy, on the left, circa 1940.

The author's family, circa 1943. Parents, Thomas Sr. and Helen, are in the center, sister Marilyn to the left, Bobby (the author) and brother Tommy to the right, and little brother Jack in the foreground.

Lt. Senior Grade Robert R. Meehan, United States Navy.

Headshot of Robert R. Meehan, 1965.

DISTRICT ATTORNEY
ROBERT R. MEEHAN

A Proven Professional

A Proven Leader

Flyer for the author's first run for Rockland DA, 1965.

US Senator Robert F. Kennedy at a MEEHAN for D.A. rally in 1965.

Newly elected DA Robert Meehan surrounded by his family. From left Mary, Kathy, Bobby (on lap), Robert, Nancy, Patty, and Tommy, with Laurie in forefront.

Dinnertime at the Meehan household, circa 1968.

Meehan Family prepares for first re-election campaign. Back row—Kathy, Patty and Laurie. Seated—Nancy, Robert and Bobby (on lap). Kneeling—Tommy and Mary.

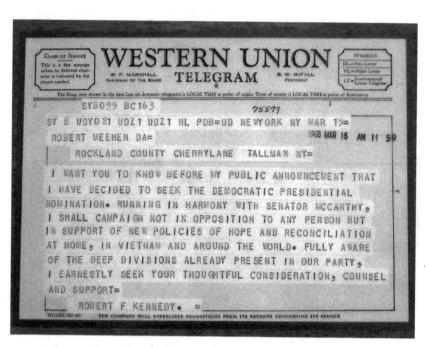

SYB099 BC163

75577

SY B UDYO21 UDZ1 UDZT NL PDB=UD NEWYORK NY MAR 19=

ROBERT MEEHEN DA=

1968 MAR 16 AM 11 59

ROCKLAND COUNTY CHERRYLANE TALLMAN NY=

I WANT YOU TO KNOW BEFORE MY PUBLIC ANNOUNCEMENT THAT
I HAVE DECIDED TO SEEK THE DEMOCRATIC PRESIDENTIAL
NOMINATION. RUNNING IN HARMONY WITH SENATOR MCCARTHY,
I SHALL CAMPAIGN NOT IN OPPOSITION TO ANY PERSON BUT
IN SUPPORT OF NEW POLICIES OF HOPE AND RECONCILIATION
AT HOME, IN VIETNAM AND AROUND THE WORLD. FULLY AWARE
OF THE DEEP DIVISIONS ALREADY PRESENT IN OUR PARTY,
I EARNESTLY SEEK YOUR THOUGHTFUL CONSIDERATION, COUNSEL
AND SUPPORT=

ROBERT F KENNEDY. =

Telegram sent to Robert Meehan from Robert F. Kennedy, sharing his plans to run for President. Sent less then three months before Kennedy's assassination, 1968.

Nancy and Bob, the newly elected President of the New York State District Attorney's Association, make their entrance at the Sagamore Hotel in Lake George, 1970. Bob's trusted assistant, Ann Hickey, is applauding in the background.

Robert Meehan addresses the audience as the newly elected President of the NYS District Attorney's Association, 1970.

Today's Man for Today's Problems

ELECT DISTRICT ATTORNEY ROBERT R.

MEEHAN

YOUR FIGHTING
ATTORNEY GENERAL

Flyer for Robert Meehan's 1970 bid for Attorney General. Campaign Manager Arnold Reif is seen in background.

Robert Meehan appearing on a Channel 4 broadcast in New York City during Attorney General race.

DA Meehan proudly served as Grand Marshal of the Rockland County St. Patrick's Day Parade in Pearl River, NY, circa 1971.

During his 1974 campaign for New York State Attorney General, Robert Meehan had the assistance and support of his entire family, utilizing the family trailer to barnstorm the state.

ELECT A FIGHTING ATTORNEY GENERAL

PRIMARY, SEPTEMBER 10th
ELECTION, NOVEMBER 5th

BOB MEEHAN

Flyer for Robert Meehan's 1974 bid for Attorney General.

New York Gubernatorial candidate Howard Samuels, left, with Nancy and Bob Meehan.

Chapter 7

Disaster

Editor's Note—The preface to this book indicates that in most cases, the names of defendants, victims, and witnesses were changed. This chapter represents the exception to this rule. The event described in this chapter was one of the most horrific tragedies in the history of Rockland County and it received significant national and regional news coverage. The names of the defendant, victims, and witnesses are well known to many people in the county. We therefore made the decision not to change the names. It was a sad time in the history of Rockland County and we continue to grieve for the lives lost and for those whose lives were forever changed.

When I awoke at around 7:30 on the morning of Friday, March 24, 1972, I was very pleased that it was warm and sunny. Nancy and I and the kids were leaving for Florida with our trailer the next morning for our first-ever spring vacation. If the good weather held, it would make the trip much more pleasant. I had just bought the first brand new car I ever owned, a 1972 Ford ten-passenger LTD station wagon to replace our eight-year-old, tired buggy. But even with that, sunshine was far preferable to rain with six kids and a trailer behind you on a 1,300-mile trip.

The trip would be fun. We were going to meet our friends from Haverstraw, Frank and Ellie McGowan and their two boys Sean and Stephen, at a trailer park on the beach at St. Augustine, Florida.

It had been a long fall and winter in the District Attorney's Office but very successful. I had been reelected to a third term as DA in November 1971 in a landslide, and there had been a conviction in an important narcotics case that I had tried myself, along with several other reasonably important cases that my assistants had handled. We also had a final appeal in Dr. Sheffield's case and he would finally be going off to jail within a few days.

That Friday would be easy. I had absolutely promised Nancy that I would be home by three o'clock to help with the final packing of the trailer so that we could start off at daybreak Saturday morning. By this time I had a history of breaking promises to get home early from the DA's Office and she had come to expect that most nights I would not be home before seven or eight in the evening. But as I was getting ready to leave for the office, I promised, this day would be different—it wasn't. Within an hour, I knew the promise would be broken and the trip itself would have to be put off.

I was getting dressed and having a cup of coffee in the bedroom and as usual listening to the local radio station, WRKL. They had world and national news from 7:30 to 8:00 a.m. and then 8:00 to 8:30 a.m. was devoted to local news. As a public official, it was important to know what had happened during the night, before I left for the office, so that local newscast was a must.

When the lead story was about a zoning hearing over in Haverstraw, I figured "it must be a slow news day" and I was only half paying attention to the radio. Then the announcer interrupted his broadcast with a bulletin.

"We've just received a phone call from a private citizen who has advised us that a school bus has been hit by a train in Congers. This is unverified. We are now attempting to contact the Clarkstown Police Department but cannot get through."

I immediately picked up the county phone beside my bed and dialed Police Radio.

"John, this is Bob Meehan. You got a problem over there? I just heard on the radio a school bus was hit."

"Damn right, the radio is alive. It happened less than ten minutes ago. Clarkstown Police Department has declared a State of Emergency. Every piece of fire equipment in Clarkstown and every ambulance in the whole county is on the way."

"John, what can you tell me? Where did it happen and how bad is it?"

"From what I hear on the radio, Mr. Meehan, it's bad, very bad. It happened over at Gilchrest Road right by St. Paul's Church."

"OK, John, I'm on my way."

"God, Mr. Meehan, I don't think you'll be able to get through. They say the roads are jamming already."

"All right, I'll do the best I can."

The next call was to Eric Vrhel. He already knew about it from the commercial radio and had tried to get through to me.

"Eric, call your friends at Deck-Air. We want a chopper on the pad, ready to go. Tell them I'll be there in ten minutes."

As I ran out of the house, I could see the shocked looks on the faces of Nancy and the kids. They had been listening to the radio in the kitchen.

I got in my county car and turned on the flashers, which I practically never used, as I headed at high speed to Ramapo Valley Airport, four miles away.

~

Less than fifteen minutes from the time of that first word on WRKL, we were lifting off in a small two-seater helicopter, heading on a five-mile trip to Congers. Within a few minutes I sighted St. Paul's and then just beyond I saw the freight train stopped across the intersection with the tail end of the bright yellow bus lying beside it, just a few yards north of the intersection.

I turned to the pilot and said, "Where the hell is the rest of the bus?" Before he could respond I looked north. "Oh my God, there it is way up the track, across the front of the engine."

There was furious activity below. I could see people parking cars in the roadway and running toward the tracks. There was an ambulance pulling out with its flashers on and two more stopped beside the tracks. There were three or four police cars and maybe half a dozen fire engines with more on the nearby roads heading in.

The main part of the bus was broken wide open with its roof off and most of its seats missing. There were men climbing over the wreckage. I could not see any bodies; however, I saw blankets on the ground beside the right of way.

It was and is, to this point in my life, the worst sight I have ever seen. I feared that if the bus was full, there could be as many as thirty or forty dead.

We set down in the field right beside the intersection and a crowd started to gather around us. They wondered who was in the chopper, but they dispersed immediately when I alighted and ran quickly toward the head of the train.

Before I got out of the helicopter, I said to the pilot, whom I knew reasonably well, "Look Charlie, get back over to the airport and get ahold of any air ambulances in the area. This looks like a major disaster." With that I got out and he immediately took off back to the airport.

As I started running up from the intersection, I saw three ambulances with two or three children in each one. It was now twenty to twenty-five minutes since impact and the local volunteer ambulances and Nyack Hospital were doing a hell of a job. I learned later that it was just under one thousand feet from the grade crossing intersection to the head of the train where the main body of the bus was, but it seemed longer, much longer that morning.

~

The first person I spoke to in an official capacity was Detective Lt. George Finlay of the Clarkstown Police Department. In a nutshell, he was my Colombo of Rockland County. I even remember saying to Nancy after seeing the pilot of the *Colombo* series, "You know something, that character Peter Falk plays reminds me of George Finlay."

But this was different from the murder scenes and narcotics raids George and I had experienced before. He was visibly shaken. He lived in Congers and he knew most of the kids and their families. He had been on the way to work when he heard of the crash and thus was one of the first on the scene. I later learned that Finlay had pulled the mangled body of a fifteen-year-old boy out from under one of the cars. The dead boy wore a blood-soaked red plaid mackinaw. George's own sixteen-year-old son had left the house for Nyack High School wearing the same colored jacket twenty minutes earlier. When he started to pull the body out he didn't then know that his own son was safely at school. He had been riding the other bus. George had every right to be shaken.

My first words to him were "How bad is it, George?"

"Well, Mr. Meehan, we've got three known dead, a couple more that I don't think can make it to the hospital, and ten or twenty more pretty bad, some with an arm or leg off."

It's an awful thing to say, especially for the families of the five who eventually died, but after seeing that bus from the air, I was actually thankful that it hadn't been worse. I was sure he was going to say that there were many more fatalities and, to this day, it is almost a miracle to me that so many survived.

There were forty-nine high school kids on that bus; three were removed directly to the morgue, two died at the hospital. Every child was injured, at least to some degree. The last ambulance pulled away from the scene at 8:22 a.m., exactly twenty-seven minutes after the bus was hit. This was a monumental tribute to the volunteer ambulance corps.

The last minutes at the scene before I left for the hospital in a police cruiser were a horror. Frantic, ashen-faced parents looking for their children. It was directed that all parents would be taken in police vehicles to the hospital.

Within half an hour I was at Nyack Hospital. All parents and relatives were sent to the cafeteria where coffee and rolls were being served by volunteers. They were instructed on the loudspeaker to wait until their names were called and they could go up to the bedside of their injured child—or worse.

~

A few minutes after I got to the hospital, Al Scott of the Medical Examiner's Office handed me a note with three names; these were tentatively identified as the known dead. I looked at the list and whispered, "Oh God, this is probably Jim McGuiness's boy." It was, James McGuiness Jr., age sixteen, dead at the scene.

I knew his father quite well. I had met him through politics and we had become reasonably good friends. When I walked into the cafeteria there were a lot of familiar faces. But with almost two hundred people in the room, I almost instantly caught a glimpse of Jim McGuiness Sr. on the far side of the room.

I had met many of the families under much happier circumstances the night of Halloween, only six months before. Jim Freeman, who was by then a former assistant district attorney, had invited Nancy and me to the St. Paul's Parish Costume Ball. It was only a few days before Election Day and we had planned to stop in only for a few minutes, but everyone was having such a good time that we stayed for a few hours. I will remember that one whole neighborhood came as "Snow White and the Seven Dwarfs" and it was Jim McGuiness who introduced me to that fun-loving group. I didn't see "Snow White" again until that morning in the cafeteria of Nyack Hospital. She was crying, but for her the sobs soon turned to tears of joy; her daughter had not been badly injured.

Jim McGuiness came over to me, as did many others; they wanted to know what I knew. I couldn't tell Jim what I knew, it would have been wrong because nothing had been verified. I said to the group, "All we know at this hour is that almost all of the children have survived."

"You mean by that that some are dead?" a woman in the crowd said.

"Yes."

"How many, God, how many?"

"Right now, I honestly don't know," and it was true. I didn't know how many might be dead upstairs in the wards and operating rooms.

Within an hour most of the parents had the word; they were at the bedside of their children or had received the tragic news. I stood beside the medical examiner, Dr. Fred Zugibe, as he gave the news to Jim McGuiness and his wife. I just bit my lip hard; it was a day for that kind of thing.

～

I later went through the wards visiting the injured children and their families. It was a time for very mixed emotions. We grieved for the dead and the dying, but there was time to rejoice for the living.

I will never forget one moment as I was walking down the corridor, and a big bear of a man came running out from one of the rooms and tearfully embraced me. "Mr. Meehan, Mr. Meehan," he said, "she's all right, my daughter's all right! She only has a broken hip. Please come in and see her." I had never met the man before that morning when I saw him at the scene and told him to go in the police car to Nyack Hospital. All I had really said as he got in the police car was "I will say a prayer for your daughter." I am not as religious a man as I should be coming from my family, but there was a great deal of religion of all faiths beside the Penn Central right of way that morning, and as I walked away from him, I did quickly and silently say one *Our Father* and one *Hail Mary* for the little girl I didn't even know.

As I went into her room, I thought *only a broken hip*, because I, like her father, had seen the devastation of the bus and any parent who saw that could truly rejoice in *only a broken hip*. The brief time I spent with that father and mother and their little girl, who smiled through her obvious great pain, is a bittersweet memory of an otherwise horrific day.

Throughout that long day at the hospital, there was only one concern on everyone's mind, the survival of the children. A helicopter ambulance landed on the lawn of the hospital and took a severely injured fifteen-year-old girl directly to New York City for specialized care. She had already lost a leg, and they were trying to save her left arm.

∿

By noon, Rockland County was inundated by the New York City and national press corps, and they, too, were only concerned with the condition of the survivors. But by late afternoon, a second consideration began to emerge: How could this disaster have happened? Why, on a bright, sunny spring morning, was a loaded school bus struck by a freight train? Was it mechanical failure? Was it human error? The public demanded to know; the public had a right to know.

That's why I rushed to the scene that morning. I'm not a doctor or an ambulance driver, policeman or fireman, and I didn't want to be in the way. However, by that time I had been district attorney long enough to know that the people of our county would very soon be demanding answers to these critical questions and I wanted as much firsthand knowledge as was humanly possible.

Who was responsible for coming up with the right answers? The answer was obvious, the *district attorney of the county*. It was my responsibility and I fully accepted it. However, I was determined to get all the help I could, all the way from the police on the scene to the National Transportation Safety Board, whose investigators were already en route from Washington to Rockland County.

I knew the first few minutes after I arrived at the hospital that the bus driver was injured, but not too severely, and that he would survive. Further, although there was great mental anguish among the crew of the train, there were no physical injuries.

A brief effort was made by Clarkstown detectives to interview the bus driver that morning, but they wisely backed off when they realized he was in pain and being sedated. The police and I made the decision not to bother the injured children that day with questions as to how it happened. For at least twenty-four hours the only question should be "How do you feel?"

~

The bus driver was Joseph Larkin, age thirty-four, of Stony Point, married and the father of three small children. Like almost all school bus drivers in Rockland County, Larkin was a part timer. He was a seven-year veteran of the New York City Fire Department with an unblemished record and had, in fact, received several citations for saving lives. I knew before I ever met him that nothing we could do could be worse for him than what had already happened. Even if it turned out that he was entirely blameless, he would have to live the rest of his life with the knowledge that he was driving when all of those children were killed or maimed.

By the next morning, Joseph Larkin had very properly retained a lawyer. We would never interview him, except at official judicial proceedings. The train crew was different. Although the chief counsel to Penn Central, Joe McGinn, was immediately in contact with us, we had the full and complete cooperation of the engineer, brakeman, and fireman who were aboard the engine that morning and saw the accident develop right before their eyes.

~

Within twenty-four hours we had a general picture of what had happened. The train crew could not be considered unbiased witnesses because they were actually involved in the collision and would, of course, have a human tendency of reporting events so as to put themselves in the best possible light. But their three stories were consistent, believable, and so very tragic.

All three were experienced railroaders. The engineer had thirty-six years on the job with only one other accident and that did not involve fatalities. The fireman and brakeman each had more than fifteen years' experience and 100 percent safety records. They told of the makeup of the eighty-seven-car freight train in Weehawken, New Jersey, which left on time at 7 a.m. for the run to Selkirk, just south of Albany. It was their regular run and they knew it by heart, especially the location of all grade crossings. The train made its usual stop in West Nyack, just three miles south of the fateful Gilchrest Road crossing.

The engineer reported that he was proceeding at about thirty-two miles per hour as he approached the Congers area. This was well within the proper speed limit and he was supported by the fact that the track between West Nyack and Congers was on an upgrade and it would have been impossible to pick up more speed than that after starting up from a complete stop with eighty-seven cars and proceeding only three miles.

The crew was also certain that they had sounded the proper train whistle warning signals, starting 1,500 feet south of the Gilchrest Road crossing. The crossing itself had no gate, no bell, and no guard. It was only marked by a STOP sign, a small, tired old railroad crossing sign, and the word "STOP" written in white on the blacktop pavement with a line about twenty-two feet from the track. However, the view from the northbound train to eastbound traffic on Gilchrest Road was unobstructed for almost 1,300 feet. This was significant. If the train had been heading south or the bus heading west, the view could have been much more limited. It was clear the train crew could see the bus if they looked in that direction and the reverse was obviously true, the bus driver could see the train *if* he looked to the south, but had he?

All the members of the train crew were not in doubt; they had seen the bus from the start. The train was proceeding at a reasonable speed toward the intersection. The train didn't stop for every grade crossing; it had the right of way. They were sure they had nothing to fear; of course the bus would stop. They were used to "cowboy" types who scared them to death by speeding up to grade crossings and then stopping short, but a school bus that was required to stop never worried them. This day would be different, as the engineer tearfully told us in the District Attorney's Office that Saturday morning.

"From the moment we came into the clearing, we saw the bus. He wasn't going that fast and we weren't worried. But as we proceeded, he showed no signs of slowing to a stop. All three of us had emergency brakes in front of us, but at first we were sure they wouldn't be necessary. Just to be safe, I pulled on the whistle again, but still nothing, the bus kept coming."

By this time this tough old engineer was in tears but he kept going. "Now our eyes were transfixed on the bus, about six or seven hundred feet south of the intersection. Acting as one, we all hit the full emergency brake to 'drop the load.' I knew we couldn't stop in time. I could now see the faces of the children looking at us and getting up from the seats nearest us, but the bus kept coming. It never stopped, it never slowed and oh, God, we hit it! And even on full emergency we kept going for what seemed an eternity, with the bus hung up on our catcher." He then put his face in his hands and sobbed almost uncontrollably.

~

By the end of the second day, I knew what the train crew had said and I knew that the preliminary report of the National Transportation Safety Board found no mechanical defect with the shattered bus, including the brakes. We also were now getting reports from parents of the injured children who told us their children said the bus never stopped, that they had all seen the train coming, that many had yelled warnings to the driver, but that the warnings went unheeded.

"Oh, God," I thought. "We are faced with a criminally negligent homicide case against the poor man." As the days went by and more witnesses came forward, it became apparent, a case of criminally negligent homicide against Joseph Larkin would have to be presented to the Rockland County Grand Jury.

By that time I had handled better than a dozen criminally negligent auto death cases, but this was so very different. In the other cases there was only a criminal prosecution because the driver was drunk or grossly reckless. One I remember well was the loss of sixteen-year-old Tommy Stewart to a drunken driver in 1970. Tommy's father, Bob Stewart, came to work for me in the following year as an investigator and I learned firsthand of the profound effect this tragedy had on all of the Stewart family. Bob Stewart told me that one of the joys of his home was the happy laughter of his wife, Marilyn. She never laughed very much after they lost Tommy. The driver in the Stewart case was a forty-six-year-old businessman with a family of his own, but his life was also shattered after spending a year in jail and living with the memory of what his drunken spree had cost in human misery.

However Joseph Larkin was different; here was a hard-working man, taking on a second job to make life more comfortable for his family and their new home in the country away from the crowds and dangers of city life. There was no hint that drinking was involved, nor was there any testimony that he drove recklessly. Hell, he wasn't even speeding. How could this have happened? A momentary lapse? A few seconds of daydreaming?

Whatever had occurred, his life would never be the same. No matter what we did, no matter what decision the grand jury and later a trial jury made, Joseph Larkin would not be remembered as a good husband and father or the brave fireman with well-deserved citations, but as the school bus driver on that fateful March day in 1972.

~

I personally presented the facts to the Rockland County Grand Jury about three weeks later. By this time every possible test had been done on the smashed bus, and the train had been put through test runs at the same intersection under the same conditions—all under the watchful eye of the National Transportation Safety Board and the press, radio, and television.

I had cases that interested the New York City press before, but usually for just a day or so, such as when Dr. Sheffield's picture was on the front page of the *New York Daily News*, but this was a continuing story. We had press briefings every day for almost two weeks. The television crews were all around us, whether at the office, in the highway garage where the bus was reassembled, or at the funerals for the lost boys.

I attended all five funerals and saw the huge outpouring of sympathy by the people of the county. Many strangers attended and I don't think it was out of curiosity. It was just that they wanted to let the families know how much they cared. There was also the added factor of "There, but for the grace of God, go I." All our children rode school buses.

The reporters were, of course, looking for new stories, for an angle, but we tried desperately not to prejudice the case or look like headline seekers. I particularly made a point of not speaking to the press at the funerals. They were there and wanted to know of any late developments, but to me those mornings outside the churches were not a time for investigations or matters of law. They were a time to mourn and a time to reflect on the uncertainty of tomorrow in all our lives.

~

As district attorney, I had three priorities. I wanted justice for the dead and injured children and their families. I wanted Larkin's rights legally protected. And I wanted the outside world to know that our county law enforcement establishment could rise to the occasion and handle this tragedy in a professional manner.

By the time we went to the grand jury, there were nineteen surviving children ready to testify, along with the train crew. We also had two vital witnesses who were identified within a few days after the incident.

First, there was an eleven-year-old boy whose home was about 1,200 feet northeast of the intersection with a perfect, unobstructed view from his second-story bedroom window. He had been looking out the window and saw the whole thing. Why? "Because I heard the train whistle and I always watch the trains pass." Very important, he verified that the warning whistle had, in fact, been sounded. He also added, "The bus kept coming and just before the tracks, I saw the red lights go on in the back, and the front of the bus went down a little but then it kept going and speeded up some and got hit by the train."

The young boy's story would be supported by students sitting in the front of the bus who said the driver seemed to realize the great peril too late, hit the brakes, realized he couldn't stop in time, and then sped up to try to "beat" the train.

The second key witness was the driver of a garbage truck. We didn't see him that morning or even learn that he had been there until a few days later. A canvass of the neighborhood next to the crossing had been done in an attempt to find more witnesses, and although several heard the whistle and the impact, no one had seen the crash. One woman who had rushed to the aid of the children told of seeing a garbage truck stopped at the east side of the intersection facing west, but that the truck backed up and left just a few minutes after the impact.

Within twenty-four hours after we learned about the garbage truck, we had the driver in the DA's Office. He was contrite and ashamed that he hadn't come forward, but he said it was the worst experience of his life and . . . "I just had to get out of there. I couldn't face it, I thought they all must be dead."

As it turned out though, he had seen the whole thing. "As I came to the crossing, I heard the whistle, looked down the tracks to my left and saw the train, so I came to a stop. When I was stopped I saw the bus coming toward me from the opposite side of the tracks and I just assumed he'd stop. But he just kept coming and I can now see the driver of the bus. He wasn't going fast, but he was looking straight ahead and showed no signs of stopping. When I realized he wasn't going to stop, I started blowing my regular horn and then I hit the air horn to try to get his attention, but he just kept coming. Oh, God, it was awful."

We correctly realized that the credibility of this "star" witness would be hurt by the fact that he didn't stay to help the injured and didn't come forward on his own, but he was an independent eyewitness and had to be called.

These were the stories that the witnesses told us in the DA's Office; what they said in the Grand Jury Room was and is still secret. I can report though that the grand jury did have an opportunity to hear all sides of the story.

~

As was announced by his lawyer at the time, Joseph Larkin waived immunity and testified before the grand jury on his own behalf.

In a case that had to be difficult for all concerned, the grand jury voted to indict Joseph Larkin for Criminally Negligent Homicide. A jury of his peers in open court would now hear all the facts and decide his guilt or innocence. It was my personal belief that he would be acquitted, but as I have said before, public confidence in the administration of justice would best be served by the decision of a trial jury.

Contrary to public opinion, the district attorney doesn't indict; his personal feelings are irrelevant once there has been a legal decision that there is sufficient evidence to present to the grand jury. In Rockland County during my years, the grand jury decided questions of fact, not I. Many times those decisions meant *no indictment* when I thought there should be one and in a few cases, like Joseph Larkin, an indictment even though that would not have been my personal decision.

In speaking to the press to announce the indictment of Joseph Larkin, I urged the people of Rockland to have compassion for all involved. "All of us need to remember that Mr. Larkin and his family must continue to live here," I said. "I am confident that the people of our county will not further prejudge him or in any way interfere with his presumption of innocence."

~

Although I had been district attorney for seven years and this case was the most famous case by far to arise in the county, I knew that I could not or should not personally handle the trial. The reason was simple; the defense attorney was Terrence Ryan of Suffern, my former law partner. It is not only conflict of interest but the appearance of conflict that must be guarded against. It would be wrong if the public in anyway perceived that the District Attorney's Office was giving anything less than maximum effort just because of who the defense attorney was.

I had run a one-man law office from the time I was admitted to practice until my upset election in 1965. District attorneys in upstate New York counties were still technically part-time in 1966 and it was all right to have a law practice on the side as long as there were no criminal matters involved. The district attorneys of many other counties had thriving practices, but I knew this would be impossible for me. I intended to give the DA's Office my best effort and I couldn't be part-time.

Therefore, I got together with Terry Ryan and we set up the new firm of Ryan and Meehan with the understanding that the partnership would take over my practice, but that I wouldn't actually work at the private office. This went on throughout the first three years that I was district attorney until I convinced the County Board of Supervisors to make the DA's job full-time. Unlike my brother district attorneys, I wanted the job to be full-time by law, and as president of the New York State District Attorneys Association in 1970, I successfully lobbied to get a law passed in the state legislature that mandated full-time district attorneys in counties with populations of over one hundred thousand. I knew I was right on the full-time issue, but I made no friends with it. In fact, many DAs didn't run for reelection over the full-time issue and the resulting loss of income.

During those three years, Terry and Kate Ryan and Nancy and I became close personal friends. They had seven children to our six, so family get-togethers were and still are a lot of fun. I just knew it would be better for the administration of justice *and* for our friendship if I didn't try the case.

∽

In the case of *The People v. Joseph Larkin*, the People would be fully and completely represented. I assigned the case to the best young trial lawyer in the office, Kenneth Gribetz.

Kenny Gribetz was only twenty-eight years old, but he had gone to work in Manhattan as an assistant district attorney for Frank Hogan right after getting out of law school and he already had as much trial experience in felony cases as many men almost twice his age. Hogan's crew weren't Boy Scouts, but they used the same motto, "Be prepared." I have never known lawyers who prepared more meticulously for trial than the Hogan-trained ADAs. Kenny was the first of many Hogan men I would work with and I was terribly impressed. I don't know why I should have been—I thought Frank Hogan was the greatest DA of all time; it was only right that his people should be of that caliber.

But Kenny, in his striving for perfection, was a nervous guy and he drove me up the wall worrying about the case. I was always saying, "Calm down, Kenny," "Take an even strain," "Do the best you can and I'll be satisfied, win or lose," but I don't think he fully shared my view and that of Grantland Rice, who said, "It's not whether you win or lose, but how you play the game." Kenny wanted to win and usually did.

∾

The trial began almost a year to the day of the tragic accident, and I believe it was handled in a highly professional manner by both sides. I have always had an ironclad rule that I would not interfere with assistant district attorneys who were trying cases. I personally tried more cases than any other district attorney in New York State during my years in office, but when I made a decision to let an assistant try an important case, that was it. If I had enough faith to give him the assignment, I had the same faith to let the assistant see it through. I, therefore, made it a rule to never go into the courtroom while an assistant was trying a case.

I broke that rule only once in nine years. It was the day Joseph Larkin took the stand in his own defense. I had to see for myself if his testimony would be the same as it had been in the grand jury.

By the time Larkin testified, the jury had already heard from the train crew, the National Transportation Safety Board experts, the eleven-year-old boy, the garbage man, and twenty-three student passengers on the ill-fated bus. Larkin told his story at the trial to a packed courtroom, with me sitting in the last row. After going through the preliminaries, he got to those fateful moments.

"I turned onto Gilchrest Road and proceeded east. I wasn't going more than twenty miles an hour. As I approached the intersection, I came to a full stop. I open the door a slight way, looked both ways, saw nothing coming, then proceeded across the tracks when suddenly we were struck by the train."

He added that he had heard no warning whistle and that he had heard no cries of alarm from his student passengers.

It was incredible; if his story was true everyone else was wrong. If his story was true, then he stopped and then proceeded in broad daylight into the path of an eighty-seven-car freight train. It just wouldn't hold water, and it didn't.

After three weeks of trial and eight hours of deliberation, a tearful jury of six men and six women brought in a verdict of "Guilty as Charged." They felt desperately sorry for Larkin, but they had to decide the facts and those facts were that Larkin had been criminally negligent. With a busload of kids sitting behind you, there is a high degree of care required; he had not met that standard of care.

A month later, Judge John Gallucci, who had presided at the trial, sentenced Joseph Larkin to five years' probation. He wouldn't have to go to jail. The judge was right. My office wanted to legally establish the blame, but we had no desire to see Larkin punished any more. In fact, we wanted him to be able to return to his job as a fireman and consented to what is known as a Certificate of Relief from Disabilities, which meant that he could still keep his civil service job as a fireman, even though he had been convicted of a felony. This was not preferential treatment; it was only seeing that justice be done.

For this case, maybe more than any other, it was hard for me to separate my role as a father from that as district attorney. My children still go off on a school bus every morning during the school year. In fact, as it has been for sixteen years, the school bus stops in front of our house. On the warm days in the fall and spring when the windows are open, I can hear the happy chatter of the kids at the bus stop and I always think it must have been the same for those young people who boarded that bus in Congers and Valley Cottage in the spring of 1972, some for the last time.

However, my children will never again cross at an unattended railroad grade crossing. On March 5, 1974, Gov. Malcolm Wilson signed into law a bill sponsored by Suffern Assemblyman Eugene Levy mandating that school bus routes may not include any railroad crossing that does not have gates and warning signals. It took five lives in Congers to make it safer, but that is how life works.

I will always carry with me the memories of the five young men who died that day: Thomas Grosse, Richard Macaylo, Robert Mauterer, James McGuiness Jr., and Steven Ward. I think of the forty-four students who were injured, many who lost limbs and will face the rest of their lives with the painful reminders of that day.

Beyond the incredible sadness, though, one of the things that I will remember most is the resilience of the young people who were directly impacted by that terrible tragedy. In the days that followed, the newspapers carried stories about children injured at the scene telling emergency responders to care for others who had more serious injuries. We heard about students at Nyack High School, upon hearing the horrific news that morning, walking across the street with their teachers from the high school to Nyack Hospital to donate blood. In the face of despair, it was the young people who taught us how to cope.

∽

That day will live with me all of my life. But there is another part of it—the legal fate of Joseph Larkin—that continues to haunt me. I believe now, and I always have, that Joseph Larkin convicted himself. He convicted himself because of his lack of faith in our judicial system and in the innate understanding, sympathy, and sense of justice of his fellow citizens.

I suppose he felt that it was the police and the district attorney who would make the judgment and if he gave them any self-incriminating testimony, they would pounce on it in their effort to get a conviction. I can understand how he would feel this way; after all, the media have been painting an increasingly sinister picture of law enforcement and the prosecution for more than a score of years now. Sure, a lot of it is deserved and when I read about rigged evidence or DAs "getting" witnesses to say what they want to hear, I am just as appalled as any citizen, probably more so because it directly affects public confidence in all of us who are elected or appointed to defend and protect society against crime. But I'll never believe that these cases are the rule and that simple justice does not prevail.

There is no statement in New York law or in the laws of any other state in this nation that a grand jury "must" indict. In fact, our law particularly commands only that a grand jury "may" indict if there is sufficient evidence to warrant it. This, of course, makes the reverse true; even with sufficient evidence, the grand jury "may not" indict, in their own sole discretion.

I will always believe that Joseph Larkin would have been acquitted if he had said something like, "Yes, it's true. Everything the train crew said, everything the children said is true. I can't explain why, I'll never know why. But I had a momentary lapse, call it a daydream, call it what you will, but I will live with that moment the longest day I live. I meant no harm to the children; I intended no harm to anyone. I ask your forgiveness; I ask your mercy so that my family and I will not have to suffer any more than we already have."

The grand jury or at least the trial jury would've had no dispute of fact to resolve, the human element would have been the only consideration.

We had done our job, the blame for the tragedy was placed squarely on Larkin; the train crew was rightfully exonerated. However, it was never for me a source of great accomplishment or pride. It was just the playing out of the final act of a Shakespearean tragedy.

More than four years have passed since that morning in March 1972. We did go on to take that trip to Florida, albeit with heavy hearts. The hurt and pain has eased for most of those involved, but for the families of the five boys *and* for Joseph Larkin, life will never be the same. I must say that it is all the more tragic that so much grief came from an unintentional momentary lapse in an otherwise exemplary life.

Chapter 8

Turn the Other Cheek

It was November 1968, and I had just been reelected by a reasonably healthy margin. It had been a disastrous year for Democrats in Rockland County. We had lost every election across the board, from president of the United States to surrogate, up until the last spot on the ballot, the office of the district attorney, where I came in with over forty-five thousand out of eighty-one thousand votes cast, or 55½ percent of the vote.

It's tough to see so many of your friends lose, but I suppose there is a survival instinct in politics, and we were relieved that I had won. A few days later, Nancy and I set off on a post-election rest trip, this time to Ithaca, New York. Ithaca is not one of your better-known November vacation spots, but there was a New York State District Attorneys Association meeting being held there the weekend after Election Day, and it was a chance to just get away. Even with an early season snowstorm and running out of gas in the middle of the night on the way up, we still thoroughly enjoyed ourselves. We had great camaraderie with the other DAs, especially Mike Dillon from Buffalo. Nancy and I always had a great time with Mike and Elaine Dillon.

On the way back on Sunday night I said to Nancy, "I know you're not going to be too happy about this, but I have one more case I have to try myself this year and that will be it for a while. But don't worry, it's one of those rare cases where you can't lose."

I was right, Nancy was not happy about it. I had tried almost a dozen cases that year, including two murders, and although it had been a highly successful year, Nancy wanted no part of another trial.

"Oh Bob, what do you have assistants for? You know what a trial means. The kids and I won't see you for two weeks and if we do, we have to walk on eggshells. Come on, the holidays are coming. Haven't we worked hard enough this year? *Please*, can one of your men do it?"

"Look Ma, I know I always say it, but this one really is different. It will be over in a week, no sweat. The guy's as guilty as sin. And I have to tell you, he's caused us enough grief in the past couple of years—I want to be there myself when we nail him."

"All right," Nancy said kind of sadly. She knew she could never win these arguments although she seriously doubted what I had said. I didn't—this was to me an exceptionally easy case.

~

Contrary to popular perception, the vast majority of criminal cases are sure winners or sure losers, and they never go to trial. Why? Because they are plea-bargained out. If we have the defendant ice cold with three or four highly reputable eyewitnesses, or evidence like a sixteen-point fingerprint identification, there will be no trial. He will either plead to a lesser offense if he has a relatively clean record or if he's been in trouble before, plead guilty as charged and throw himself on the mercy of the court.

On the other hand, if the prosecution's case goes sour, a witness changes his story, a new and different expert opinion is obtained, or a myriad of other problems occur, the prosecution takes a plea to any minor charge the defendant will go for. Or, if the prosecutor comes to believe the defendant is, in fact, innocent, he moves to dismiss the charge before trial.

That leaves for trial only the cases that are close questions, ones that can go either way. Ninety-five percent or better of criminal cases that actually make it to jury trials fall into this last category. The other less than 5 percent are sure winners, hardened criminals where the DA has a strong case and won't give an inch in a plea bargain. The defendant knows that even if he pleads guilty, the judge will throw the book at him. He's got nothing to lose, so he rolls the dice. He goes to trial, hoping for a miracle, a mistake by the prosecution, a fluky verdict . . . anything to save himself from heavy time. This was just such a case.

~

The week before Thanksgiving 1968, Nick Manzino went to trial with absolutely nothing to lose. At thirty-eight years of age, he had a prior record of fourteen arrests, but only two convictions, one misdemeanor, and one felony that occurred thirteen years earlier, when he was twenty-five years old. However, he was what is called "known to the local police." That meant that we were certain he was up to his neck in crime in our county, but couldn't prove it. My view of those cases was always, "Take an even strain. One of these days we'll get him. His day will come."

Nick Manzino's day came in the early morning hours of April 20, 1968. At 1:20 a.m., a lone masked bandit entered the lobby of the Holiday Inn in Nanuet, New York. He left about six minutes later with about $2,700 in cash in his pocket, the *property* of the Holiday Inn, and successfully made his escape in a vehicle that was not identified.

There had only been two people on duty at the hotel when he entered: a twenty-six-year-old clerk named Matthew "Matt" McCartney and a sixty-seven-year-old janitor, Bruno Johansen. McCartney offered no resistance and was unharmed when the police arrived about five minutes later in response to his call. Johansen was less fortunate. By chance, he walked into the desk area from a back room, just as the masked man was emptying the cash drawer. He apparently put up no fight, but the startled thief turned and struck him in the head with the butt of his pistol. It was a severe blow; it would be eight months before Johansen was out of the hospital and able to return to work.

～

The police investigators who responded to the scene were under the command of Clarkstown Police Detective Lt. George Finlay. As I mentioned before, I suspected that the writer of the *Columbo* TV scripts must have seen George in action. He could be very laid back and ultra-polite to witnesses as he asked "just one more question," the one that often nailed them to the wall. I've even seen him in a trench coat.

Witnesses like Matt McCartney, at the Clarkstown Police Station that morning in April 1968, were George's specialty. By 4 a.m., McCartney was spilling his guts.

"Nick promised that no one would get hurt. He promised, he promised!"

It seems that Nick Manzino frequented the bar in the Holiday Inn and as a "big spender," impressed young McCartney who had never been in trouble before in his life. Before McCartney knew what he was doing, he had agreed to give Manzino the protection of not trying to hit the robbery alarm if Nick came to "see him" early some morning. For this consideration, Nick would pay him 25 percent of the take.

We now had a good confession out of McCartney, but since he was an accomplice to Manzino, and Johansen couldn't identify Nick, we needed more if we were to get the man we really wanted.

Within an hour of breaking, McCartney was working fully and completely with Finlay. It had been prearranged that after the robbery, the two would meet at a rest stop on the New York State Thruway in Sloatsburg at noon the next day, where Manzino would pay McCartney his quarter share.

The meeting would go forward as planned with only one difference; Detective Finlay would be in the trunk of McCartney's car when he entered the rest stop. McCartney had a 1965 Buick Sport Convertible with a radio speaker in the center of the rear seat. The speaker itself was removed, but the grill cover was left in place. Finlay could see clearly up into the interior rear of the car, but he couldn't be seen even if you looked right at the speaker cover.

∼

At noon that day the meeting took place in Sloatsburg. It was too good to be true. Manzino got into the front passenger seat in clear view of George and said, "Everything okay? The police give you a hard time?"

"No sweat," answered the surprisingly cool McCartney.

"Well look, I got about $2,200 and change, but you did a good job—here's an even $600."

Manzino then handed McCartney $600 in $20s and $10s. Of course, we knew the actual take was $2,700. He wasn't too bad a guy; he was only cheating McCartney out of about $75.

Within three minutes, Manzino was out of the car, back in his own car, and on his way. Within six minutes, the backup men, Detectives Russ Smith and Joe Mercurio, had Manzino spread-eagle over the hood of their unmarked police car. After being advised of his Miranda rights, Nick, of course, didn't go for spit. He wanted to talk to his lawyer.

That was the case as I entered court on Monday, November 18, 1968. Manzino had been indicted for First-Degree Robbery and First-Degree Assault. He had inflicted serious physical injury and used a deadly weapon in the course of a holdup.

I had only six witnesses: Johansen and his doctor (to prove how serious the injury was); McCartney, who put Manzino in the middle of the whole thing; and Detectives George Finlay, Russ Smith, and Joe Mercurio. While McCartney may have been an accomplice, his testimony could be corroborated by the three detectives. Finlay saw and heard the "payoff" and Smith and Mercurio saw Manzino enter the Thruway rest stop, get in McCartney's car, and found more than $2,000 in cash in small bills on him when he was arrested.

There were only two physical exhibits for evidence, the $600 taken immediately from McCartney and the $2,120 found in Manzino's wallet.

The defense attorney was Maurice Phillips of Spring Valley, an extremely capable courtroom litigator. As we began to pick a jury, I thought to myself, "I don't give a damn who the defense attorney is, it could be F. Lee Bailey guided by the ghost of Clarence Darrow. Manzino's still going down."

I've always felt the jury selection was one of the most important parts of any case; after all, those are the twelve people who will make the ultimate decision. But this was different. Just before going to court, I had a cup of coffee with Ann Hickey and said, "You know, Annie, I'll take any twelve people they put in the jury box. No one, but no one, is going to acquit this guy."

I could see that Ann was surprised. Although she wasn't the principal person on any case, she played an important role in *every* case. She never went to court, but she was always there for the preparation, the self-criticism afterward, and the long vigils of jury deliberations.

"Boss, are you sure you're not being overconfident? The sheriff's deputies tell me Manzino is strutting around the jail acting like he's got it made."

"Don't worry, Annie, this one is different. We've got him on ice."

Jury selection took less than a day and I was true to my word. Each side had twenty peremptory challenges; Phillips used six and I used none. There was only one juror where I had any doubt, and, of course, the jury selection rule is "when in doubt, get him out." I broke the rule. I left a Presbyterian minister on the jury. The minister was a young, personable guy and he answered all the questions in a totally satisfactory manner.

"Yes, he could convict if the evidence warranted it. Yes, he understood that the presumption of innocence could be overcome or else no one would ever be convicted of anything. Yes, he knew that the prosecutor's burden was to prove guilt beyond a reasonable doubt—not to a mathematical certainty." In almost all cases, that would be impossible.

Thus we began our trial that Tuesday morning with a jury of nine men and three women; one of the men—a minister. I was confident, even though the night before in the office Investigator Herman Van der Linde, an old pro whom I respected, said, "Meehan, the DA, leaves a minister on his jury? You must be off your skull!"

"Herman, have faith!"

By Wednesday afternoon we were recessing for the long Thanksgiving weekend and I rose and said, "The People rest." The witnesses had all come across beautifully; it was like the pieces of a fine clock meshing together.

Phillips hadn't hurt any of our witnesses on cross. He was sympathetic to Johansen, who couldn't identify Manzino and totally respectful to his doctor, who described the poor man's head injuries. He was just as respectful to Detectives Finlay, Smith, and Mercurio. He treated them as good police officers, fine men doing their jobs.

McCartney was different. He was painted as a man responsible for a felony who was "beating the wrap" by implicating poor Manzino. But even with that, McCartney's story wasn't broken at all in the brief half-hour of cross-examination. Phillips could depict McCartney as evil as he wanted to, and that didn't change the eyewitness testimony or the passing of the money and the conversation in the car.

Maurice Phillips said the defense would call witnesses and thus the case was adjourned until Monday morning, the 25th.

~

It was a pleasant Thanksgiving. As usual we had eighteen to twenty family members at our house for dinner and football, both on television and in the yard. (Happily, the infamous and notorious "Mud Bowl" between the Eagles and Lions that day did not delay the feast that Nancy had worked so hard to prepare.) Nancy was surprised and pleased that I really wasn't worrying about the case on trial. By this time she was used to spoiled dinners and working weekends during trials. I even began to sense that my wife thought I was overconfident.

Monday morning it was back to the Manzino case and my first big shock of the trial. Phillips had only one witness to call. "The defense calls Nicholas Manzino."

To my complete surprise, Manzino was an excellent witness on his own behalf. He was soft-spoken, humble, and to my chagrin quite believable. Phillips very wisely went right to his client's two prior convictions. He knew we couldn't mention the twelve other arrests without a mistrial, so he zeroed in on the convictions and to some extent used them to his advantage.

"Yes, I was a bad kid," Nick began. "I was always in trouble and life was rough. I went in the Army to Korea, but when I got back there was no job and I got in trouble. But I learned my lesson and now they're picking on me because they know I had a record when I was young."

Then Phillips took him through the events of the evening, with Manzino declaring he was home alone in bed by midnight. "I'm sorry I don't have any witnesses, but that's the God's honest truth." What about the next day at noon in Sloatsburg? He readily admitted meeting McCartney in the car and giving him the $600. Well what about him saying, "Everything okay, the police give you a hard time?"

"Sure, I said it. I knew the Holiday Inn had been held up the night before and I just wanted to find out if he was all right."

"Why is it that you gave Mr. McCartney $600?"

"I owed the kid $500 and a guy from Syracuse who owed me money paid me back $2,200. I gave the kid $600 because he had been nice to me a few times, giving me a room on the arm once in a while when I had something hot going for me in the bar."

Manzino was not painting himself as a pillar of the community, but he sure sounded believable. But then he went too far.

At the end of his direct examination, Phillips asked, "Nick, you said you were in the Army in Korea. Will you tell us about that?"

"Well, I was over there from '51 to '53 and saw a lot of action." He said it in a completely humble manner and didn't seem to want to pursue it, but Phillips did.

"What type of discharge did you receive?"

"Honorable, sir."

"Did you receive any medals? And, if so, will you tell us about the circumstances."

"Well, I was at Pork Chop Hill and our platoon got cut off and our radioman got shot, and I pulled him back across the field. I guess they thought I was brave or something because they gave me the Silver Star."

By this time the courtroom was in dead silence as Phillips continued.

"And, Nick, for your conduct at Pork Chop Hill, were you recommended for any other medals?"

Nick put his head down rather sheepishly and said, barely audibly, "Yes, sir."

"Nick, please this is important," Phillips continued. "What medal was it that you were recommended for?"

A seemingly long silence and then another low, but this time clearly audible answer from Manzino, "The Congressional Medal of Honor, sir."

"Your witness," Phillips concluded as he turned toward me and then sat down.

I asked for a brief adjournment and got it from Judge Gallucci and was on my way back up to the District Attorney's Office almost at a dead run. We had been hurt and hurt bad. The story about the loan repayment could probably be cracked, but the war stories were damned impressive; the kind of thing that "reasonable doubt" is built around.

Within minutes, Ann Hickey was on the phone to the Department of the Army in Washington. "Damn it," I said. "Why couldn't it be the Navy? I could call the Third Naval District at Church Street in New York City and have his record read to me in ten minutes. It had to be the goddamn Army. I don't even know where the hell they keep their records."

Within the hour, I knew all about Army records. Army Second Lt. Peter Thayer would be catching the one o'clock air shuttle from Washington to New York. He could be picked up at the Eastern gate at LaGuardia and be brought back to Rockland County with a high-speed police escort by later in the afternoon.

Lieutenant Thayer had a folder with him, but it would still be a few hours before he arrived. However, I already knew the contents of the folder as I reentered the courtroom after the brief recess to commence cross-examination of Manzino.

I began by questioning him about the loan. When had McCartney loaned him the $500? He didn't recall. For what reason was the loan made? "Well, I was short."

"Did you sign any type of note?"

"No, it was just a friendly loan."

"Oh, it was a friendly loan. Was McCartney your friend?"

"Yes."

"Well, why do you suppose he's framing you now?" He didn't know and he hemmed and hawed without giving an answer, but he was still keeping his cool.

"Who was the guy from Syracuse?"

"I don't know his name, he's just a guy I met in Spring Valley."

"Do you know his address?"

"No."

"Did he sign any note for the loan you gave him?"

"No."

"Another one of those friendly loans?"

"I suppose so."

"All right, you're saying that you loaned $2,200 to a guy who's name and address you don't even know at about the same time you were hitting this kid McCartney up for $500; you want the jury to believe that?"

"Well, I'm telling the truth!" Unfortunately for me he did sound like he was telling the truth, and was a little hurt that I didn't believe him.

~

Then I went to the "war stories." I went into them in more detail than Phillips had, going through his Army service from the day he "enlisted." He recounted his battle experience and then I asked him to tell me if there had been any kind of ceremony when he got the Silver Star. Oh, there had been, it was small, just his company "and some general who came over."

About the Congressional Medal of Honor, how did he know he was up for that?

"My captain told me, he saw the whole thing and he recommended me and he told me the general was going to recommend it too."

"How long was he your captain?"

"Almost two years."

"Did you like, respect, and admire the captain?"

"Yes, sir."

"And what was his name?"

For the first time Manzino seemed to break a little. He couldn't remember the captain's name. After fumbling a little, he blurted out "Captain Jones! That was it, Captain Jones." This time he hadn't impressed the jury. He came across as having just made the name up.

Having now properly set him up, I went for the jugular. I went over to the prosecutor's table, open a file that actually had nothing to do with Manzino or his case. I took out some official looking papers and held them in my hand as I continued questioning Manzino.

"Now, Mr. Manzino, isn't it true that you were *drafted* into the United States Army on May 3, 1951, and isn't it true that you reported for induction at the Draft Board in Spring Valley, New York, early that morning?"

"Yes, I guess that's true."

"Well, didn't you say you had enlisted?"

"Yeah, but I guess I was wrong."

"Further, Mr. Manzino, is it not true that after reporting for induction you were taken by bus to the United States Army Training Center at Fort Dix, New Jersey, where you were formally sworn in that day?"

"Yes," the answer was weak and barely audible.

"Continuing, Mr. Manzino, isn't it true that you commenced basic training at Fort Dix the following day?"

"Yes."

"And, Mr. Manzino," I continue, my voice rising, "is it not also true that you never finished basic training, that you were hospitalized on July 9, 1951, and isn't it further the truth that you received a general medical discharge from the United States Army on the seventh day of August, 1951, and that you never set foot on the Peninsula of Korea in your entire life?"

There was silence—Manzino didn't answer. Finally I said: "I am waiting for your answer, Mr. Manzino."

"Well you got some papers there, I don't know what they say, I suppose that could be right."

"You suppose, what do you mean you suppose? Do you suppose the stories about Pork Chop Hill are a pack of lies?"

Again he didn't answer. After Judge Gallucci directed him to answer, his final answer was a very weak, "I guess so." I asked no further questions. I sat down. After a brief recess in which Phillips conferred with Manzino, he asked no further questions. The defense rested. The case was over except for summations.

~

Lieutenant Thayer did arrive later that afternoon but he never had to testify. The point had been made. The lieutenant had the very official looking service jacket of Private Nicholas Manzino, US Army. I had learned the significant dates from Lieutenant Thayer on the telephone and had prepared a memo that I placed on top of an equally official-looking file that I had used in court.

Actually the file I used in court looked both official and familiar—because it was. It was the service jacket, returned upon retirement of Lt. Senior Grade Robert R. Meehan, USNR 1105/573148. Lieutenant Meehan *had* been to Korea.

Summations were not that long. I didn't harp on the war stories. I just said to the jury, "It's up to you. Can you believe this man?"

The jury got the case after Judge Gallucci's charge at about 5:30 that evening. The old court reporter Joe Komonchak said, "They should be back with *guilty* before it's time for dinner." They weren't.

The hours went by slowly and as they did my concern grew. How could they possibly acquit? Our witnesses had all held up, the defendant had literally been destroyed on the stand. At 10:30 that night, the jury asked for a redefinition of reasonable doubt. Bad. I was now very worried, that's always a defendant's question.

At 12:30 a.m. they were locked up for the night. The next day they resumed deliberations at 9 a.m. At three o'clock that afternoon, the jury came in with its verdict.

"We the jury find the defendant *not* guilty on both counts."

By that time I was ready for it, but it was still a shock. Judge Gallucci seemed really taken aback. It was the only time in all the years I've worked before Judge Gallucci that I ever heard him tell the jury he disagreed with their verdict.

It was the only case I ever had, win or lose, where I felt the jury system has failed. But I still stood up in open court and congratulated Mr. Phillips and shook Manzino's hand. Manzino himself seemed to be in a happy state of shock and actually was very pleasant.

~

Outside the courtroom, I said to Eric Vrhel, "Get ahold of one of those jurors. Find out what the hell happened." Eric was back to me in ten minutes, by which time I was standing talking to Herman Van der Linde and Werner Loeb. Werner was then chief assistant public defender and would later become one of my best assistant DAs.

Eric said, "Herman was right, it was the minister. The first vote was 11 to 1 for conviction, five minutes after they went out. It was still 11 to 1 when they went to bed last night. He convinced them all today. They all knew he was guilty, but the minister said he deserved another chance—and, get this boss, the minister went after you personally in the jury room for destroying Manzino's reputation on the service record in front of all those people."

Herman just smiled and I slowly shook my head with a very weak smile. Werner, who is Jewish, then broke us all up.

"Bob, you made a mistake. You should've had a rabbi on the jury. He believes in *an eye for an eye, a tooth for a tooth*. A minister, he'll just turn the other cheek."

Chapter 9

That's Peggy O'Neil!

Eric Vrhel came to work for me January 1, 1967, the same day that Ed McElroy did. I lost Ray Lindemann when he was elected sheriff, but I gained two new men, doubling the investigators staff.

For Ed, coming to the DA's Office was much easier than for Eric. McElroy fit right into the mold of Ray Lindemann, and Lindy's predecessor, Bill Sterns. Ed, Lindy, and Bill had all worked in local police departments, were well respected in local law enforcement circles, and knew just about every cop in the county on a first-name basis. When they went out to the local police stations, they were always well received and got the full cooperation of the department. Eric was different—he was an outsider; he had to prove himself.

Eric grew up in the Scranton/Wilkes-Barre area of Pennsylvania and moved to Rockland County in the late 1950s when he married a local girl, Peggy Snyder. He was literally a "jack of all trades." As a boy in Pennsylvania, he had done everything from becoming a pretty good farmer, to an auto mechanic and he even tended bar at his father's tavern. He had a hair-trigger mind, but also loved to work with his hands.

Eric served in the United States Marines in the mid-1950s. He moved to the Suffern area after getting married, and further developed his many skills. He drove trailer trucks, worked as an ironworker, and became an accomplished carpenter, plumber, and electrician. He worked for two years as a police officer for the borough of Upper Saddle River, New Jersey, and then left to take a management level position at the Ford Motor Company assembly plant in Mahwah, New Jersey.

While working for Ford, he started his own licensed private investigation business and that's how I first came to know him. I was in private practice on Cherry Lane and he only lived a mile away. He started doing investigations for me on auto accident and criminal defense cases. I was pleased with his thorough investigative work, but I think it was our common interest in construction and automobile repairs that caused us to become personal friends.

He lived in a house that he had personally built in 1958, and I must say I was very impressed. The house was not big or lavish, but it was solidly and beautifully built, with the attention to detail you never see in a development house. Soon after we met, he bought the lot next door and was commencing to build another house, this one far bigger and much grander than the first. I used to like to go over and watch him and sometimes help. I never claimed to be in a league with Eric as an artisan, but he taught me a lot and helped me develop into a hell of a good amateur builder.

~

Strangely, it was just as much his construction skills as his investigative ability that caused me to hire him at the DA's Office. At that time Rockland, along with Suffolk, were the fastest growing counties in New York State. The Tappan Zee Bridge opened in 1955 and in the next ten years, the population of Rockland County more than doubled.

This building boom brought with it many good things . . . new wealth, new and better recreational facilities, and good neighbors who chose to escape the city of New York and came to love our county. But as night follows day, with the good came the bad . . . the chiselers, the home-improvement swindlers, the fraudulent door-to-door salesmen, among others.

This was a job for a good DA's Office, but it wasn't being done in Rockland or any other suburb. The laws were poorly drawn, but just as important, the DAs didn't understand the types of people they were up against. Too often the con men were called in by the district attorney and proceeded to con the DA. I was determined not to allow this to happen in Rockland. After all I had campaigned and largely been elected on a promise to fight consumer fraud. When it came to construction, nobody was going to be able to con Investigator Eric Vrhel.

Eric was with me less than six months before he proved himself to me. He led a crackdown on fraud and it was his knowledge of building methods and procedures that led to our first conviction of a public official in April 1967, a building inspector on the take who had been turned in by a good witness. The trial would have been lost without Eric sitting beside me, feeding me the technical information on plumbing that became vital to the case.

The problem was that Eric's part of the work didn't get headlines. I knew he was doing the job, but the public and, more importantly for him, the local police did not.

Ed McElroy had his murders, robberies, and rapes, and everyone knew about them. Not so Eric. It was a few years before Eric got the chance to prove his worth to the county at large.

~

Eric's first locally notorious case began one evening in my Cherry Lane home in the early fall of 1969. Eric came over and said he wanted to talk to me alone. It was important, so I shooed the kids out of the den where we had all been watching *Get Smart*, so that we could have a private talk. Eric began, "I was just up at the Tallman Pancake House and this swimming pool builder, who I met a couple of years ago, came up and asked me if it was true that I was now working for the DA's Office. I told him I was and right away he wanted to know if I wanted to 'turn a fast buck.'

"It seems the son of a good friend of his was picked up in that drug raid a few weeks ago and he's willing to pay off to fix the case."

"Son of a bitch," I responded. "Who was he? Did you get the name of the kid? Hell, I think we picked up thirty-eight in that last raid."

"His name's Ike Siedler. He's still in the swimming pool business. He wouldn't go for the name of his friend. I couldn't push too hard. I wanted to string him along."

I didn't know who Siedler was, but I was personally angry. I may not have been the smartest DA around, but I had a reputation for being an "untouchable" and this guy had some nerve thinking he could fix a case in my office.

Before Eric left that night, we had agreed that he would get back to Siedler, act interested, find out how much money was involved and who was involved. This time however, Eric would be wired for sound.

Electronic gear was nonexistent in the Rockland DA's Office in 1969, so the "wiring" meant that Eric would tape his own little recorder around his waist with a microphone under his shirt and tie. It was also agreed that the case would be discussed with no one, not Mac, not Annie, no one. Need to know was the rule.

Eric met Siedler the next morning and before noon he was in the office with the tape of the conversation. I was impressed by Eric's voice on the tape, he was doing a fine con job on Siedler; he really sounded like he was out to make that fast buck.

Siedler identified his friend as Dr. Isadore Markowitz, a psychiatrist from Monsey whose twenty-two-year-old son, Nathan Markowitz, had been arrested in the recent drug raid. Siedler said his friend would probably be willing to go to $5,000. It turned out that, for Siedler, it wasn't all friendship; he wanted 25 percent of the take.

As per my instructions the night before, Eric insisted that he meet and talk directly with Dr. Markowitz and that any payment would also have to be direct. Siedler went for this with no trouble at all. It was arranged that Eric and Ike Siedler would meet the doctor for breakfast the next morning at the same pancake house where Siedler first approached him.

By mid-morning the next day, Eric walked into my office with a really dynamite tape. When Eric arrived at the pancake house, Siedler and Markowitz were already there, so he switched on his recorder immediately. Siedler came over to meet Eric at the door and immediately said, in a whispered voice, "Ask for six, we can settle for five."

There was no audible response from Eric, but his quick mind was already working. There was the exchange of greetings as Eric was introduced to Dr. Markowitz and also the ordering of coffee and toast. This was followed by about eight or nine minutes of irrelevant small talk, including the general weather picture. Finally, Siedler broke the ice.

"Well, we all know what we're here for."

"Right," Eric responded. "Just what are you looking for?"

Dr. Markowitz didn't mince words. "My boy's in trouble. Ike here tells me you can take care of it, and I want to know how much you want to do it?"

"Let's get this straight," Eric said. "I checked it out; your boy, Nathan, is charged with criminal sale of heroin. He faces up to fifteen years. Do you want to get him off with a light sentence or do you want the case against him killed altogether?"

"I want it killed altogether and I'm willing to pay. Just tell me how much," Markowitz said.

"OK, the only way to do that is to have the evidence destroyed and that means I've got to pay the evidence room man too. This is going to cost!"

"Damn it," Markowitz said impatiently. "How much?"

"Well a thousand for him and the other guys, and I'll need five more, that means six thousand altogether."

"Does that include Meehan?" Markowitz said.

I could tell Eric was a little taken aback but quickly responded, "I'm not saying, I'll just guarantee you, you pay me six and your kid walks away from the whole thing—no time, no record, no nothing."

"All right, you've got a deal. I can have the money for you in two days."

The conversation continued concerning the place and time of the payment. It was agreed that it would be 7:30 a.m., two days later, but Eric wouldn't agree to a location. Instead, he said he would call Siedler at 7 a.m. that morning and give him the location. I could hear the sneer in Eric's voice as he said, "You are nice guys but I'm not going to give you a chance to set me up." Smart move; let them think he's worried about being double-crossed, instead of giving them time to think that they are being set up themselves.

I think the thing I remember most about that tape-recording was the very last words on it. The three were apparently walking out together when Siedler whispered to Eric, "We made a very bad mistake. We should've asked for ten, he would have gone for it!" Some friend.

⁓

The decision of where the meeting would take place was mine and I decided on the parking lot of the Howard Johnson Motel and Restaurant in Nanuet. There were three principal reasons: First, the motel rooms overlooked the parking lot for an excellent hidden camera location. Second, backup men could sit in the restaurant and have a good view while mingling with the heavy breakfast crowd. And third, I could bring George Finlay and his Clarkstown detectives in on the case. The Howard Johnson was in their territory.

That Friday morning I sat in the Clarkstown Police Station waiting for the meeting to take place. By that time I had learned from experience, but reluctantly, that I shouldn't be at the scene myself. I must leave that part of the job to trained investigators. However, through moving pictures, I would later see the whole thing from start to finish, in living color, no less.

The prearrangements were made. Eric would arrive in his private car at 6:30 a.m. and park in a good location for visibility. Detective Russ Smith of Clarkstown would be in a second-floor room of the motel with the camera and train his lens on Eric's car through an opening in the drawn drapes. Two plainclothes detectives, including Ed McElroy, would be inside the restaurant. George Finlay, on his own improvisation, would be dressed as a Howard Johnson busboy, complete with a white uniform and paper hat, and would be sweeping the sidewalk. When Siedler and Markowitz arrived, Eric would get out of his car but not move toward them; instead he would wait for them to come over to him. When they gave Eric the envelope, he was to open it, do a fast check to see that there was a substantial amount of actual cash in it, scratch his head as a signal, and then step back. George Finlay would then come forward and draw his gun, at which time Eric was to draw his gun and Siedler and Markowitz would be placed under arrest.

A few days later, I saw the developed movie; it was beautiful. It starts with Siedler and Markowitz arriving in Siedler's car, entering the parking lot and pulling up right next to Eric's car. The two get out and Eric gets out, and they walk over and both shake his hand. Dr. Markowitz immediately reaches inside his jacket and pulls out what turned out to be sixty $100 bills and puts them right on the hood of Eric's car, no envelope, no nothing. Eric looks startled, but gives no signal. At this point, into the picture from the left, pushing a broom furiously toward them, comes George Finlay. Finlay is only about five feet away when Eric finally scratches his head, and George immediately drops the broom and pulls out his service revolver.

"Police officer, you're under arrest," he shouts. Well if you ever saw two frightened guys, it was Siedler and Markowitz. Eric didn't pull his gun immediately, but when he did, I think they were even more surprised. I learned later that they initially thought he was being arrested too, and when Dr. Markowitz learned that Eric Vrhel was in on it, he was furious, *furious with Siedler* who apparently sold him a bill of goods about how Eric could be trusted.

∼

By Friday noon the exciting part of a case that only began on Monday evening was over. But for Eric, with only a fraction of the effort that he had put into so many other cases, he had arrived. This was his case; he had pulled it off and local law enforcement respected him for it. Dr. Markowitz and Ike Siedler were indicted for bribery and I must say we had the nearest thing to an airtight case I ever had. You, therefore, might think it strange, but I didn't pursue it all the way. Many may think I was too soft on Markowitz but I allowed both Siedler and Markowitz to plead guilty to a misdemeanor and receive fines and a short jail term.

My reasons were simple. I was dealing with a forty-eight-year-old professional man who had never been in any trouble with the law in his entire life. He had an outstanding reputation as a psychiatrist and I knew that a felony conviction at that time meant automatic forfeiture of his license to practice medicine. I felt, forgetting fine or imprisonment, that was too great a penalty for him—and for his patients—to pay. After all, no matter how much he insulted me and my office, no matter how important it was to rid society of this type of pervasive evil, it still boiled down to one thing, a father trying to help his only son. There was no motive to buy influence, to corrupt government, or obtain a personal financial benefit, as is the case in more than 99 percent of briberies.

I had a somewhat dimmer view of Mr. Siedler, but his record was also clean and it would have been difficult to prosecute the middleman to the full extent of the law and let the actual briber off so easy.

Markowitz did have a hearing on revocation of his license after the case was over. We did not press that it be revoked, and he did not lose his license. To me the key was that his crime had nothing to do with the practice of medicine. Later, when Eric had another "doctor" case, I was consistent. His crime went to the heart of practicing medicine and we went after that doctor's license with a vengeance.

∿

Eric's next big case came just about a year to the day later. Like the Markowitz case, it was over in a few days, but that's where the similarity ends.

In the summer of 1970, Eric took over our newly organized Narcotics Unit in the office. Now his work would be much different than it had been in the past. This required undercover street work, haunting the bars and other likely places for narcotics sales, irregular hours, strange attire, and everything that went with actually establishing a second identity. I have always considered this to be the worst job in law enforcement, and I don't recommend it to a family man. It can have disastrous personal effects.

Eric took on his new assignment with great vigor and dedication. He worked day and night arranging narcotic buys, anywhere from $10 for marijuana to $300–$500 for relatively large amounts of heroin or cocaine. He was good at it and by early September had won the confidence of a small-time local pusher. Then one night the pusher said that his supplier from New York City was coming to bring a package and Eric talked him into letting him go along.

When the meeting took place, the man from New York City was furious that a stranger had been brought along, but Eric handled that well and within an hour they were friendly and discussing business. The dealer from New York was a short stocky, black man, about forty years old, who was introduced only as *The Judge*. Apparently, his associates from the low world gave him the moniker because they thought he was very smart. A mistake—he wasn't!

By five o'clock that morning, Eric had convinced The Judge that he could handle "half a key" of heroin; that he had a contact from Buffalo who would be down the next day and take the whole thing. Before that initial meeting was over, they had agreed on a price, $12,000, and that a delivery and payment would be made within forty-eight hours.

∽

When Eric reported the story to me, I was highly skeptical. We had a lot of two-bit pushers in Rockland County, but no one big and I guess I had become convinced from reading stories, watching television, and so forth, that these guys were very smart. As I learned in the case of The Judge and others that followed, I was wrong!

Eric knew exactly what he was talking about when he said "half a key." This was half a kilogram or roughly one and one-eighth pounds, just enough to bring him under the then newly passed New York State narcotics statute. Before the new law was enacted, no matter how much narcotics were sold, it was still only a Class C Felony, punishable by up to fifteen years—the same penalty whether you sold $10 worth or $10 million worth of hard drugs. Under the new law, sale of a pound or more meant a Class A Felony and automatic life imprisonment.

Cynical as I may have been, we went forward with preparations. Investigator Charlie Purcell of the State Police and Detective George Finlay of Clarkstown were brought in on it and we arranged that the sale would take place in a room at the Holiday Inn in Nanuet. Three rooms were arranged for; the one in the middle for the meet and backup protection on either sides. Uniformed men with walkie-talkies were in marked cars about a quarter-mile away, standing by ready to block the two exits from the Holiday Inn if necessary. This type of preparation was elaborate but not difficult to make. We did, however, have one very big problem, as I said to Eric. "Where the hell are we going to come up with $12,000? This guy may be dumb, but I assume that he's going to want to see the 'bread' before he comes up with the hard stuff."

In my last years in the District Attorney's Office, we had worked out a "banking" plan for show money, but not so in 1970. Therefore, we worked it out as best we could. We only had about $200 left in our investigative fund. I took $300 out of my checking account, with the admonition, "I better have it back by Friday or I won't be able to make my mortgage payment!" Eric personally came up with $700.

This meant we were dealing with just 10 percent of what we needed. Although we could package it with wrappers of $20 bills filled mostly with singles and make it look like a lot more, it was up to Eric to make sure The Judge never really got to count it.

∾

Investigator Bruce Conklin of the New York State Police was assigned to be "the man from Buffalo." I was pleased. We were on new and possibly dangerous ground, dealing with "weight" dealers from New York City. With Bruce, my fear of harm to our men was greatly reduced. Conklin was young, soft-spoken, but very tough. If there was to be a fight or gunplay, I would always recommend being on Bruce's side. I never saw Conklin abuse a prisoner physically or verbally. I did, however, see a narcotics defendant go after Bruce once in the squad room at the state police barracks. Before it was over, the defendant had plenty of time to reflect on the error of his ways—from a hospital bed.

Eric arranged to meet with The Judge and two days later at about two o'clock on a bright sunny afternoon, Eric and Bruce went to meet him at the bar of the Holiday Inn.

We were sure the dealer wouldn't come alone; he would have some protection with him. We were half right—he didn't come alone, but I would hardly call his associates protection. He was accompanied by two people, a twenty-six-year-old black man who couldn't have been more than five feet, four inches, and 130 pounds at best, and an eighteen-year-old rather plump but pretty girl, who was also black.

Although I was right about The Judge wanting to see the money before showing the heroine, from the outset we had the upper hand. Bruce made it clear "I'm not showing you a fucking cent until I frisk you and your friends here. I'm not about to be ripped off."

The Judge seemed almost offended that they would even consider a rip-off, but readily agreed to a search, without even raising the question, "How about searching your group, too?" This was extremely fortunate since both Eric and Bruce were armed.

They went directly from the bar to the room where The Judge and his male companion were both thoroughly searched. The girl's handbag was searched and her flare-type slacks were checked for an ankle holster, but that was about it.

The next move was an idea that was pure Eric Vrhel. The Judge wanted to see the money. Eric had the money neatly wrapped with $20 bills on top of singles in a cigar box. He walked right over to The Judge, opened the cigar box and there, lying across the top of the money, was an open switchblade knife. As he held the box with his left hand, Eric grabbed the switchblade knife and stuck it hard against The Judge's gut as he said, "You black bastard, you touch one dime of this without coming up with the stuff and you're a dead man."

The Judge was so shocked, he immediately backed off and was totally on the defensive. Eric's play had worked beautifully. The Judge was so anxious to show that he was acting in good faith, he did none of the things we assumed a big drug peddler would do to protect himself.

After checking out the money, The Judge's small male friend left and five minutes later was back with a brown paper bag, inside of which was a clear plastic bag filled with the heroin. Bruce went into the bathroom where he had his field test kit taped inside the toilet tank. It checked out, the heroine test was positive; not as pure as The Judge had bragged that it would be, but the real stuff.

Bruce stepped out of the bathroom with his service revolver drawn, and on the signal, Eric did the same. Within three minutes the room was filled with police. The Judge and his friends were initially so scared that they were going to be murdered by a couple of rip-off artists that they were almost relieved to find out that they were being arrested by the state police and the District Attorney's Office.

I had been in one of the marked cars with the uniformed men, about a quarter of a mile away, and we arrived at the room about five minutes later. I'll always remember approaching that room. All I could hear was the sobbing cries of the young girl saying over and over again, "He made me do it, he made me do it!"

I, of course, had no sympathy for The Judge or the man with him, but I must say I felt sorry for that young girl. I was sure she didn't really know what she was getting involved in and we later took this into consideration when we let her off with less than a year in jail.

The case was a cause célèbre and good for my office and the state and local police, but for Eric in particular this was another big notch in his belt; the "outsider" had really arrived.

There was only one flaw in an otherwise perfect case. As I said to Eric the next day, "How could you do it? My number one frauds man! You, sir, have been the victim of a consumer fraud! Your friend The Judge short-weighted you. There was only fifteen and a half ounces!" Eric and I laughed, but that was one short-weighting where it really paid off for the thieves. The Judge, aka Harold Russell, and his accomplice, Grover Moore, are now both serving fifteen-year sentences at the New York State Prison at Auburn, New York. But had it not been for their consumer fraud, they would be in for life.

～

The last of the trilogy of Eric Vrhel cases began for me like the first, in my den on Cherry Lane. But it was to last much longer than the others and be another one of my personal maximum efforts.

It was early evening on a cold, snowy night in mid-February 1971 when Eric arrived. He wanted to see me alone; he had something interesting to show me. He didn't say a word; he just showed me three prescriptions, one for Seconal made out to a Peter Grimaldi, the second for Biphetamines for Michael Cutter, and the third for Darvon made out to William Tyler. All three were on the printed prescription pads of Dr. Samuel Kass of Spring Valley. I was impressed.

The names Grimaldi, Cutter, and Tyler were by then familiar to me; they were aliases that Eric used in his undercover narcotics work. The name of Dr. Kass was also familiar. We had a tip the summer before that he was selling prescriptions, but we hadn't been able to break into his circle until that evening in February.

Eric had been what we called "on the street" for almost a year at that time and he had developed some pretty good informants. One of those informants was an attractive twenty-two-year-old girl named Catherine Bartley, but to me known only as *Candy Bar*.

Candy Bar had made the first contact with the good doctor and within two weeks, she brought Eric in and introduced him as a friend, named Phil Terry, who just came up from Florida and had his own little rock combo.

The doctor was careless to say the least. Within fifteen minutes he was writing prescriptions for him. The price was simply $10 per narcotic prescription and $5 for other prescription drugs. He made no effort to examine Eric or to open any type of medical file on him. He just asked what drugs Eric wanted and what names he wanted on the prescriptions. After taking $25, his only comment was "Don't get these filled at the same drugstore." I then told Eric, "Look, this is a real breakthrough, but we don't have a case against him at all yet."

"Let's face it," I went on, "it's your word and Candy's against his. He's a medical doctor, and we lose. He may not have patient files on your names yet, but he'll sure as hell have them fast if we bust him. He'll say it's not his fault if patients give phony names. A jury wouldn't waste an hour with this one. They'll acquit in less time than it took you to get those prescriptions!"

Eric agreed and so we sat there and laid out our plan of attack against Dr. Samuel Kass. Eric would go back again, but from now on he would be wired for sound. By this time, the DA's Office did own some sound gear, but it wasn't much more sophisticated than Eric's little tape recorder we used a year and a half earlier with Dr. Markowitz. So a week later Eric was back in Dr. Kass's office with Candy Bar. This time he bought five prescriptions under five different names for $35. However, the recording was problematic. The recorder had been too high on Eric's chest and his heartbeat interfered with the sound. I also learned that Dr. Kass spoke in a low voice and it was hard to pick up all his words. This was an issue that was to continually plague the case. After all, Eric couldn't pull a "Maxwell Smart" and say, "Please speak into my tie."

Eric returned each Thursday for the following three weeks, but not with Candy Bar. Each time I had him take a different man from a different law enforcement agency: one state police investigator, one deputy sheriff, and one investigator with the State Organized Crime Task Force. I wasn't going to rely on the tapes alone. I wanted the credibility of all of these law enforcement agencies to back us up. After all, a man's license to practice medicine was going to be on the line.

By the end of the last visit, we had twenty-nine prescriptions—sixteen for narcotics and thirteen for other dangerous prescription drugs. We also had some pretty strong incriminating statements by the doctor, but the quality of the tapes, due to his low voice, was still poor.

~

We also had another problem, the law itself. In one of those quirks of the law, the state legislature in enacting the new Penal Law of 1967 had *forgotten* to put in a penalty for the sale of prescriptions. Prior to 1967, such an act by a doctor was a felony punishable by up to five years in prison on each count. Although the new Public Health Law still spelled out the offense, there was no penalty for it and the only thing that stopped Dr. Kass from walking away scot-free was what is known as the saving clause: "If no other penalty is prescribed by law, it shall be a Misdemeanor punishable by up to one year in prison, a $2,000 fine, or both." Since I felt twenty-nine years in prison and a $58,000 fine was more than sufficient, I wasn't upset by the flaw in the law except for one thing, a felony conviction would mean automatic forfeiture of license; a misdemeanor meant a possible loss of license. I knew this would be important. It was.[1]

When Dr. Samuel Kass was indicted in April 1971, he made the usual protestations of innocence and it was nine months later before we got all the pretrial business behind us and could finally go forward with the trial.

The most significant issue in the trial, which I personally handled, regarded the tapes. Eric and the other investigators involved, of course, could remember what had been said and, therefore, listening to the tapes, they could pick up the soft-spoken words of Dr. Kass. The big problem

---

1. See the notes section, p. 239.

was that a jury hearing the tapes for the first time, and not knowing their content in advance, would be hard-pressed to understand Dr. Kass's own words. We, therefore, made very careful typewritten transcripts of the tapes and by following the written transcript while listening to the tape, it was actually very easy to understand what Dr. Kass was saying.

The only problem was getting the trial judge, John Gallucci, to allow the jurors to have written transcripts in their hands as they listened to the tapes. His first inclination was not to allow them because they might violate the defendant's constitutional rights. I won that battle of the tape transcripts during the trial in January 1972 for one reason. I had been on *The Barry Gray Show* a little over two years before and had read fellow guest Giraud Chester's book, *The Ninth Juror*, in preparation for the show. In the book, Chester described the prosecution's successful bid to get written transcripts before a jury due to the poor quality of a defendant's taped confession.

I called the office of Manhattan DA Hogan, and they supplied me with the trial judge's opinion when he allowed the transcripts to be used and also the decision of the Appellate Division when they upheld the conviction on appeal.

Dr. Samuel Kass was convicted on twenty-three of the twenty-nine counts. The jury had bent over backward to be fair. They acquitted on six counts when the name on the prescription was the same name the investigator used in introducing himself. I also talked to one of the jurors afterward and he said, "We never would have convicted without the tapes and to tell you the truth, it was easy to understand the tapes with the transcripts, without them we would have been no place."

We never did get Dr. Kass's license revoked even though he did get a year in the county jail. I must say though, that it was not for lack of trying. We felt that this case went to the heart of the practice of medicine, that the doctor had proven himself unfit to continue in his profession and that the people of Rockland County had a right to demand that he no longer practice medicine. Fortunately for Dr. Kass, his case came up just before the national awakening to professional and white-collar crime brought on by Watergate. A panel of medical doctors meted out his punishment: three-month suspension of his license. They should have been ashamed of themselves for selling their own professional standards so short.

∾

There is one other point I believe should be mentioned. Our success in the Markowitz and Kass cases had one thing totally in common; they both depended on electronic sound equipment for their success.

That turned out *not* to be the blessing we originally thought it would be. The local press was very praiseworthy of our successful use of the equipment, and the county legislature, with little resistance, appropriated the money for newer and more sophisticated equipment. We used the new equipment on several cases starting in early 1973 and felt that we had really professionalized the office. But then things changed and changed drastically. In July 1973, Alexander Butterworth told the world about sound equipment in the Nixon White House . . . and the public mood changed. For some reason, the use of tape recordings in law enforcement became confused in the public mind with treachery, violations of privacy, and cover-ups. Defense attorneys suddenly acted shocked to hear that defendants and witnesses were taped without their permission. Hell, the Markowitz and Kass tapes would have been somewhat hollow if we had announced in advance that we were taping them.

It also became terribly wrong for a law enforcer to make a misrepresentation of his position, lest the defendant be entrapped into incriminating himself. I wouldn't have had much to prosecute if Eric had felt compelled by the post-1973 legal morality to say to Dr. Kass, "By the way I should tell you that I am an investigator for the District Attorney's Office."

The cardinal rule to remember is that it is *not* eavesdropping if one party to the conversation is aware of the taping. After all, a person can testify as to what was said in his presence. What better evidence than a recording of *exactly what was said*, no chance of puffery, no chance of slanting the story, just the exact verbatim conversation.

Even the very liberal Supreme Court Justice Earl Warren, during the 1960s, recommended use of modern electronic investigative techniques instead of station house confessions. I look forward to the day when the public will again distinguish between the proper use of electronic equipment and investigations, and the improper use of it as was the case in the Nixon White House.

As I think back to those cases, I think of only one person, Eric Vrhel. He had proven himself worthy of my complete trust. To Eric no one is above the law, he is the very definition of an "Untouchable."

Of course there were many other cases that Eric made in the 1970s, but most of them were straight sale of narcotics, and, therefore, relatively simple cases. As evil a crime as the sale of hard drugs is, it is reasonably easy to litigate, and I usually left those trials to the junior assistants. It was routinely just three witnesses, the undercover man who made the buy, the backup police officer who witnessed the pass, and the lab technician who analyzed the suspected narcotics.

~

For one special reason, I will mention the only one of Eric's routine narcotics cases that I ever tried myself. It was the summer of 1973 and I decided to personally handle the case because I wanted to get a feel for that type of trial. But probably more important, Arnold Becker was appearing for the defense. I wasn't going to miss another opportunity to face my friend Arnold in court.

The trial lasted for a week, exceptionally long for a narcotics sale trial, but considering that "Bulldog" Becker was appearing for the defense, not long at all. Although Arnold fought us at every turn and genuinely had me worried, by the time the jury got the case on a Friday afternoon at about five o'clock, I was feeling pretty confident. At 9:30 that evening they were back. "We, the jury, find the defendant, Timothy Callaghan, guilty as charged on both counts." It had been rather long deliberations for what appeared to be an airtight case. I found out a few hours later what had given the jury pause.

After the verdict, several of us from the DA's Office went over to the Barrister, a tavern across the street, to have a drink to celebrate the victory. We also often did this when we lost; it's just a sense of relief that another trial is over.

We sat down at a table and I immediately recognized two men standing at the end of the bar as having been jurors on the case. After a few minutes, one of them came over and he stuck out his hand and said, "I want to congratulate you on a good job. You know it's harder than we thought it would be to actually convict a guy."

"I'm glad to hear you say that," I said. "This is a tougher business than most people realize."

"That's right, Mr. Meehan, and for several of us, one of the toughest things was his grandmother. She was so loyal and she was there every day. We felt so sorry for her."

My only response was kind of a quizzical, "His grandmother?"

"You know, Mr. Meehan, that sweet little old Irish lady who sat in the back of the courtroom all by herself every day."

"Oh," I said with a slight smile as Annie, Eric, Eddie, and Herman also smiled. "That's not his grandmother, that's Peggy O'Neil, Number One court watcher in Rockland County."

The juror looked surprised, but he didn't pursue the subject and I made no attempt to explain who this wonderful old lady was. In a moment he left and rejoined his fellow juror at the bar.

"Boss," Ed said with a broad grin, "she damn near beat you!"

"No way, Mac, the day *Peggy O'Neil* beats me, that's when I cash in the chips."

~

Everyone associated with the Rockland County Courthouse in those days knew Peggy O'Neil. From the sheriff's deputies to court attendants to the judges, they all loved her. But there was no question, I was her favorite and everyone knew it.

Most days during trial, I was too busy to even eat lunch, but occasionally I did and several times I took her out to lunch and she seemed to so enjoy it. Although she played no part of any case, she was there through so many great moments of those years. I think her story is worth a few minutes telling—and I know the story.

She grew up in Newburgh, New York, another brick town, thirty miles to the north in Orange County, and was orphaned by the age of fifteen. Her mother died suddenly of a heart attack when she was only eleven and then her father was a casualty of the Great Influenza Epidemic of 1918.

On her own at that tender age, she made a life for herself and eight years later she graduated from nursing school in New York City. That same year, 1926, she ran into an old boyfriend from high school in Newburgh, and thus began a love affair that would last for nineteen years until his death at the close of World War II. Talking to her over those lunches so many years later, I realized that in kind of a nice way, the love affair had never ended.

They were married in 1928 and when she was widowed at age forty-two, there were four children, the oldest a junior in high school. There were tough years after that, but by the time she came to our courthouse in the late 1960s, the four were grown and settled in life, college graduates, all through her efforts. Now she had time to herself, to do the things she wanted to do and she literally loved the action of the courthouse.

Actually, her name was Helen O'Neil, but if you were Irish, young, and pretty, and your last name was O'Neil in New York City of the 1920s, the classic song "That's Peggy O'Neil" became your moniker. For Helen, it stuck.

The old boyfriend she met in 1926 was one of those tough Irishmen from the brickyards of the Hudson. His name was Tom Meehan, my father. Of course, *Peggy O'Neil* is my mother.

Chapter 10

The Dutchman

I met Herman Van der Linde in the late winter of 1968. We had been approved for a new assistant district attorney for the office and Herman was coming in for an interview. He didn't know it when he walked in, but in my mind he didn't stand a chance.

I had been elected district attorney when I was thirty-five and all of my new staff members were guys younger than myself. I was convinced that young, energetic, and aggressive assistants who were out to make a good reputation for themselves would end up giving the District Attorney's Office the best kind of image.

Herman did not meet these specifications. He was fifty-one years old, and to me at the time, that seemed much older than it does today as I fast approach the midcentury mark myself. He was also a retired New York City detective lieutenant. No good! That probably meant that he had worked very hard for a long time and now he was looking to take it easy. Besides, a New York City detective must be a very conservative, law-and-order type who couldn't look at cases objectively. How very wrong I was.

Herman had joined the police department in 1942 and retired after twenty years, in 1962. However, he started law school while still on the job. He graduated and was admitted to practice the same year he left the NYPD.

The six intervening years were spent in general practice in The Bronx and although I didn't think he ever made a great deal of money, he did develop a reasonably good criminal practice, defending the same kind of people he had spent twenty years going after as a cop. To me this was a plus; I always felt my own years as a defense attorney helped me take a more even view of the Office of the District Attorney.

Herman, who had come from Holland as a small boy, was a big, jovial man, about six feet tall and 225 pounds, and on the surface was very easy-going and fun-loving. It didn't take long for me to find out that below that surface was a very serious guy with a legal mind that could only be described as brilliant. Although he didn't start law school until 1957, it was obvious that he had been "studying" law since his earliest days as a policeman.

Together with his wife, Katherine, and their two teenage sons, Jerry and Jimmy, and a four-year-old daughter, Kathy, the Van der Lindes moved from The Bronx to Rockland County in 1963. By that day in 1968, he and the family had become active in community affairs and were very well liked in Rockland County.

I figured the interview with Herman would take fifteen or twenty minutes tops, and then a few days later I would send him a "Dear Mr. Van der Linde" letter. Three hours later we were still talking and two significant changes had occurred. First, Herman had an excellent shot at the job and, second, my stereotyping of New York City policemen was forever at an end.

I didn't offer him the job on the spot but told him I would give him very serious consideration, which I did. The next day I called my friend, Burt Roberts, who was then the chief assistant district attorney in The Bronx. Within two days, Burt was back to me reporting that Van der Linde was aces. Both police and prosecutors who had worked with him, or against him, as was the case in his last years in The Bronx, said he was a good lawyer and a "straight shooter." I made the decision. I would hire Herman Van der Linde.

∾

Within two weeks, Herman Van der Linde was on my staff; within a month I knew I had made the right decision, and within a year I was wondering how I ever got along without him.

It turned out that this man, who I had believed would be too hard-headed, was far more liberal than I. He had had as full and complete an appreciation of the terms "proof beyond a reasonable doubt" and "presumption of innocence" as any prosecutor I had ever met.

Herman worked for me for six great years and carried the ball on some of our most interesting and complex cases. He didn't personally try as many jury cases as I did, but he won *every* one and the juries loved him. He knew how to put in just the right amount of humor to liven things up while still doing a professional job. With the organized crime and narcotics investigations that he handled, Herman gained an excellent reputation in the county and I came to admire and respect him very much. I will also add that everyone in the office, especially the investigators and secretaries, were crazy about him. He could be oh-so serious on a case, but he was streetwise and had a real feeling for people. And Herman was the life of the party at all our DA's Office social get-togethers.

As I now look back over those wonderful years with Herman, one case immediately comes to mind above all others. Ironically, it was the only one we ever seriously disagreed on. It not only demonstrated his belief in the presumption of innocence, it was also a true measure of the man.

∾

It all began on the last day of January 1970. It was a bitter cold morning and the ground was covered with white from a snowstorm earlier in the week. At about 6:30 a.m. on that Saturday, I got a call from the Orangetown Police Department. They had an apparent homicide on Route 9W in Grandview-on-the-Hudson. By that time I had officially named Herman Van der Linde chief of investigations. So before I left the house for Grandview, I called Herman.

"Herman, it looks like we've got a strangulation down on 9W in Grandview. I'm on the way, I'll see you there." By the time I arrived at the scene twenty minutes later, Herman was already there.

A 1966 Chrysler four-door sedan had gone off the road and down a steep embankment toward the Hudson River. The underbrush and heavy snow had stopped the car about 120 feet from the edge of the highway. In the backseat of the car was the fully dressed, but dead, body of Mary Murphy.

Mary Murphy had been an attractive, twenty-one-year-old Caucasian girl from The Bronx. We learned before the day was out that she had died of manual strangulation and that she had had sexual intercourse in the last hours of her life. As we went down the steep embankment by the use of a heavy rope that the police had tied to a telephone pole, we first saw the car with the trunk lid open. On closer inspection, we found that the latch that holds down the trunk lid had been unbolted and that the latch and the two bolts were lying on the floor of the open trunk. Also lying on the trunk floor were a small half-inch open-end wrench, a partially used book of matches, and three used, burnt-out matches.

As we moved further along using the rope tied to the side of the car, we could look in and see the lifeless form of Mary Murphy curled up on the backseat. No one else was in the car at that time and we, of course, did not touch the body, because we were still awaiting the arrival of the coroner.

We looked over the car very carefully before going back up the embankment. The only other factor that was to prove significant was that there was a large toolbox of auto mechanic's tools on the right side inside the trunk. It was open and it did contain a full set of ratchet wrenches.

When Herman and I made our way back up the road to the highway, we met Detective George Barnes of the Orangetown Police Department and Ed McElroy of my office, who had just arrived at the scene from the police station. They gave us the first outline of what was to prove one of the most bizarre stories I had ever heard.

~

At about 6:05 a.m., the Orangetown Police Desk received a telephone call from a private resident of the area along Route 9W where the car was found. It seems that one Walter Mulligan had come to their door in shirtsleeves in the bitter cold morning and reported that he and his girlfriend had been kidnapped in The Bronx and he was now afraid that the kidnappers had murdered her.

By the time I first talked to Detective Barnes, he had taken a preliminary crime report from Mulligan and he had more details. According to Mulligan's report, he and Mary Murphy were engaged to be married. They had gone out on a date on Friday night and after stopping at several bars in The Bronx, they had gone to Van Cortland Park for a little necking or petting or whatever term was in vogue in 1970.

As they sat necking in the front seat of the car in the darkened park with the motor running to keep the car warm, two men in stocking masks approached the car from the driver's side. One of them pointed a rifle or shotgun outside the window, right at Mulligan. Mulligan opened the door. They made him get out and open the trunk and, after putting a bag over his head, put him in the trunk. A frightened Mary Murphy was kept in the front of the car.

Mulligan's story continued that they then were driven someplace for about fifteen or twenty minutes. After the car stopped, he was taken into what he thought was the basement of a house and made to completely strip and sit totally naked, with the exception of the bag over his head, on a cold and dirty wooden bench. He couldn't see a thing and he didn't hear Mary cry out or say anything, except to ask to go to the bathroom. After they had been in the house for about half an hour, he never heard her voice again.

After about an hour, according to Mulligan, he was made to dress but was not given back his jacket. He was taken out, put back in the trunk of the car, and again driven off. This time he said they drove for well over an hour, stopping only once very briefly, he believed to pay a toll.

Soon after that the car came to a complete stop, he heard the car doors open and close, and then the car started turning and moving very slowly. Suddenly the car lunged forward and, as Mulligan said, "I thought the car had been pushed off a cliff." When the car finally came to a rest and he realized he wasn't really hurt, there was complete stillness. He said that after a few minutes he started crying out for Mary, but there was no response. After a time, he thought of the tools he kept in his trunk and, using matches in his pocket for light, he got out the open-end wrench and was able to remove the bolts from the latch and open the trunk. After getting out, he said he took one look at Mary in the backseat of the car, feared that she was dead, and made his way to the nearby house where the call to the police was made.

~

Barnes, McElroy, Herman, and I then headed for the police station to interview Mulligan, but not before we went down to take another close look at the car. When we got to the station, the four of us had a strategy session before talking to Mulligan. I led it off.

"All right, the three of you together can question him. You know my rule against lawyers on initial interrogation, but Herman, you're different. Before you start, let's keep one thing in mind—we are either dealing with the tragic victim of a crime whose fiancée was just murdered, or we've got a murderer on our hands."

Before they started that interrogation, we all knew certain facts that made us suspicious.

First, to get the latch bolts loose in that position with a little wrench was possible, but not probable.

Second, the first officers to go down the hill to the car saw *no* footprints in the reasonably soft snow, either behind the car or on either side of it. How did he get out of the trunk, check to see if Mary was alive and then go up to Route 9W without leaving footprints in the snow?

Third, if he was in the trunk with no coat on and moving around enough to get the latch off, how come his white shirt was clean with none of the dirt and dust that was all over the trunk?

George Barnes and my men would treat him with the respect a victim of a crime deserves, but still try to obtain answers to all the questions in our minds.

I met Mulligan briefly just before that interrogation began. He was twenty-one years old, six feet, three inches tall, well over two hundred pounds, and very Irish looking with jet-black hair. I told him I was sorry about his fiancée and introduced my men who would be questioning him, along with Barnes, whom he had met earlier.

The thing that impressed me most at that time and throughout the next two days was his ice-cold, calm attitude. He showed no emotion whatsoever and, as my men reported to me, he related the story as if he were reporting the details of a minor fender bender accident to an insurance adjuster.

With Mulligan's consent and knowledge, his interviews that day and the next were tape-recorded so I had the opportunity to listen to the monotone, unfeeling account of such a great human tragedy.

～

The story that he told throughout those two days never varied, with the exception of becoming even more detailed. When he was let out of the trunk, he walked with his head still concealed by a canvas bag, "like a bank money bag," over what he thought were wooden planks, and then down eight or ten steps into a cellar that was "warm, but very dusty and dirty." He had been made to sit naked on the very dusty bench and the soles of his feet became "dusty and dirty" as he sat there on the bench.

That Monday was the date of the annual winter luncheon of the New York State District Attorneys Association in New York City and, as a vice president of the association, I felt compelled to at least make an appearance. I, therefore, departed for the city at about 11:30 a.m., leaving Herman in charge.

At 2:30 in the afternoon, I got a telephone call from Herman. He had made the decision to let Mulligan go. His story hadn't been shaken, and although we were highly suspicious of him, it was far less than sufficient evidence to hold Mulligan. Mulligan had agreed to come back in the next morning.

∼

That afternoon, the *Journal News* gave the killing a Page One headline with an article that included a picture of Walter Mulligan. By nine o'clock that evening one of the readers of the paper had been in touch with George Barnes—what he had to say was highly significant.

It seems that one Charles Hudson, age forty-six of Orangeburg, was driving south on Route 9W at about 5:15 that morning. He was a bartender at a tavern in Nyack and it was not unusual to be traveling on that route to his home at that hour. Hudson reported that as he drove south on 9W, he saw a "dark-colored sedan, probably a Dodge or Plymouth or even a Chrysler" stopped on the pavement in the southbound lane with its lights on, and a tall man standing beside the car on the driver's side. The tall man looked like the man whose picture he has seen in the evening newspaper.

The next morning we were all back at the Orangetown Police Headquarters hard at the investigation. As requested, Walter Mulligan was also back at the station house by 9:30 a.m. By 10:30 a.m., he was in a lineup, being picked out by Charles Hudson, as the man he saw standing beside the car at 5:15 a.m. the previous morning.

It was a good lineup and a solid identification, but we knew it would be trouble. After all, he saw only one picture in the newspaper the night before. Had Mulligan's right to a fair lineup been forever prejudiced?

After another full day of questioning, Mulligan's account of the event was unshaken. We found a remarkable consistency in his stories. This made us even more suspicious. In true life, an honest man never tells the same story the same way twice. He's not memorizing a story; he's remembering an event.

∽

At five o'clock that afternoon a decision had to be made. It would be a tough one, but by that time I was getting used to difficult decisions. Barnes, McElroy, Van der Linde, and I sat down and went over what we had by the end of that second day. It added up to the following:

First, Mulligan definitely placed himself at the scene in Grandview, but locked in the trunk and innocent of wrongdoing.

Second, the first two officers at the scene swore there were no footprints on the hill or by the car until they made them.

Third, Mulligan said that when he got out of the car, he went around by the driver's side door, opened the door and looked in at Mary. The police had approached from the passenger side and so when the first pictures were taken over an hour later, there were still no footprints on the left or driver's side of the Chrysler.

Fourth, laboratory analysis had been done on the latch bolts and the half-inch open-end wrench. There were no metal fragments from the bolts on the wrench. However, one of the sockets in the toolbox, the half-inch socket, did contain metal fragments identical to the latch bolt, *and* we could prove that the socket and ratchet wrench couldn't be placed on the bolts *with the trunk lid closed*.

Fifth, we had an eyewitness, Charlie Hudson, who told us he saw Mulligan up on the highway when the Chrysler was still there.

Sixth, by analyzing the sperm found in the body of Mary Murphy, we could type the blood of the male participants. It was O+, the same as Mulligan's. There was only *one* type found. If there was more than one rapist, they both had to have the same blood type as each other and as Mulligan. Possible, but not probable.

We were divided as to whether we should charge Mulligan. Barnes and I thought we should, McElroy wasn't sure, and Van der Linde was sure we should NOT charge him.

Herman was adamant. "Boss, where's your motive?"

"Hell, Herman, you know I don't need a motive. The law doesn't require one."

"Well, in a case as thin as this one, it sure would be nice."

"Goddamn it," I said, "I know it would be nice, but we don't work with what's nice, we work with what we've got. If you told this SOB's story to a horse he'd kick you! He's alone in the car with his girlfriend, she's strangled, and he comes up with an alibi that we've destroyed. She's murdered, he's at the scene, his alibi is a proven phony. For Christ's sake, if he was innocent, he would've told the truth. He's lying and you know it. For my money he's guilty."

Herman didn't back down an inch. "Look Bob, if you want to charge him with falsely reporting an incident to the police, okay. But murder? No way! All you've proven so far is that he wasn't in the trunk. I agree his story won't hold water, but that doesn't prove he murdered Mary Murphy or anyone else."

Van der Linde wasn't through yet. "And you talk about motive; you don't know his motive for murdering her and I don't know his motive for making up that hokey story. But until I hear a motive, this guy's got my benefit of a reasonable doubt."

He didn't have mine. I was fully aware of a long line of cases that said in essence, "Proving a false alibi does not *alone* prove the crime." But I also knew that in none of those cases were they able to place the defendant at the scene of the crime. Those defendants may have lied about where they were and what they were doing but that wasn't evidence that they were at the scene and had an *opportunity* to commit the crime. Not only did we demolish Mulligan's alibi, we had also placed him at the scene.

Now the decision whether or not to formally charge a man with a crime, usually made at a police station, is a very *undemocratic* process. It is not done by majority vote. It is the sole decision of the district attorney or the senior assistant DA present. You listen, you take advice, but the decision and the responsibility for it is yours.

That evening the responsibility was mine. For the strangulation death of Mary Murphy, Walter Mulligan was charged with First-Degree Manslaughter. I would give him the benefit of the doubt that he hadn't planned this. He hadn't intended to kill her, but in the heat of lover's passion he had in fact strangled the life out of her.

~

Twelve days later, the grand jury of Rockland County agreed with me and Walter Mulligan was indicted for Manslaughter One. But before that, one interesting thing happened. The Wednesday after the killing, funeral services for Mary Murphy were held in The Bronx. The public defender, Arnold Becker, was initially representing Mulligan and he made an application to allow Mulligan to be taken under guard from jail to the funeral. We did not oppose, and Mulligan did, in fact, attend the funeral under the guard of three sheriff's deputies. Also accompanying Mulligan on that journey to The Bronx was the chief investigator for the public defender, Richard J. Van Zandt.

When Dick Van Zandt got back, he came up to see me in the DA's Office. "Look," he said, "we fought in court before and we'll fight again and I've heard a lot of crazy stories from defendants, but this one is different. I beg you to take a hard look at it. I am morally certain this guy is innocent!"

I was impressed; Dick had never before come to me like that and he never did again in the three remaining years he spent with the Public Defender's Office. Now two people whom I so admired disagreed with me. My decision became even more lonely.

~

After Mulligan was indicted, I told Van der Linde and McElroy that I wanted them to stick close to this one. If we were to convict at trial, we needed every scrap of evidence we could obtain to build our case.

Six days after the indictment, they came up with a very significant piece of evidence. It did not build our case. In fact, based on it, I consented that Mulligan be released on a very minimal bail bond.

In a routine check of sex crimes in the area, my men had come up with a report regarding an unsolved rape case from December 1969. It had taken place in the town of Greenberg in Westchester County, and for me, it was shocking to read.

A young coed from the University of Texas was home for Christmas vacation and was out on a date with her boyfriend. They parked for some lovemaking at about midnight in a deserted Westchester County park. Two men with ski masks approached their car and made them get out at gunpoint, using "a rifle-type weapon." They were then made to enter another car, but before they did, bags were placed over their head, "canvas bank or post office type bags." They were then driven for about half an hour before the car stopped and they were forced to get out. They were taken into the basement of a house and both made to strip of everything they were wearing except the bags that were kept over their heads. They said that as they walked to and from the house, they walked on "what seemed like wooden planks." Further, that the basement was about ten steps down and was "filthy dirty."

The girl was raped three times. Afterward, they were made to dress and were returned to the same park where they were tied to a tree and left otherwise further unharmed. After working themselves loose, they immediately reported the crime to the police.

I was impressed; no two stories could conceivably have been so similar without a direct relationship. Mary Murphy had been the victim of the same criminals as the girl from Westchester County. But did this clear Mulligan? There was still one big question on my mind and although I consented to Mulligan's release, I would not move to dismiss the manslaughter charges until it was answered. Was Walter Mulligan a participant in the Westchester crime? Did he use the details of that crime to cover himself when he had raped and murdered his own fiancée? I was now reasonably convinced of his innocence, but having probably made a monumental mistake in indicting him, I wasn't going to make another mistake and dismiss the charges until I was sure.

Of course, if the case dead-ended at that point we would definitely dismiss, but I wanted it solved not only for our sake, but for Mulligan's. When the day came to dismiss, I wanted to be able to say categorically that he was innocent. I would need more facts before such a statement could be made. Herman Van der Linde was in charge of getting those facts.

∼

By this time Mulligan had hired a private lawyer to replace Public Defender Arnold Becker. I, therefore, called in his new lawyer, Arthur Spring, from Westchester County and put my cards on the table. Artie Spring had been an assistant district attorney in Westchester County and I knew him well. I also knew that he was a savvy guy who could work with us as long as he knew we were now actually trying to clear his client.

After Herman and I filled Spring in on what we had, he agreed to talk to his client, and the first and most important question was, "What was Mulligan doing and where was he on the night of December 19, 1969, and who were his witnesses to prove it?"

We got an answer back later that same day. It wasn't much help. After wracking his brain to remember what he had been doing on a night two months before that had no special significance at the time (try it, it's damned hard), he finally recalled going to the movies and then out to a bar for a few drinks. He had a witness all right, obviously it was his fiancée, Mary Murphy. We would have to look further for the truth.

Herman and Ed spent many days and nights prowling around the bars in The Bronx and cruising through Van Cortland Park during the next few months. They had the full cooperation of the 50th Precinct of the NYPD and a maximum effort was made. But after three months of endless record checking and surveillance of the area, they were still batting zero.

Finally, a break came in early May. A young couple was alone in their car at about 1 a.m. in Van Cortland Park. The driver's side window was open and the boy in the driver's seat thought he heard a noise behind the car. He looked out the back window and saw two figures approaching the car and quietly turned on the key and put the car into drive gear. Suddenly a man ran up to the open window with a long gun in hand and a stocking mask over his head. As the man told him to get out, he floored the gas and sped away, almost hitting a tree. A gutsy guy who had taken a hell of a chance, but he and his girlfriend came away unscathed and went immediately to the local precinct house.

By luck, Van der Linde and McElroy were in The Bronx that night and within a half hour of the report, they were at Mulligan's house. He was in bed and he was calm. His mother and father both swore he never left the house that evening and they had all gone to bed between 11:30 and 12; they remembered because the eleven o'clock news had just ended.

Herman called me at home at about 2:30 that morning and filled me in on what happened. "Bob, I'd bet my life on it. That boy was in bed, you could tell by his eyes, by the way he talked and everything else about him." The parents were just as believable.

Before I got off the phone with Herman, it was arranged that we would all meet with the couple who had *almost* been victims in The Bronx at nine o'clock that morning. It may seem strange, I was being positively proven wrong, but I was elated. I couldn't get back to sleep (a rarity for me) and I ended up getting up at about 5:30 a.m. (an even greater rarity for me).

The couple was in their late teens, and both were both very sharp and helpful. They had been parked almost half an hour when the aborted attack took place. One thing that had made the boy alert and sensitive to the slight noise behind the car was the fact that the car had driven by slowly at least twice and possibly three times and it had made him nervous.

"Of course I remember the car," the young man said. "It was a red compact, and I won't swear to it but I'm almost certain it was a Chrysler-made car, probably a Dodge Dart or a small Plymouth." All right, this was a heavy lead but we wanted more. My next question: "Did you get any kind of look at the two men?"

"Well I saw two figures behind the car but I didn't get a look at one of them at all, and the other one who came up on my window had a stocking mask over his face."

"Did you get any look at him at all? Remember, the moon was almost full last night. For instance, do you know whether he was tall, short, old, young, black, or white?"

"Oh, he was definitely a white man."

This, of course, was helpful by itself, but he was able to give us more. He wasn't sure of his height because he bent over the window, but he was heavy set with a full face, had black or dark hair, and looked quite young. Herman and I looked at each other and without saying a word we both knew, he was describing Mulligan—or he was describing the same man standing beside the car on Route 9W that Charles Hudson had described, a man who looked like Mulligan.

We then tried an interesting experiment. We set up a "photograph lineup." This consisted of ten pictures of young men, all eighteen to twenty-five years old, all with dark hair, and all on the heavy side. One of the pictures was that of Walter Mulligan.

The young witness was then shown the ten pictures with an explanation.

"Look son," I said, "I want you to look at these ten pictures. This is not an identification we would ever use in court, because you didn't get a good enough look at the man. We just want to use it as a guide to check through the records. Do any of these men look like the man you saw with the gun last night?"

"I really can't tell," he answered.

"All right, which one of these ten looks most like the man you saw?" This question asked by me would legally destroy a lineup procedure if you were trying to nail a defendant. Our purpose was just the reverse, we were trying to prove that Charles Hudson's identification had been honestly mistaken.

After about three or four minutes of poring over the pictures, the young man pointed and said, "Well, this one is the nearest." He was pointing at the picture of Walter Mulligan.

~

On the way back to Rockland County that day with Herman and Ed, I said, "Herman, I don't know where you get that sixth sense, but you've got to admit, this one is a bitch. The Mulligan kid, in his ice-cold manner, tells a pretty hokey story and then one of the guys who did it turns out to look a hell of a lot like him. I will still feel better when we nail the bastards who did it."

That day was a long time coming. Throughout the rest of the spring and summer, hundreds of mug shots of known sex offenders were checked out. Anyone who looked remotely like Mulligan was checked out as to what type of car he owned or drove, but this proved fruitless. An alarm was out for the red compact and patrol cars in that area of The Bronx checked out and stopped dozens of such cars. The officer would get the name of the owner and then check it against our file, but this led to nothing.

The break came in early September 1970. At about midnight on a moonlit night, an NYPD patrol car saw a 1965 red Dodge Dart enter the south side of Van Cortlandt Park and drive slowly up the lane. The officer noted the plate number, but didn't stop or pursue the Dodge. The plate number was called in as they sat parked at the south side of the park. About ten minutes later the Dodge cruised slowly toward the exit of the park and this time they could see there were two men in the car. Then the car made a U-turn and went back up another lane. Just then the identification on the ownership of the car came back on police radio, "Joseph Pillatello, DOB 11/26/35, 555 E. 14th St., Brooklyn, New York, no wants."

The officers decided that they would enter the park and check out the car and its occupants. The Dodge pulled over and stopped with no difficulty. Pillatello was driving and the passenger was Jack Gordon, age thirty, also of Brooklyn. Luckily Pillatello did not have his auto registration with him. This gave the officers cause to take them to the precinct house. They knew it was Pillatello's car; they had already checked that out, but both officers—who were well aware of our case—were impressed with one thing. Pillatello was older at thirty-four, shorter at about five feet, eight and half inches, but he looked an awful lot like Walter Mulligan.

Pillatello and Gordon griped a little but did accompany the officers in the patrol car to the precinct house after locking the Dodge Dart.

Back at the station, Detectives William South and James Carroll were on duty. They took one look at Pillatello and were interested. Within half an hour, South and Carroll knew that Pillatello had three prior arrests on sex-related charges and one conviction, dating back twelve years. We later discovered that Pillatello's was one of the files that had been pulled out when we were looking for the rapist. But that twelve-year-old mug shot of a twenty-two-year-old Italian kid who only weighed 135 pounds at five feet, eight and half inches was hardly worth checking out.

It's amazing, but Pillatello didn't look that Italian; as it turned out his mother was Irish. Mulligan was what we used to call as kids "Black Irish." Now this was not in any way meant as a slur, my father was "Black Irish" with jet-black hair and deeper tone skin that took such a good tan in the summer while most Irish just get a good case of sunburn. This dates back hundreds of years to the Roman and Spanish soldiers who came ashore in the south of Ireland. The long and short of it was that Pillatello, now at 195 pounds, looked a hell of a lot like Mulligan.

While Pillatello sat in the station house swearing it was his car and that the registration was at home, detectives South and Carroll rode over to Van Cortlandt Park. They didn't have a search warrant for the car and they weren't sure they had the legal grounds to get one, so for now they were just looking.

South and Carroll had worked closely with Van der Linde and McElroy on our case and they knew all the facts. They looked over the locked car with flashlights for less than a minute. Ten minutes later, they were back in the station house calling Herman. They now had enough for a search warrant! After filling Herman in on what had happened, Carroll said, "Lindy" (all NYPD guys called Herman "Lindy"), "guess what I saw on the backseat of the car? Two canvas bank moneybags!"

Three hours later, armed with a search warrant signed by a Supreme Court judge, South, Carroll, Van der Linde, and McElroy searched Pillatello's car. In the trunk they found a 30.06 rifle and three stretched women's stockings. By noon that day, Pillatello's companion Jack Gordon, confronted with the evidence, admitted that he had been in on the December attack in Westchester and the aborted attack in The Bronx in May. But he swore he had no part in the attack on Mulligan and the murder of Mary Murphy in late January. He did say, however, that Pillatello had told him about it and had said he never meant to kill her. He was just trying to hold her down to rape her with his forearm across her neck and that he had "accidentally" choked the life out of her. Gordon didn't know who had been with Pillatello that night and Pillatello never told him.

~

That afternoon Gordon led us to the scene where he and Pillatello had raped the Westchester girl. By that time I had joined Herman and Ed. As we drove up to the location, it seemed all wrong, but not for long.

It was a huge Quonset hut in The Bronx that housed the Tryon Stone Company. We entered through a small door in the back, which was locked, but by pulling it up a little and prying on the lower corner, it opened very easily. Inside were rows of piled stone and between them *wooden planks* to walk on and there, sitting in the corner of the huge enclosure, oddly enough, was a one-and-a-half-story wood-framed Cape Cod house. We followed the planks to a back outside cellar door, opened the door, and descended into a very dusty cellar.

It turned out that twenty years earlier, the stone company bought the property for their business and they were going to bulldoze the house, but then thought better of it and built the structure around the house so they could use the house for offices.

It also turned out that Joseph Pillatello had been employed by the Tryon Stone Company from 1960 to 1967.

~

The pieces had fallen together. There was a case—*in Bronx County!* My buddy, Burt Roberts, who was then Bronx County District Attorney, held a big press conference to announce the indictment of Pillatello. He praised the NYPD, my men, and me for breaking the case and clearing an innocent man. Burt is a colorful guy and the press conference was jam-packed and resulted in a lot of publicity for all of us, *all favorable.* I felt a little guilty looking so good after such a big mistake.

But now I was ready for a day that I wholeheartedly, if somewhat ironically, looked forward to. Ten days later on a Monday morning in Rockland County Court, I stood up before a crowded courtroom and told Judge John Gallucci, "The People move to dismiss all charges against Walter Mulligan. This is not the usual case of dismissal where we believe there is a technical bar to guilt or a failure of evidence beyond a reasonable doubt. This is the case of a *totally innocent man* and I accept full responsibility for the heartache and injustice we have caused Walter Mulligan. The heartache of the loss of his fiancée—the injustice of being falsely accused of this terrible crime."

Judge Gallucci was very nice about the matter and said that having read the grand jury minutes and the entire investigative report leading to the arrest and indictment of Walter Mulligan, he was satisfied that the District Attorney's Office had "acted in good faith." This was important to me.

Art Spring went much further. He gave me probably the finest tribute I had ever received in a courtroom. Spring talked about things like "the finest tradition of prosecutors—justice above convictions—a credit to the legal profession," and so on. I was embarrassed.

I stood again and said, "I appreciate your remarks, Mr. Spring, but they should be directed to my chief of investigations, Herman Van der Linde, and my chief investigator, Ed McElroy. The victory of justice today is theirs and theirs alone. I pride myself on one thing only—having the good sense to have men like Herman Van der Linde and Ed McElroy working for me."

~

Before I close the book on Mulligan I suppose there are some questions that are left unanswered. Why the particles on the ratchet wrench and not the half-inch open-end wrench? Why no footprints in the snow? Why did Hudson refer to the "tall man standing beside the car"? And what about O+ blood type of the semen?

Actually, the only answer we ever found to these questions was that Pillatello had O+ blood. The rest we don't know and we probably never will. Were the laboratory, the policemen at the scene, and Hudson all mistaken or was Mulligan in fact guilty of falsely reporting a crime? Was Herman right? Had we proved just that—for some unknown reason, perhaps a sense of guilt for not defending his fiancée or whatever a mind can conjure, had Mulligan staged the crash down the hill?

I don't know and I'll probably never know, but that is the way almost every case ends in real life. The TV movie drama is written so that there are no loose ends, the questions are all answered, and they all fall neatly in place in 120 minutes, less time for nine commercial breaks. Life is not like that. Think of your own life. Oh God, if we could only answer all the "whys" of our lives!

At the time the charges were dismissed, I never mentioned or even alluded to these questions. Why try to make the poor guy look guilty of a petty crime when he had been falsely accused of a major crime.

However, three years later these matters had to be brought out in court. Mulligan sued the County of Rockland and District Attorney Robert Meehan for $1 million for malicious prosecution. We had to show the "good faith" Judge Gallucci spoke of. We did, we won, the civil suit was thrown out. I was glad to be exonerated of wrongdoing but I still felt sorry that young Mulligan got nothing for the pain caused to him—but that is the law.

I even felt sorry for him after I read his civil court papers that said, "The district attorney was questioning me and he said, 'If you don't come clean, you're going to fry.'" It was easy to disprove the statement since I hadn't even questioned him, but when the line was printed in the local newspaper, my only response was, "I'm afraid that Mr. Mulligan has seen too many James Cagney movies."

And so the sad case of Walter Mulligan was over. I could not undo the months of suffering that he had undergone with a few words in a courtroom, but I could and did vow to never let such a thing happen again. I don't believe it ever did happen in the remaining five years that I was District Attorney of Rockland County. Sure, some defendants were acquitted after trial, some won technical motions to dismiss—a DA who never lost would be a horror! But there was never in my mind another "totally innocent man" indicted in Rockland County on my watch.

≈

Herman remained with the DA's Office until late 1973. During those years Herman and I became closer professionally and personally. The man, who to the outside world was a big, happy-go-lucky, and terribly funny Dutchman, was in reality the conscience of the DA's Office.

He would walk into the office with a beautiful drunk act that broke us all up (I actually never saw him have too much to drink) and then sit down and legally and factually tear a weak case apart. When I was working too hard late at night or taking myself too seriously on a case, it was Herman who would break the tension. "OK, Clarence Darrow, we shall now adjourn to the Barrister (our favorite watering hole) for further study of this matter."

It wasn't a matter of avoiding work—because Herman knew how to work and work hard—he just knew when we were no longer accomplishing anything.

In late 1973, Herman returned to what I always believed was his real professional calling, defending criminals. A former assistant district attorney and close personal friend of Herman's, Frank Barone, replaced Arnold Becker as public defender. Frank made Herman "the offer you couldn't refuse" and so the Dutchman left us. I was sorry to lose him, but glad for Frank because Herman would be such a big help and would bring the "heart" that is so vital to a good Public Defender's Office. Becker had Van Zandt; Barone now had Van der Linde. One an investigator, the other a lawyer, one young, the other somewhat older, but oh what "heart" they both had! Where had Dick Van Zandt gone?? He became the newest investigator for the Rockland County District Attorney's Office.

I, of course, saw Herman often during that last year before I, too, left the District Attorney's Office. But it was never quite the same and I truly missed having the Dutchman around. I had always hoped that someday, somehow, we could work together again. That will never be. Herman Van der Linde got into his car to go to work at the Public Defender's Office on a cold morning in midwinter of 1976. He never got out of the driveway. A heart attack and he was gone. I shall never forget him.

Chapter 11

Attention to Roll Call

By far, my toughest year in the District Attorney's Office was 1973. It was the time of our biggest involvement in organized crime cases and also a series of political cases. The organized crime cases made strong enemies out of a lot of big shots in crime, not only in Rockland but also in Westchester, and for this I was pleased. It further built the "Untouchable" image that I was so proud of.

The political cases were different; it made mortal enemies out of former friends. The Republicans said I was only going after them for political reasons; the Democrats acted as though I had betrayed them. It was hard not only for me but for Nancy and the kids, especially when we found that people we thought were our good friends would now no longer speak to us.

However, the hardest thing that happened to my family that year, and in all of my years as DA, occurred on May 10, 1973. I really don't like to talk about it and anyone who knows me personally, professionally, or politically knows that I seldom do talk about it. It was an event that received as much publicity as anything I have ever been involved in, but I still think of it as a personal thing and of its personal effect on the family. And that is why I find it difficult to talk about.

As I think back I realize, however, that I could not tell my story of the DA years without relating the events of that night and morning.

～

I had spent the evening at the Annual Men's Club Dinner of the Nanuet Hebrew Center with my great friend, Max Cohen. When I left the dinner at about 10:30, I decided to take a ride back over to the courthouse because I knew the jury was out for deliberations in the case of John Cruz, the guard alleged to be responsible for the "Boys' Night Out."

It was already a very foggy night as I approached the courthouse in my almost brand new county car, a 1973 Chrysler, and I was well aware of driving carefully in the fog with this first really nice car the county had ever bought for the DA's Office.

The lights were on in the courthouse and I learned from Assistant DA Werner Loeb, who was handling the case, that the jury had asked a lot of questions but was still hard at deliberations.

Judge Ted Kelly was presiding that night and the usual procedure in Rockland County was to lock the jury up for a night's sleep at a nearby motel if they hadn't reached a verdict by midnight.

This night was to prove different. At about eleven o'clock, the foreman sent out a note asking for the rereading of some of the testimony. It was well after midnight when the court reporter finished the rereading and the judge was ready to lock them up at that time, but the foreman rose and said, "Couldn't we have until about one o'clock? I think we can reach a verdict." The judge agreed.

Finally at about 1:30 a.m., when there was still no verdict, Judge Kelly called them in. They would be locked up for the night. By the time the jury filed back in, the courtroom strangely had many spectators. Apparently, as the local bars and taverns in New City closed, people on their way home stopped to see what was going on at the lit-up courthouse at that hour. Therefore, I saw many strange faces in the courtroom as Judge Kelly told the jury to go and have a good night's sleep and then recommence deliberations in the morning.

Outside the courtroom, in the passageway, I talked to Werner Loeb, Hal Seidenberg, who was the defense attorney, and Gil McCormick, who was then a partner of Seidenberg. We talked for a few minutes about the case and then I went up to the District Attorney's Office with Werner.

I telephoned Nancy from the office and said I would be home in a little while. I remember Nancy saying she was going to bed but that she would leave a dish of vanilla ice cream for me in the freezer. (I was and still am a late-night ice cream addict.) I then went down to the back of the courthouse where I always parked my car and got in the new Chrysler for the nine-mile trip home. I had a Police Radio in the car but, as was often the case, it was turned off. I usually listened to commercial radio. That was the last time I would ever drive a county car without the Police Radio on.

∾

It would be longer than the usual seventeen or eighteen minutes because by now, the fog was very heavy and I wanted to be extra careful with that new car. I took my usual route home through the back roads of New City and Spring Valley. New City can be reached from my house by staying on the main roads of Route 59 and Route 304, but I always preferred to cut back through the apple orchards. I had learned that way of going to New City from my father back in the 1930s, before those back roads were even paved.

With the exceptionally heavy fog, I crawled along New Hempstead Road doing not much more than fifteen miles per hour, then curbing around where New Hempstead met Union before turning right on Brick Church Road. After the short drive on Brick Church, I went left on Route 306 and drove a few hundred yards to Viola Road.

There is a traffic light at the intersection of Route 306 and Viola and as I was approaching it, I could just barely make out that it was green through the fog. There were no other cars in sight behind me or to either side on Viola Road.

It was still green as I came to the intersection and turned right on Viola. I would be going straight on Viola for about a mile to College Road, passing some newly constructed, unoccupied houses on the left and the old apple orchard on the right.

I had just made the right turn to head west on Viola when suddenly, seemingly out of nowhere, headlights from another car appeared behind me. It was still just as foggy and I'm sure I was doing less than twenty miles per hour, but the car behind me was coming up fast and I believed it was going to pass me. This was fine with me and I just went slightly to the right to give the passing car room, but it seemed to be coming very fast and very close to the left side of the Chrysler. In that split second, I thought, "Oh no, a drunk driver and my new car!"

The car never touched the Chrysler although I thought it was going to, so as it started to pass, I pulled hard right and braked. Just as the car came even, I heard what I will always believe to be *two* loud shots and at the same instant glass shattered into the car and I saw a hole in the forward part of the driver's side door glass, about the size of a small grapefruit.

The other car continued forward at high speed and all I remember about it is that I'm *sure* it had the new New York plates, which were just being issued around that time, namely, blue numbers on a yellow background, and I *think* it was a larger model car with large vertical type taillights. I never actually saw the plate numbers because it was too far away before I ever looked and to tell you the truth, I wasn't being a good witness—I was badly shaken.

~

One thing I was instantly certain of, I had been shot at. As I sat there beside the road in that fog I couldn't think what to do. Should I go forward, which was the direct and shortest route to the Ramapo Police Station? Or should I turn around and go the other way in case whoever it was had stopped and might be coming back or waiting for me?

I must have sat there for thirty seconds although it seemed longer. I kept saying to myself, "What should I do, what should I do?" Then I finally remembered the radio, the Police Radio.

I turned on the radio and called Ramapo headquarters as I shot forward, driving at high speed, fog or no fog. I don't remember to this day exactly what I said on the air, but within seconds the patrol cars were on their way and talking to me to let me know they were coming. By the time I got to College Road, I had been instructed to turn left and head toward the station, but I saw another Ramapo police car head out west on Viola, I guess in pursuit of the car that had fired at me.

As I headed down College Road, I noticed that the whole piece of glass in the driver's side door was shattered and the pieces were falling out, making the whole even bigger. When I got to the corner of College Road and Route 59, two Ramapo police cars were waiting for me and I pulled in and stopped at the DeWaard Piano Store. Lieutenant John Boyd ran over to the car and asked if I was all right and I said I was. He then told me to get out and one of his men would drive the Chrysler to the station.

It was ridiculous but I kept saying, "John, I'm OK. I can drive the car." But as I said it, I realized that my hands were trembling on the wheel. John was really nice and I remember him treating me almost like I was a kid, saying something like, "That's alright, Mr. Meehan, everything's OK.

Just let one of my boys drive it in." He wasn't being condescending, he was just acting like the pro he has always been.

～

Within a few minutes, I was in the Detective Squad Room of the Ramapo Police Department. Within half an hour, almost everyone involved with law enforcement at the town and the county level was there. I did a silly thing at that point. I decided I better call Nancy in case someone called her and had the report wrong, but I decided I wouldn't tell her the truth, it would only worry her.

"Nance, I'm OK but I'm down at Ramapo PD. I had a little accident with the car."

It must have been the tone of my voice, but Nancy wasn't buying my story. "What's wrong? Are you all right? Now tell me really, what's wrong?"

I then told her the truth, that I was perfectly all right, but we believe shots were fired at the car on Viola Road. I didn't tell her that we knew this for sure because I had not yet received a report of a bullet hole or a bullet being found in the car. Since both passenger side windows were closed, if I had been shot at, there had to be an exit hole or a bullet in the car.

It was only a few minutes later that Chief Joseph Miele personally told me of finding an apparent bullet hole by the armrest on the passenger side of the car. When this was confirmed, it showed that the bullet trajectory was just inches forward of my chest. The braking and turning to protect the new car from the "drunken driver" saved my life, or at least spared me a good slug in the chest entering from the heart side.

I stayed at the station for over two hours, going over the case again and again with Chief Miele, Chief of Detectives Bill Sinclair, as well as Herman Van der Linde, Eric Vrhel, and Ed McElroy from my office. Nancy had wanted to come to the station, but after Eric assured her I was all right she stayed at home and waited.

My brother Jack, a trustee in the nearby village of Suffern, was informed about what happened and raced down to the station. After assuring him that I was okay, I handed him the very difficult task of driving to my mother's Suffern home to let her know about my near miss before she heard it on the news.

～

It was after 5 a.m. when several of us went up to my house, including all three of my men and Chief Miele. Nancy was, of course, waiting up and although she made coffee, I remember I had a couple of Scotches to calm my nerves as we all sat in the den.

To me one of the most unfortunate parts of the whole thing happened next. My son, Tommy, who was then just shy of eleven years old, slept at the exact opposite end of the house from the den. Tommy was and is a very sensitive boy and he had a habit of playing the radio in his room at night; not rock 'n' roll, not even music, just one station—WCBS News. Unlike his father, Tommy is a very early riser. He is almost always up at 6 a.m.

Just after six o'clock, Tommy came running into the kitchen where Nancy was standing alone, pouring more coffee. With an ashen face, Tommy said, "Mom, they just said on the radio that Dad was shot."

Nancy immediately yelled out to me and grabbed Tommy and said, "Oh, no, no, no. Daddy's all right. He's right here."

When I got to the kitchen, I didn't know what had happened but I could see that Tommy was biting his lip to keep from crying. When Nancy told me, it was my turn to bite my lip.

That is the memory of that night and morning that shall live with me always and that is the reason I wanted so desperately to crack that case. Do what you want to me, but hurt my children and I shall never forget or forgive.

At this point, Nancy got Patty, Kathy, Laurie, Mary, and Bobby up, and we sat as a family so I could tell them what had happened, assuring them that with my men and the police, we had nothing to fear.

My only injury were cuts on the left side of my neck from the shattered window, and although I was still having little glass fragments come to the surface for about a month, it wasn't painful and not very noticeable.

I told Nancy that the best thing for the children was just not to talk about it anymore and, as children do, they would soon forget. However, that proved impossible. There were too many changes in our life to let them forget.

~

That day was a hectic one, but I was determined to go to the office at the usual time to let the people of the county know I was okay. I remember pulling into the rear driveway of the courthouse in the DA's car with Mac at the wheel and Frank Errico literally riding shotgun. (He had a long gun straight up in front of him.) As the car came to a stop we were immediately surrounded by both still and television cameras. It was just the start—by noon the office was jammed with local and New York print and TV press along with the wire services.

When we first got up to the office, the girls were all a little weepy and Annie, Val Peterson, and Jackie Mollica all gave me a kiss—not the usual morning greeting. I must say that the whole thing was rather embarrassing; everyone was treating me like a martyr or a hero or both, and it was obvious I wasn't either. I was only one thing—lucky.

I rarely held press conferences, but by eleven o'clock we decided we better talk to all of them at once, so we did a press conference in my office at noon. I really only remember one question that I was asked and that is only because of a memorable telephone call I received that evening.

The phone rang at about 7:30 and Nancy answered. The phone was literally ringing off the wall and I wasn't taking most calls, but Nancy knew, without asking, that I would take this one.

"Bob, it's Mr. Hogan."

With my extraordinary respect for the Manhattan DA, of course I took the call. "Bob, this is Frank Hogan. I just watched you on the television news and I'm calling to inquire as to the state of your health, which I trust is still good."

I assured him that I was fine and then he added, "Robert, my lad, I've been increasingly proud of you, and the job you're doing up there in Rockland. But the thing that impressed me most tonight was your continued total honesty and that you haven't lost your sense of humor. I love that answer when you were asked, "Do you think they're trying to kill you or just scare you?""

My answer at the press conference had been, "Well, I don't know, but if they were just trying to scare me, *they succeeded!*"

~

Sheriff Lindemann and Chief Miele, as the head law enforcement officials involved, made a decision to guard the house night and day. The kids were watched getting on the school bus and returning. Sheriff's deputy cars were stationed outside of Suffern Senior and Junior High Schools, and Cherry Lane Elementary School, and staff members were given special instructions for checking my children's arrival, departure, and whereabouts during the day.

My chief investigator, Frank Errico, set up around-the-clock body-guard arrangements for me. This actually wasn't new for district attorneys; in fact, it had been the rule in New York City and larger counties such as Nassau for years. But it was new for Rockland, new for me, and I didn't like it.

I had always been impressed with the Secret Service protection of presidents and I never in any way thought of it as something distasteful. However, in 1972, the only prominent person in America whom I considered a personal friend, Senator Henry M. "Scoop" Jackson of Washington State, was assigned Secret Service protection during his bid for the Democratic presidential nomination. When he visited Rockland County one day, I rode with Scoop as he drove in from LaGuardia Airport in a secret service car. We got to talking about the Secret Service protection and he said, "Bob, they are all sharp and wonderful guys, but believe me it's not what it's cracked up to be. Talk about lack of privacy, this is really tough, especially for Helen and the kids." I didn't fully realize what Scoop meant until May 1973, and I must say that having a guard all the time that last twenty months as district attorney was something no one in the family enjoyed.

I can't say for sure about the kids, but I know this, that shooting and the security that followed completely changed Nancy's attitude toward the District Attorney's Office and really toward any type of public office. In the past, she has always been happy to stand with me for whatever I wanted to do and what type of work made me happy. After that, she still outwardly supported me in all my efforts, but I knew for a fact she was glad when I finally left the DA's Office.

~

As always, there was a silver lining. In the case of the shooting, it was my old friend, Dick Van Zandt. He had just transferred to the District Attorney's Office as my newest investigator a few months earlier and during those first few months of security, he was the one assigned the most. It meant that Dick was around the house when I was home a great deal of the time and the kids, especially the younger ones, loved Dick and were convinced he was the funniest man they had ever met.

Dick took the work very seriously, as the consummate professional he is, but he still found time to make the kids happy and definitely lessen any tensions they may have had.

The Sunday after the shooting was Mother's Day and we had my mother and my brother, Tom, his wife Karen, and their two small children over for dinner. We also had my "bodyguard" Van Zandt. Right before four o'clock in the afternoon, the phone rang and Dick took the call. He then took me aside privately and said, "Bob, NYPD just got an anonymous telephone call that they relayed to Ramapo PD. Some guy says there's a bomb in your house and it's supposed to go off at four o'clock."

"Hell, Dick," I said, "it's got to be a crank because of the publicity we've been getting."

"Bob, the caller said, 'DA Meehan's house on Cherry Lane in Tallman.' We can't take any chances. We've got to clear everyone out, let me handle this."

And he did. He just marched into the den and using one of his many comic dialects—this time an imitation of the German sergeant in *Stalag 17*—said, "Attention to Roll Call. Everybody out of the barracks! Ve vill now adjourn to Herr Vrhel's house for zee zoup and ztrudel course!"

The kids didn't know what type of foolishness was going on and thought it was some kind of a joke, but within less than a minute my six kids, Tom's two kids, and the rest of us were filing out of the house, into my station wagon and Tom's car, and pulling away for the one-mile trip to Eric Vrhel's house where they spent the next two hours. Patty, who was then seventeen, was the only one who seemed reluctant. But I just said, "Humor him, Patty, you know my crazy friend, Mr. Van Zandt. He's just having fun. Just play his game." She did. Other than Patty and Kathy, whom I told later, the other kids never even knew why they left. All they know is they had a good time. No "zoup and ztrudel" but plenty of ice cream and cake from Peggy Vrhel.

Needless to say, it was the crank call that I thought it was, but it was also another one of those wonderful things I shall always remember about Dick Van Zandt.

∼

The investigation into the shooting went on for several months under the personal direction of Herman Van der Linde. Dick, Eric, Ed, and Frank

Errico also put many hours into that investigation, but nothing really significant occurred until early September of that year.

At the time of the incident, I had been heading up a joint investigation with the New York State Task Force on Organized Crime and the United States Attorney's Office of the Southern District of New York on the possible infiltration of organized crime into Rockland County. This was certainly a motive that was explored and I was grateful for the many people who urged me to stay strong and continue the investigation. I did.

However, I had always believed that it was some sort of nut, disgruntled by one of the hundreds of cases that I had handled by that time. DAs do get shot and killed from time to time. It's happened in Georgia and Tennessee within the past ten years. Remember, if you handle a few thousand criminal cases, it only takes one defendant or his relative or friend to cause you grief. It's the nature of the business, not necessarily an indication of a *conspiracy* or that you were "too good" a DA or even "too bad" a DA.

No one has ever been arrested or charged concerning that attack on me in May 1973, but certain information was developed by the New York City Police Department in September 1973 that we have every reason to believe points to the perpetrators. But first to dispel some vicious rumors that were afield in the county in 1973—it had nothing whatsoever to do with the political investigations that were going on at the time and it was not anyone I had ever met.

The NYPD informed us that an unidentified person had been overheard bragging in a bar in New York City that he had been the one who took a shot at the Rockland County DA. "My only regret is that I missed the son of a bitch." He was heard to tell the same story in the same bar a second time, only this time he identified by name a person who had been with him.

Herman took the investigation forward and found out the braggart was, in fact, related to a person who had been charged with a crime during my years as Rockland District Attorney. Further detailed investigation established that the suspect *probably* had been in a bar in New City on the night in question with another person with the same first name that he had used in telling of the incident. We realized it was possible that the suspects could have been among the late-night spectators awaiting the "Boys' Night Out" verdict at the New City Courthouse on that foggy night.

Unfortunately, it never went further than that. The identification in New City was far less than positive, and besides New City is almost six miles from the spot on Viola Road; that's not exactly putting the suspects at the scene of the crime.

We recovered a .32-caliber bullet from a headliner inside the car where it had lodged after ricocheting off a metal support of the passenger side armrest, but we could never trace a .32-caliber weapon, or any weapon for that matter, to the suspect.

Years ago, suspects like that would've been brought to the station-house and "grilled" for hours in the hopes of eliciting a confession. But I realize that was wrong. I've been convinced since September 1973 that Herman had been successful in identifying the assailants. But I also knew that the evidence was too thin to hope for a conviction. If we were right about the perpetrators, that is what we called a "crime of opportunity." I was there, they were there, this was their chance. I hope and trust that I don't present such an "opportunity" in the future.

As the years pass, the memory of events fades. We never talk about the shooting and Nancy has even gotten back to not being desperately worried if I am an hour late getting home.

For me, it just strengthened the view of life I've always had. *It can happen here.* You can be a victim, a school bus could be destroyed in your county, the girl down the street could be raped, your district attorney could be murdered. You cannot dwell on the possibility of such calamities, but you also must be prepared to face what life hands you. I firmly believe that this will make you appreciate so much more each day that God continues to bless you, your family, and your friends.

Chapter 12

"Press Secretary to Whom?
Running for What?"

The District Attorney's Office should not be a political office. The problem is that you can't be a district attorney in the state of New York unless you get elected.

Therefore, the task is difficult; you must try to be a good politician when you're running and then completely eschew politics once you are elected and begin the task of running your office on a day-to-day basis. The dilemma is that being a good politician, you try to make friends. Being a good district attorney, you invariably make enemies. As I think back, I'm not so sure I was a good politician, but I must've been a fairly good district attorney because I sure made a lot of enemies.

I guess the thing that hurt me as a politician was that I really didn't like running for office. Some men and women just love running for office. They enjoy the limelight of the campaign. Having your picture in the newspaper, being quoted, being on the radio or on television is a cherished part of the experience. Sad to say, there are some who don't even care what office they are running for, just as long as it's important or at least more important than the one they've got now. It never even crosses their mind whether they would be any good at the job or even whether they'd be happy doing it.

I ran for only one reason, to get the job. I wanted to be district attorney and I literally loved the job. When I ran for New York State Attorney General, it was the same thing. I felt that I would be right for that job. I certainly didn't do it for the thrill of running a statewide race in New York because, believe me, it's no picnic.

Now the irony of all this is that the two races I most enjoyed were both races where no one gave me a chance to win the office: My first race for district attorney in 1965, when I pulled off the upset, and my first race for attorney general in the 1970 Democratic primary, when I got clobbered.

From the beginning in 1965, I thought I could win the DA's race and it was almost fun that no one else thought so at first. I was meeting new people every day and it was a challenge to try to win them over. Since I definitely liked people, this was easy. What became difficult in the later years as district attorney was the succession of functionary appearances that meant I was constantly seeing the same people. I liked my political friends and some became personal friends, but still, I missed meeting new people and making new friends.

The 1970 attorney general's race gave me that new breath of political fresh air. Once I crossed that Rockland county line, heading north, south, east, or west, I was totally unknown. This was a brand new challenge and I loved it.

~

The "Meehan for Attorney General" campaign of 1970 had to be the smallest, worst-financed, statewide operation in New York history. Since I had to be in the DA's Office almost every day, my personal time was limited and with a budget that was almost nonexistent, I had a paid staff of zero. The campaign headquarters was the den of my house on Cherry Lane. Our newspaper, radio, and TV budget was easy to keep track of—it was also zero.

When I began the AG campaign in early January of 1970, I was, however, running to win. My design for victory was reasonably simple. At that time Arthur Goldberg was being drummed as the Democratic candidate for governor and I assumed (totally incorrectly as it turned out) that with all his credentials such as justice of the Supreme Court of the United States, secretary of labor under Kennedy, ambassador to the UN under Johnson, and so on, he would be a great candidate.

It also appeared that the candidate for lieutenant governor that year would likely be Basil Paterson from New York City. Arthur Levitt, also from New York City, would of course be renominated for state comptroller and every one of about six candidates vying for the US Senate nomination were from New York City, except Dick Ottinger who was from nearby Westchester.

That left one more spot on the ticket, attorney general, and if my calculations were right, the spot had to go to a candidate from upstate New York (north of the New York City border) to balance an otherwise totally New York City ticket. Wrong again, but still that was the premise of my race. I thought I was qualified to be attorney general because of my years as district attorney and the fact that I was president-elect of the New York State District Attorneys Association, but most of all, I was an *upstater*.

Now this was something of a problem because most people I met weren't sure where Rockland County was. It wasn't too much trouble in New York City because they all knew it wasn't one of the five boroughs and since it probably wasn't on Long Island, it almost undoubtedly was upstate. Long Islanders were even better because they knew for a fact it wasn't on Long Island and, therefore, it had to be upstate.

When it came to Albany, Utica, Syracuse, Rochester, and Buffalo, they just took it on faith that Rockland was upstate because nine out of ten people hadn't the foggiest idea where Rockland was. But were those upstaters ever nice to me! Starting from a zero base outside Rockland in January, I got 32 percent of the vote at the Democratic Convention in early April at Grossinger's in the Catskills. This represented more than two-thirds of the upstate vote since I only got three votes from the entire New York City delegation: one in Brooklyn, two in Queens—all three committing the mortal sin of voting against their county leaders.

~

My campaign entourage that year consisted of myself, Eric Vrhel, who gave up all his free time to travel with me on nights and weekends, and two other people. The first was our pilot, Aero Thompson (a hell of a name for a pilot, but true), a good-looking blonde kid about twenty-two years old. Hiring Aero was one of the few expenses of the campaign. We had worked out a low-cost lease of a Cessna Cardinal four-seat single-engine plane out of Ramapo Valley Airport. We went everywhere in that little plane and I loved every minute in the air.

The fourth member of our group (which was all we had room for in the plane) was Arnold Reif of Sloatsburg. When I think back to the campaign, Arnie is the one I remember best. We had only met and become friends a few years before, but he got into that campaign with both feet.

Arnie is seven years younger than me, I'm Irish and he's Jewish, but we look a great deal alike and most people we met around the state were sure we were brothers. For Arnie this was just fuel for his cutting, Don Rickles–type of insulting humor. Believe me, during that campaign 90 percent of that humor was directed at me, while most of the other 10 percent was black humor about the inevitability of that plane crashing. He would greet me at the airport with something like "Well, here we go again, another flight in this death trap, eating cold fried chicken and trying to pawn off Pinocchio here as a real live candidate."

The trouble with the airplane jokes was the worse the weather got, the worse the jokes got. Aero was trying to be a serious pilot, but even he broke up over some of that black humor, which is too bad to even repeat.

Another butt of Reif's jokes were the other candidates on the circuit. I personally was running against Adam Walinsky, a former Kennedy man whom I greatly admired. I suppose he did invoke the names of John and Bobby Kennedy a bit too much, but it was his Bobby Kennedy–style of speech and mannerisms that Arnie was always riffing on. In a primary, you see your opponent and the other candidates often, sometimes four or five times a week, because you're going after the same vote. I think Adam and I got along quite well, but not so Reif and Walinsky.

Arnie was constantly needling him with things like, "Hey Adam, if you use that line again tonight about 'getting the state moving forward,' I'm going to throw up." It was silly but it seemed to genuinely bother Adam and I always had to assure him, "That's just Arnie's way, Adam."

Arthur Goldberg was also a special favorite of Arnie's. I came to realize that Goldberg was probably one of the worst candidates I have ever seen, but I still have deep respect for the man's ability based upon his past achievements. Arnie did not.

One night after a candidates' forum in Rochester, there was a small reception for various candidates and Arnie said, loud enough so anyone within earshot could hear, "Gee, Ambassador Goldberg was great tonight. Listening to him speak is about as interesting as watching paint dry." I just cringed and turned away hoping that no one would realize Arnie was with me, but he wasn't through yet.

"If Goldberg can win this nomination and keep coming across like he did tonight, I think there's a good chance that Rockefeller will carry Canada."

In defense of Arnie and Mr. Goldberg, I will say that his analysis of my speeches in the plane on the way home was just as cutting—and he *liked* me, at least I think he did.

~

Arnie was the only one in our campaign who actually had a title, and he was everything—campaign manager, advance man, public relations man, press secretary, and caterer.

By caterer I mean that we never ate in a restaurant and it was always Arnie who was running to get us something to eat as Aero was warming up the plane. His personal favorite was fried chicken and I believe that during that five-and-a-half-month campaign, I ate more fried chicken than I had in my whole life, before *and* since. After a while the inside of that plane smelled like you were standing in line at Colonel Sanders, all compliments of Arnie Reif.

I guess it was his press secretary hat that I remember best. It did get better as the campaign went on, but in the beginning no one in the news media had the vaguest idea who I was or what I was running for.

I remember one time listening to him on the telephone making an advance call to Syracuse, trying to drum up some media coverage for me. I could only hear his end of the conversation:

"This is Arnold Reif, Press Secretary to District Attorney Robert Meehan of Rockland County, Democratic candidate for Attorney General."

(Pause) "Arnold Reif, R-E-I-F."

(Pause) "Robert Meehan." (Pause) "M-E-E-H-A-N."

"He's Rockland County District Attorney." (Pause) "R-O-C-K-L-A-N-D . . ."

At this point I interjected, "Arnie, if he asks you how to spell Robert, hang up."

Nothing seemed to deter Arnie; he just made another joke and plowed forward. In fact, thanks to Arnie, most of the upstate media people ended up treating us very well. To prove the point, on the day before the primary in June, we made a dawn to late night aerial tour of upstate and he got me on fourteen different TV stations and even more radio stations, as well as coverage in every major upstate newspaper.

It was effective coverage; we carried forty-one of the fifty-four counties north of the Westchester line. There was just one little problem. We lost the City of New York by a 3 to 1 margin and therefore, the overall primary by 2 to 1. We couldn't break the New York City media; there's only one way to do that—*buy it* and that we couldn't afford.

∽

By 1971, I was running for my third term as Rockland County District Attorney. I was proud to receive the largest vote of any candidate in the history of the county, and yet I remained wistful, cherishing the memories of that crazy airborne spring of 1970.

And so, in 1974, I made the decision to run for attorney general again and I had high hopes. At the Democratic Convention held in June in Niagara Falls, we were able to parlay my upstate support into some city support and I won the nomination at the convention with 56 percent of the vote, even though I did not receive a single vote out of The Bronx or Manhattan delegations. I'll always appreciate the way those upstate delegates fought for me with the Brooklyn and Queens delegations and got me just enough votes to put me over the top at that convention.

I was now on what I considered a very strong Democratic Party–endorsed ticket with gubernatorial candidate Howard Samuels, lieutenant governor candidate Mario Cuomo, and US Senate candidate Lee Alexander. I was also pleased that the primary had been moved from June to September, giving me more time to make my case to the voters.

This time around, I decided to add our family trailer, decked out with "Meehan for Attorney General" signs, to the campaign transportation budget, and Nancy and I and the kids spent a memorable summer vacation barnstorming upstate. We were able to generate some nice publicity each time we pulled into a new city. The press seemed to get a kick out of watching all the kids pile out of the station wagon with the "Meehan for Attorney General" trailer in tow.

I was also pleased that, for the most part, the whole family really got into the spirit of the adventure. As we wound our way through cities like Utica, Elmira, and Syracuse, Nancy and the kids would sit in the front row and cheer me on as I spoke to local supporters. On one memorable occasion, Bobby, all of eight, stood up in the middle of my remarks and made a beeline for the back of the hall, obviously to use the bathroom. I couldn't help but to poke a little fun, saying to the crowd of about two hundred, "Hey, I guess my speech isn't that interesting." Bobby was mortified and I was called on the carpet by the other kids for embarrassing him.

My children had inherited my love of television, particularly crime dramas. One in particular that had caught our fancy was called *Owen Marshall, Attorney at Law.* This gave rise to a family charade that we affectionately called "Owen Marshmallow." Whenever someone in the family (almost always me) committed a transgression, they were put on trial, with various family members, including Nancy, serving as prosecutor, judge, jury, and of course, Owen Marshmallow for the defense.

And so, as we drove out of Elmira that afternoon, I found myself on trial for the crime of Misdemeanor Humiliation in the First Degree. Tommy, serving as DA, completed his closing argument with "When you gotta go, you gotta go." My defense could never recover from that. I was found guilty and was sentenced to stop at the nearest ice cream stand for double scoops all around.

∾

Despite these happy memories and the chance to meet some amazing people, looking back, I wish I hadn't run that second campaign for attorney general. To make that race, I had to give up the renomination for District Attorney of Rockland County, which was also up in 1974. That year, I raised my total wins in the attorney general primary to fifty-one out of fifty-four counties north of Westchester, but the city results against the popular, likable, and well-financed Bronx borough president, Bob Abrams, were the same. In what ended up being a tough year for party-endorsed candidates, Samuels, Cuomo, Alexander, and Meehan all went down to defeat in the September primary. Thus ended the political career of the Hayseed DA.

∾

In retrospect, I suppose I should say, "I have no regrets," but that would not be the total truth. Sometimes I wish I had stayed where I belong in Rockland County. There are so many people all over upstate New York who were wonderful to me and to my whole family, but it's not fair when you have six school-age children to be running all over a state the size of New York. I was reaching for the brass ring when I couldn't even afford the ride on the merry-go-round.

There has been a great silver lining to all this, however, and that is the time that I can now spend with Nancy and the kids. Bobby, who was born just after I was elected district attorney, finally knows what it is like to have a father around more often. And as the older children go through their teenage years, it is nice to be able to spend more time with them before they head off to college and lives of their own. Gone are the fears that gripped the Meehans, especially the little ones in 1973. So life has really continued to be very good to my family.

I'm also glad to report that Arnie and I have continued to be close friends. Having shown his acid-tongue political style, I think it's only fair to say a bit about his personal style. He is really a wonderful and kind person, which I have seen demonstrated time and time again. He lives with his wife, Nancy, and their two lovely daughters, Susan and Gina, in the little village of Sloatsburg, population 2,500, on the Rockland-Orange county line. He is unquestionably one of the most popular guys in the village and he, in fact, was elected a trustee of the village of Sloatsburg in 1975. Arnie is also president of the local volunteer fire department and everyone considers him a great neighbor, especially in time of trouble.

Arnie has always been something of a paradox. Once you learn that he is only kidding, after he has insulted everything about you, he will quietly proceed to help you in any way humanly possible. That is when you realize how great it is to have him as a friend.

For me this is particularly significant. When I was DA so many fair-weather friends were falling all over me telling me how great they thought I was and what a wonderful job I was doing. I never see or hear from them nowadays. Arnie, whose comment on a big win in court would be something like "Dumb luck, how many jurors did you have to reach?" is still around. He never forgets us and going to see the Reifs or having them over is always a pleasure for all of the Cherry Lane Meehans.

$$\sim$$

As I look back now at my active years in politics, I of course think, "What did I do wrong?" There was the obvious mistake of being politically poor, but I have another theory. I had the wrong heroes.

Most politicians I've met seem to try to pattern themselves after famous Americans. Abe Lincoln is far and away the favorite, but Horatio Alger runs well too. In the past score of years, the Kennedy "image" has come on strong. I especially remember the 1970 state campaign where many candidates for state and local office were outdoing themselves trying to sound, and yes, even look like Jack or Bobby Kennedy. Some pulled it off pretty well; others were grotesque.

My problem was that although Jefferson, Lincoln, Truman, and Kennedy are my political heroes, none of the men I tried to pattern my style after were presidents. In fact, they weren't even real people for that matter. For me it was the damned movies.

My four heroes were, in no particular order, but standing above all others, Captain Edward Kinross, the British destroyer captain of *In Which We Serve*; Father Francis Chisholm in *The Keys of the Kingdom*; General Frank Savage, the group commander in *Twelve O'Clock High*; and Atticus Finch, the Georgian lawyer in *To Kill a Mockingbird*. Why these four? What was the common denominator? Other than the obvious fact the Gregory Peck played three of the four roles, I believe I now know.

Think about it for a minute. All four of my heroes faced their own losses.

As A. J. Cronin's priest, Gregory Peck was sent on a remote mission to China while his boyhood friend became Bishop of Tynecastle in their native Scotland.

Playing the Eighth Air Force general, Peck's character had a break-down and couldn't lead the last critical mission over Germany.

Peck won the Academy Award as the country lawyer—who lost his case.

As for Noël Coward, the very first line of *In Which We Serve* is "This is the story of a ship." He was the captain of HMS *Torin*; the *Torin* was torpedoed and sank.

Chapter 13

Annie

It was about a week after Election Day in November 1974, and I was sitting in my office alone, going over the serious felony cases to be presented to the grand jury, as I had for so many years before. But it was an empty feeling. I began to realize, "These won't be my cases. By the time they come to the tension and excitement of trial, I'll be gone."

The election of November 1974 had been a great success for Democrats, both statewide and locally. Hugh Carey, whom I had come to know reasonably well during the long primary season, had been elected governor and in Rockland County, Kenny Gribetz won the district attorney's race by about nine thousand votes. However, it was personally a very hard time for me. I was entering the final days in the office I loved so much.

I guess I had to admit to myself that although I would desperately miss the cases, it was working day in and day out, night in and night out with *my* people that I would miss the most.

By that time everyone working in the office had been hired during my years. The last two holdovers from the previous district attorney had retired in early 1974. We had started with ten people and as I prepared to leave, we had thirty-two. I had a special feeling for so many of them, and for others who had come and gone during those nine years.

Mention a case, any case, and I associated it with one of my people. If it was Rivera and Biggs, it was Lindy; Sheffield was Mack; Dr. Kass was Eric; Mulligan was Herman; the bus was Kenny, and so on and so on.

I suppose it's a bad thing at age forty-four to be reminiscing about the past, but my mind really wandered through the cases we had tried over the years, and I started making a little scorecard of just who had been the most important to the successes of those years. There were so many people to consider.

Just then Bill Frank walked into my office with the newest assistant DA, Jimmy Mellion, who had just passed the bar exam. Bill Frank had only been with me for a year and a half but I already knew he was one of the finest young men I had ever hired. Like Kenny, he came from four years in Hogan's office in New York and I was particularly pleased that he was to become chief assistant district attorney under Kenny. Although only twenty-eight at the time, Bill already had a level of judgment, maturity, and calmness that would be so helpful in keeping the highly charged Kenny Gribetz on an even keel.

"Chief," Bill began. (I really liked to be called "Chief." That was what Bill and everyone else in Manhattan called Mr. Hogan, and every time he said it, I took it as a compliment.) "Young Jimmy here is preparing a burglary case for grand jury and he's got fingerprints and he's not sure how to handle it. I told him to see the Chief, he's the expert."

I kind of laughed and said, "Expert! Jim, you should have seen me on my first case with prints, I didn't know what the hell I was doing!"

At that point, Bill broke in. "Wait a minute, Chief, I read the transcript of that Ritter trial. You knew exactly what you were doing."

"Oh yeah, by the time we got to trial I did. But if you've got a few minutes, I'll tell you how it all began."

So we sat there for almost an hour. I hope it helped Jimmy with his case. I know I enjoyed that hour.

∼

It was the fall of '66. I was in the middle of picking a jury on my first murder case and I arrived home at about midnight. As was not too unusual in those days, Nancy and I were having dinner at 1 a.m. on the morning of September 7, 1966, when the phone rang. It was the desk sergeant of the Clarkstown Police. There had been a murder in the Clarkstown section of Spring Valley. Within half an hour I was at the scene on 2nd Ave. in Spring Valley.

It was a particularly heinous killing. A twenty-six-year-old divorced mother of four preschool children had been brutally stabbed to death in her bed, while her four children slept in the next room. There were seventeen stab wounds in her head and chest, but it was the deep cuts on her hands where she had apparently struggled to keep the lethal weapon away that were the most pathetic to see.

The officer in charge when I arrived at the scene was then Detective Sergeant George Finlay, my first case with my pre-*Colombo, Colombo.* George filled me in rapidly. We had the murder weapon. It was a butcher knife found beside the murdered girl's bed, apparently taken from the kitchen of the apartment that was on the first floor of an old two-story frame house. Entry had been through the back ground-floor bathroom window. The screen had been forcibly removed and the window was open. Both doors to the apartment were locked and bolted from the inside when the first officer arrived at the scene. Other than the blood-splattered bed, the apartment was neat and orderly and nothing appeared to be missing. There was a pocketbook on an end table in the living room containing $18 in cash and there was $6 dollars in change in a jar on the kitchen counter near the drawer where the butcher knife was ordinarily kept.

Burglary was ruled out because if the young woman had been awakened by an intruder and confronted him before he could steal anything, she would not have still been in bed in the bedroom in the front of the house at the opposite end of the apartment from the kitchen and bathroom. This appeared to be a premeditated murder. Whoever entered that apartment did so with the intent to murder poor, frail little Mary Ritter. He didn't need to bring a weapon; he already knew where one was!

~

Mary's upstairs neighbor and good friend, Muriel Tillman, had heard the screams in the night and called the police. Muriel was there when Patrolman Flip Sullivan broke down the bolted door and ran to assist the dying woman. When Sullivan turned on the light and they saw the horror of that bloody scene, Mary's eyes were still open and she was nearing her last breath. Muriel cried out, "Who did it, did Michael do it?"

Her weak and only response was "I don't know but he was wearing glasses." Within a minute she was unconscious, within fifteen, she was dead.

There was only one suspect, Michael Ritter, age twenty-seven, the former husband who in life she had mortally feared. Muriel Tillman told us that night at the police station of how Mary had lived in constant fear of Michael, of how the inside door bolts were put on with the help of Muriel's husband, Bill, all to protect against Michael. She went on and on, telling what Mary had told her of Michael's threats as recently as the day before.

When I talked to Mary's mother and brother at the police station in the early morning hours of that day, it was the same. Through their grief, they described the fear and almost panic that Mary felt toward Michael. As I listened to those stories, I could have cried for Mary's poor distraught mother, but I was also thinking like a prosecutor. "Oh my God," I thought to myself, "none of this will ever be admissible. They are all private threats. What she told them in life is now hearsay. Only that 'dying declaration' to Muriel Tillman and Flip Sullivan will be admissible, and that only said, 'but he was wearing glasses.'"

~

Michael Ritter did wear glasses, but when he was picked up less than two hours later, he was clean as a whistle. He looked like he had just taken a shower. There was one problem for him, however, his right hand had a severe cut between the thumb and index finger. To us, the injury was suggestive of thrusting a knife into an object and having it slip since there was no hilt. To Ritter it was nothing. The case of Ernesto Miranda had been the law of the land for eighty-five days and Ritter already seemed fully aware of its implications. He wanted his lawyer; he wasn't saying anything. It wasn't up to him to explain away the cut; it was up to us to prove that the cut occurred as he plunged the knife into his defenseless little ex-wife.

Although we couldn't legally question Ritter, we could have him medically examined and we did. Yes, the butcher knife *could have* caused the injury. "Could have" is not the same as "did," a good piece of evidence, but only that.

A legally authorized search of the little summer cottage where Ritter lived alone produced almost nothing. No bloody clothes, no shoes that fit the tracks in Mary's backyard. Just a wet shower stall and two seemingly unimportant packs of cigarettes found on his kitchen counter. They became important later when we found out that he had gone to a neighbor at about one o'clock in the morning to bum a cigarette. A strange thing to do with two packs in the house in clear view, but not so strange if you're trying to *establish an alibi*.

By dawn we had already talked to the lawyer who handled Mary's divorce from Michael. Legally he was more help than Muriel Tillman or the distraught family of Mary Ritter. He was able to testify to threats against Mary made by Michael *in his presence*; one of them in the passageway outside of family court. *Admissible!* Statements made by the defendant in your presence—exceptions to the hearsay rule.

All right, with what we heard from Muriel and the family, the bad cut on his hand, the clumsy attempt at an alibi with the cigarettes, and the lawyer statement, we were sure Michael Ritter was our man; but I was just as sure we couldn't prove it in a court of law. I wasn't even sure I had the right to hold him much longer.

A lot of people say things to their soon-to-be former spouses outside the courtroom. People also cut their hand preparing a chicken. Are you going to lock up a guy because he asked for a cigarette when he had some in the house? Thus far we had NOT placed the defendant at the scene of the crime.

At 6:30 that morning a paid defense lawyer who was called by Ritter, said to me, "Meehan, charge my man or let him go. If you don't I'll get a writ!"

"Get your fucking writ, this guy's going no place." I'm sorry to report that I was pretty hot by that time and had reverted to the brickyard language that my father so disliked. But I also knew I only had two and a half hours until county court opened and the defense could indeed get a writ of habeas corpus. As I scurried about trying to come up with an eyewitness from the neighborhood or any other type of incriminating evidence, Old George Finlay (he's two years younger than I, I just think of him as "Old George"), assisted by a fine young detective, Ron Purdum, was busy dusting the entire scene for fingerprints. I wasn't hopeful.

My reasons for not putting too much stock in prints was that in less than nine months in office, I had already learned that developing latent prints was about a thousand times more difficult than I thought. I also knew by this time that the blood-soaked knife was valueless for prints. Ritter had visitation rights for the children and had been in that apartment about once a week that summer. If we found his prints, so what? Again, I was wrong.

∾

At about seven o'clock that morning, Finlay came to see me at the stationhouse with John Slater, head of the Bureau of Criminal Investigation (BCI) at the Sheriff's Office. I knew who Slater was, but had not worked with him before.

Finlay said, "We've got two prints in the bathroom, one on the screen that probably won't help us and what looks like a 'fresh' palm print on the windowsill, which indicates the arms and body are toward the outside. It looks like pressure was exerted and we might be able to make a positive on it."

Ritter had already been printed, but not his palm prints. A few minutes later, over the strong protestations of his lawyer, who I regret to say I continued to heap verbal abuse on, Ritter had both his palm prints taken. It was less than forty-five minutes later that Slater, the best fingerprint man in the county, reported back, "They match. I've got over twenty points of identification."

I interrupted my story at that point to say to Jimmy Mellion, "You know, Jim, at that point, I wasn't even exactly certain what was meant by 'points of identification' except that I heard you needed twelve for a positive."

Twenty sounded very good to me. I said to Finlay, Slater, and Clarkstown Police Chief Ernie Wiebecke, "That's it, we'll charge the son of a bitch—Murder One." As I said those words, I knew we still had problems. There seems to be no exact science of when fingerprints were placed, so "fresh prints" wasn't all that it seemed. I could also just hear the defendant on the stand, "Oh, I'm sure that's my palm print. I was in the bathroom a lot and maybe when the window was open in the hot weather, I leaned back against the sill when I was watching the kids take a bath."

I didn't voice that doubt at the station. In my opinion, *we did* have a prima facia case. I would learn more about "fresh prints." I would rely on a theory that I always had as a defense attorney and now as a prosecutor, "The truth will out." If he was guilty, as I was morally certain Ritter was, the more facts we got, the more the truth of that guilt would come out.

Michael Ritter was arraigned in Clarkstown Justice Court on a charge of First-Degree Murder at 9:15 that morning. I remember leaving court and saying to his lawyer, Jerry Kornfeld, whom I didn't know well, "Mr. Kornfeld, I don't regret anything that happened to your client this morning, but I do regret treating a fine member of the bar as shabbily as I did you. I apologize." Jerry's answer was, "The heat of the battle, Bob, no apology necessary." A real pro.

So the battle began. Within a week Ritter was indicted—one count Murder in the First Degree. This case would never be compromised or bargained. Ritter would be convicted of Murder One . . . or he would walk.

We gave the case a top priority; everyone who knew Mary Ritter in any way was interviewed. Did they ever hear Michael threaten her *in their presence*? The answer was uniformly "no." She only told of the threats that they never actually heard.

Within a week, we got information indirectly helpful to our case. Ritter had been in the United States Air Force and had gotten a Dishonorable Discharge. My years in the Navy had taught me that "DDs" don't come lightly. Ritter deserved his. He had been convicted of two First-Degree Burglaries—burglary of a private residence where physical injury had been caused. The first time he used a gun butt on a man's head; the second time it was a pipe on a woman's head. The burglaries had occurred when he was stationed with the Air Force in England.

Within twenty-four hours, I was in touch by telephone with Superintendent Geoffrey Crossland of Scotland Yard. I must have talked to him twenty times in the next five months and although I never did lay eyes on him, he was fully prepared to go to Rockland County to testify and, believe me, he would have done my favorite British character actor, Jack Hawkins, proud. "Superintendent Crossland here." I loved the guy; it was like my late-night movies come to life.

What it meant legally was that Michael Ritter *probably* would not take the stand in his own defense. Prior records—and this one would have been damaging—are only admissible *if* you take the witness stand in your own defense.

With all of our investigation, the British connection and all, I was still damned worried. Jerry Kornfeld's partner, Tom Newman, had now taken over the case for trial. Maybe Ritter couldn't tell his little story about the bathroom, but Tommy Newman would. It could be a beautiful part of his summation.

Then, about three weeks later, in came George Finlay and John Slater. George began, "You know, we'd really like to try to do something with that print on the screen."

I looked quizzical and said, "I thought you said it was no good. I looked at it and I could see the nine finger outlines, but I thought the surface was too rough for positive."

John spoke up and said, "Well in a way you're right, Mr. Meehan. On eight of them you're definitely right, there's nothing there. But on number *nine*, I think if you had the right photographic enlargement equipment you could make it."

John went on to say that his equipment was good but not good enough, and I responded, "Well where is the equipment that is good enough? We'll get it."

"Mr. Meehan, the only place I know is the FBI lab in Washington and they have a hard rule, they won't work a print that someone else dusted and tried to make."

I wasn't about to miss an opportunity to get a guy for murdering his wife based on a fingerprint identification on number nine, third finger, left hand. I immediately picked up the intercom, "Annie, get me the chief of the FBI Identification Unit in Washington, DC." Within twenty minutes I had the FBI on the line and within another ten I had *conned* him out of the rule. "Sir, a vicious murder case is at stake, rules are made to be broken." When I got off the phone, I said to John Slater, "How soon can you leave for Washington?"

The bathroom window had a full-size double window screen. The double turning locks that held it in place had long since been broken and it was actually nailed in place. The latent prints were in the best possible spot, on the inside of the lower crossbar where someone would have had to apply great pressure with their finger on the *inside* of the screen and their thumb on the outside as they pried off the screen. It would *not have been possible* to leave prints on that part of the crossbar with the screen *in place*. The print would have to have been made by the person who removed the screen.

The first thing I did was head home to Cherry Lane. In the garage I got my skill saw and headed right back to the DA's Office. There in the evidence room, I proceeded to set a forty-five-degree angle and carefully cut the bottom wooden crossbar off the screen. My carpentry skills were finally paying off in the DA's Office.

John and I then carefully placed the wooden crossbar in a large cardboard box, suspended at either end so that the important "latents" wouldn't be disturbed.

~

John Slater and I caught the noon Eastern shuttle from LaGuardia to Washington National Airport. By 1:45 that afternoon we were showing our precious piece of green painted wood to the FBI agent in charge of laboratory, Peter Byrnes.

As I said to Jimmy Mellion, "I'll always remember that brief conversation between John Slater, Byrnes, and myself."

After Byrnes had called in one of his best fingerprint identification men, Phil Reese, and they both had carefully inspected the crossbar with a magnifying glass, they kind of frowned at each other. I was worried so I piped up and said, "Well I realize it's difficult, you don't have to be positive. If you could find a few points of identification, if you could say it looks a lot like his, it sure would help!"

Byrnes looked at me as though I had just committed the worst mortal sin. "Sir, in this business there are only two findings on latent fingerprints: *Positive* or *No Identification*. There is nothing in between!"

The next two and a half hours, sitting with John Slater, felt to me very much like sitting in the Father's Room of Good Samaritan Hospital in Suffern, waiting for Nancy to have a baby. When the identification man finally came back, he didn't say "boy" or "girl," just "*Positive*, eight points, but positive."

I was thrilled but still worried. What about the books that talked about the importance of twelve points? Byrnes almost took me by the hand and said in a rather fatherly tone, "Mr. Meehan, I don't give a damn how many points, it's either positive or no identification. This one happens to be positive." I knew we had Ritter.

~

The trial was set for the first Monday in January 1967, and I was busy putting all the evidence and exhibits together, while fully aware of the fact that the fingerprint evidence was the key to the case. When I got around to meeting with John Slater to discuss exactly how we would put in the fingerprint testimony, the first question I asked John was "Let's see, John, you've been a police officer since 1946, you've been with the BCI since 1957, and you've been chief for a while now. How many times have you testified on dusting and identification at trials before?"

"Well, Mr. Meehan, I've testified in grand juries, but I've never testified at a trial before. Hell, they all plead guilty!" He was right. Fingerprints are the great tool of burglary investigations. No one saw the burglar enter, no one saw him leave, he had no business being there; a print sinks him! It is damning evidence, so he pleads guilty, taking the best deal he can get. Even in the robbery cases where the perpetrator confronts his victim, if we know whose fingerprints to compare with, we usually get an eyewitness identification in a lineup and the fingerprints lose their significance if any positives are developed. And few positives are developed.

I have since learned that if I were to take ten automobiles and the fingerprints of the ten men who drive them regularly, I would be lucky to get a positive identification on ONE of them. The rest, even with top experts, would be unidentifiable smudges with the only real hope being a thumb on the glass of the rearview mirror. I honestly believe that television and the movies have overstated the ease of obtaining latent fingerprints to the point where jurors are disappointed and feel we've fallen down on the job because we didn't come up with an identifiable print, when there was none to be had.

Fingerprints in a murder case? It practically never happens! Why?— Because the victim almost always knows the killer. In my cases, more often than not, they are related. If the killer had a right to be on the premises, if he had been there or if at least we couldn't prove that he did not have a right to be there, the print became valueless.

The case of Michael Ritter was the exception—we had a murder and the verdict hung on the fingerprint testimony. I'll always remember sitting at four o'clock in the morning in the kitchen of John Slater's house on Brewery Lane in New City, going over book after book on fingerprints and fingerprint testimony. He knew fingerprints, backward, forward, and sideways. I knew how to present evidence. Our problem was to bring the two together.

∾

When John Slater took the witness stand, he sounded so much like an old hand at testifying that Tom Newman, a sharp defense lawyer, never even asked how many times he had testified at trials before. Clearly he was afraid of the answer. The FBI identification man, Agent Phil Reese from Washington, was great, but actually no better than Slater. We had systematically nailed Ritter to that screen.

Tom Newman put up a valiant fight and systematically shut down every point, including, as I had anticipated, the palm prints on the windowsill. He even got Slater and Reese to admit on cross that those "fresh prints" could be "two hours to two months old or even older." But the one thing he couldn't break were the prints on the screen crossbar. In fact, his inability to crack those prints led to one of the most dramatic points of the trial.

The big screen, less the crossbar, was on display in the courtroom. At almost the end of his summation on the last day of the trial, Newman picked up that large screen and actually threw it across the room at the cardboard box still containing the crossbar. As the screen landed hard, he roared, "And that's what I think of your amateur carpenter DA and his stupid screen!"

During that same summation, Tom had referred to my office and the Clarkstown police, who attended trial that day, as "the vultures, eager to be in on the kill." He accused us of violating every legal right the defendant ever had and, letting his Irish Catholicism come through, said, "Mr. Meehan and his men have violated the canons of human decency. Don't let Mike Ritter suffer for their sins."

When his summation was over and the jury filed out for lunch break, I walked over to Tom with a mock frown and said, "I can forgive you for everything you said about me, I can forgive you for all but one thing, Tom; you broke my screen."

Michael Ritter was convicted of First-Degree Murder. He is now in his tenth year of a life sentence at the New York State Prison at Attica, New York. He was in the yard that day in early September 1971, when all hell broke loose. He was severely injured but he survived. I'm glad he did. I am very well aware of the two sides to the burning issue of capital punishment, but since I am the guy that had to convict them, I'm a little more sensitive to the issue than most.

"Jimmy, the moral to the story is what they still teach Boy Scouts in this country. 'Be prepared,' read the books, find out, never walk into a courtroom unless you've made yourself enough of an expert on any given subject that the jury will at least *think* you know what you're talking about."

～

When the session ended and Jim Mellion and Bill Frank left, Ann Hickey came into my office and said, "Boss, I haven't seen you look so happy since you lost the primary." I proceeded to tell her that I had been talking about prints and I got carried away talking about the Ritter case.

She smiled and said, "I'll always remember how upset you were with that one woman juror on the Ritter case. You were so sure she was the one who was holding out for acquittal when they locked them up for the night. It turned out she was for conviction from the first vote."

So Annie and I sat there talking about a case that had happened eight years earlier just like it was yesterday, and that too was a pleasant interlude at a difficult time.

After Ann gave me a few messages, she left the room and I glanced down at the little scorecard I had been fooling with before Jim and Bill came in. I then realized, who am I kidding? Who was there on the very first day in January 1966 and who would be there on the very last day? Who had typed out the notes for the summations on the Ritter case and every other case? Who was the first to know that we would move for indictment against a public official? Or, other than Nancy, know I would make a run for attorney general?

In good times and bad, in triumphs and tragedies in the Rockland County District Attorney's Office, it was *always* Annie. God knows what with Ronkie and her mother dying during those years, she had her share of tragedies, but she never entered that office without a smile and a kind word for everyone. If a woman came into the office to get her husband out of the drunk tank, Annie would treat her the same as she would the president of the Bar Association.

She made me look good. After all we were public servants, and when the public contacted me, they talked to Annie. It was more than once that people who were annoyed or upset with me said something like "Well you can't be all that bad with a secretary like that."

She not only had her special winning way, but she literally ran that office. I loved investigations and trials but she was ready, willing, able, and actually *liked* to do things like payroll, purchasing, personnel records, and so forth. In the eyes of the other departments of the county, I was a reasonably good administrator; without Annie I would've been an utter failure.

But above all things, she was what held us together as a family. She knew and remembered everybody's birthday. If someone's child was hurt, she came in with a present; if their wife was sick, she took care of the children or cooked the meal—or both.

In the office, she invariably knew who was down. I remember Eddie McElroy sitting at his desk one morning after we lost a rather tough jury verdict. He was uncharacteristically sullen and downcast. A few minutes later Ann went over to his desk in the squad room and handed him an envelope labeled "Sr. Investigator Charles E. McElroy—Urgent." "Eddie," Ann said, "This was just hand-delivered to the front desk. It looks important so I brought it right in."

As Ann turned and went back to her desk, Ed opened the "important" communication. Within a minute, he was heading into my private office, grinning from ear to ear, as he said, "Look what that dumb broad of a secretary of yours just handed me." I looked at the note inside that envelope, it read: "Dearest Honey Love, I just love that red tie you're wearing today. Oh God, you are handsome! (Signed) A secret admirer."

As Ed left my office, the downcast mood was gone; he was smiling broadly. Annie had again worked her magic.

That's why for that time in my life, I can say that I'll never forget Eddie or Eric or Dick or Lindy or Herman. Working with the old pros and all the great young assistants was a true privilege. But most of all I'll remember Annie.

∿

So after nine wonderful years, I left the District Attorney's Office. I believe that the main reason I have written these chapters is to show that prosecutors, too, can be human. Obviously the press cannot report the behind-the-scenes drama that occurs during each case, but we also don't want to be portrayed as "wooden."

For instance, I was always proud of being called "The Fighting DA" in Rockland. In fact, I nurtured that image. In 1968, my reelection signs, posters, bumper stickers, and so on, all had one slogan: "Reelect Your Fighting DA." In 1971, there was only a one-word change to "Reelect Rockland's Fighting DA." I suppose it may sound conceited, but I believe I deserved that image. But what does it mean? Politicians are always saying that they are "fighting" for this or that and it loses its significance, but to me it meant one thing. Not that I would enjoy locking up my grandmother and throwing away the key or that I had a killer instinct in court or obviously not that I was actually involved in a physical fight; my last fight of that kind was during the Korean War.

It meant to me that I was willing, when I was convinced that the cause was just, to take on what I well knew could become a legally "lost cause." I often said to my assistants and to judges, "I would rather lose this case than take a plea to a misdemeanor." I know they didn't believe me when I said it, but I meant it all the way. Conviction rate percentages were not that important to me. I learned that from the best prosecutor I ever knew, Frank Hogan.

Let me illustrate my point. Let's say the police make one hundred arrests, all on good, legal probable cause. Seventy-five are good solid cases with no legal technicalities. On the other twenty-five, you are morally convinced of guilt, but you are also certain that you're in for a real legal battle. The DA, with his vast prosecutorial discretion, can play it safe and only present the seventy-five that are sure winners to the grand jury for indictment. He'll have far fewer jury trials. Because of the certainty of conviction, most of the defendants will take a plea. And the ones he does have will—with rare exceptions—result in convictions. His conviction rate, if he's very careful, can actually be at, or very close to, 100 percent. The other twenty-five get a slap on the wrist in justice court with no felony conviction, or even walk free altogether.

Now the "Fighting DA" would be different. He would present all one hundred cases to the grand jury and, assuming the good probable cause I spoke of, all would be indicted. There would literally be five times as many trials. Let's assume he is a good fighter and, of the twenty-five more difficult trials, he wins 68 percent of them. That's seventeen plus the easier seventy-five by plea or verdict, for a total of ninety-two convictions or a conviction rate of 92 percent. Who is the better DA, the safe guy with 98 to 100 percent, or the fighter at 92 percent?

I realize many in this era of defense consciousness would say the "safe" guy is the fair guy. Sure, eight people were put through a trial and acquitted, but they won didn't they? They were *cleared* by a jury of their peers. That's the American way.

I could only be the fighter. I couldn't forget the victims of those other twenty-five crimes; they too must have their day in court. Those victims deserve a firm but fair shake, too. I believe that I always gave it to them. The Fighting DA is not necessarily a mean, unfeeling person.

So I hope that I will be remembered as a DA who cared, not with the stilted image that the public may have perceived, especially in the statewide press when I ran for attorney general. I remember they would refer to me very officiously as "the veteran Rockland prosecutor" or "president of the District Attorneys Association." Those one-liners say so little about the person behind them.

~

One little story about the DA's Association might tell more about the title of this book. It was the night before I was sworn in as president of the association in June 1970 at our convention at the Sagamore Hotel at Bolton's Landing on Lake George. There was a party going on in my room at about one o'clock in the morning. I was relaxing with my shoes and jacket off and my collar open. The secretary to the Rensselaer County District Attorney had never met me before and she came up to the room with her husband and with her DA, Gus Cholakis, and his wife. By that time I knew Gus well and also liked him very much.

About twenty minutes after they arrived, Gus came over with his secretary, Tess, by the hand and with a big smile. "Tess, I want you to meet the new president of our association, Bob Meehan from Rockland County."

I responded, "Hi, Tess," and Gus said, "I figured I better introduce you. Tess just said to me who is that Clem Kadiddlehopper character in the corner with the holes in his socks?"

Of course it was me. I did have holes in my socks. I guess I always will.

Epilogue

Robert R. Meehan died on Sunday, February 29, 2004. Leap Day. The six of us children figure he planned it that way. Dad loved numbers; statistics, odds, percentages, box scores. He was always calculating something. We suspect that he loved defying the odds to pass away on a date that only comes along every 1,461 days. So Leap Days can be a little hard, but they only occur every four years.

Dad so treasured his days as *Rockland's Fighting DA*, but soon after he stepped down, he was happily tackling other challenges. He was appointed New York State Special Assistant Attorney General for Medicaid Fraud in 1975, where he was able to expose and prosecute elder abuse in nursing homes across the state. In 1982, Governor Hugh Carey appointed him to serve as a Rockland County Court Judge to fill the post vacated by the retiring Judge John Gallucci. He was subsequently elected to serve two terms and during this time also served as an Acting State Supreme Court Justice. Dad loved being a judge, and he truly relished being called *Judge Meehan*. There were so many great stories from his years on the bench, but alas, we never found a manuscript about those adventures! Dad retired in 2000 but continued to serve as a New York State Judicial Hearing Officer.

Mom and Dad had many more wonderful years together, traveling and spending time with their children and grandchildren, before Mom—Dad's beloved Nancy—died of cancer in 1997. The six of us children all went on to fulfilling careers and had families of our own. Pat made our parents so proud when she became a pediatrician, and Dad was thrilled when Tom became an officer in the United States Navy before going on to a career in computer technology. Mary and Bob both pursued careers in education, focusing on the needs of children with developmental disabilities. I found my niche in the communications field, writing speeches and other documents for elected officials, college presidents, and not-for-profit organizations. However only one of us, Laura—to whom this book is dedicated—chose to follow in Dad's footsteps. After graduating law school, Laura served as an Assistant District Attorney in Orange County, New York, and later as an Assistant New York State Attorney General, initially working in the same Medicaid Fraud Control Unit run by our Dad. Sadly, Laura died in 2018 from complications related to a heart condition. She never had a chance to read Dad's book, but we know she would have loved it!

After Mom passed, Dad missed her terribly, but he was able to fill the void with the help of wonderful friends, including Ann Hickey, Al and Renee Weiner, and Zeena and Jack MacLean. But most of all, Dad loved playing *Papa* to his grandchildren. At the time of his death, he had ten grandsons and six granddaughters. After Dad's passing, Bob had two more sons, and named one Robert R. Meehan III. It is noteworthy that one of his grandsons is hoping to carry on Papa's legacy and is about to graduate law school.

As Dad's health failed, he got in the habit of spending the winters with Mary and Bob and their respective families in San Diego. His doctor was happy that he was away from the harsh northeastern winters, and Dad was thrilled to spend time with his California grandchildren.

Before he left for California in December 2003, Dad had something very important to take care of; he needed to apply for an absentee ballot in order to vote in the New York State presidential primary, scheduled for March 2, 2004. It probably goes without saying that Dad ALWAYS voted. He impressed upon all of us that voting is more than a right or a privilege; voting is an obligation that we must pay if we want to live in a free country.

However, the 2004 presidential primary was more important to Dad than most elections. When the War in Iraq began in early 2003, he was very upset. As a naval officer who served in the Korean War, Dad knew about the horrors of war and could not understand the justification for sending American troops to die in a country without provocation. Dad was eager to vote for someone new to set the country on a different course.

As Dad was enjoying his visit to San Diego in January 2004, he went out to lunch with Bob at the Outback Steakhouse, wearing his beloved USS *Bradford* Navy baseball hat. Seated at a nearby table were a small group of aviators from the aircraft carrier USS *Nimitz*. Seeing Dad's hat, the fliers told the waitress that they would like to pay for Dad and Bob's meal. Dad was very touched by the gesture and asked the gentlemen to join them. For the next thirty minutes, Bob recalled, Dad was in his glory talking with the aviators about Admiral Chester Nimitz, for whom their ship was named, and his role in directing operations against the Japanese in the Battle of Midway.

The next day, Dad's health took a turn for the worse and he was admitted to the hospital with congestive heart failure. Thus began the final leg of his journey.

As his health deteriorated, Dad became concerned that he wouldn't get a chance to vote in the presidential primary. He became very focused on receiving his absentee ballot in the mail. Mary would look for it each day and would hate to tell him that it hadn't arrived.

Finally, at the end of February, the ballot showed up. Mary brought it to Dad and he asked her to help him sit up and hand him his black Flair pen. When he had finished filling out the ballot, Mary noticed a perceptible level of calm sweep over Dad. They talked for about thirty minutes, and then he drifted back off to sleep. At Dad's request, Mary then headed straight to the post office to mail the ballot.

A few days later, while in Hospice care, Dad slipped into a coma. Some of us, myself included, had already flown out to San Diego to say goodbye. My sister Laura and Ann Hickey had not yet had that chance and they immediately booked flights to see Dad before he passed. On the morning of Saturday, February 28, while their planes were in the air, the hospice nurse called Mary to say that Dad was slipping away. Fearing Dad would be gone before Mary could make the twenty-minute drive to get there, the nurse put the phone to Dad's ear so that she could say goodbye. Mary had a different message. "Don't you dare let go yet, Dad!" Mary told him firmly. "Laura and Ann are on their way! You have to hold on for them to get there!!"

When Mary arrived at the hospital, the nurse told her that after she had hung up the phone, she watched in wonder as Dad's condition improved. While he did not awaken from his coma, his vital signs began to stabilize. Laura and Ann made it to Dad's bedside that night.

Early the next morning, with Laura by his side, Dad quietly slipped away. Two of his final acts were to demonstrate his love for his family . . . and to cast his vote. It was the fulfillment of an ordinary commitment at the end of an extraordinary life.

Acknowledgments

On behalf of my father, I include perhaps the most important acknowledgment of the contributions of my mother, Nancy Thayer Meehan, who passed away in 1997. While I have no direct knowledge of her involvement or any assistance she would have provided to my dad while he was writing the book back in 1977 and 1978, I am 100 percent certain that she played a pivotal role. She always did.

I have no doubt that my mom typed the manuscript, provided advice and encouragement throughout the writing process, and invented all of the fictitious names for the defendants, victims, and witnesses, as described by my dad in his preface.

My parents were a team who supported each other unconditionally. I know my mom loved working on this project with my dad, and somewhere they are celebrating together the publication of this book and the fruits of their efforts made so many years ago.

To those who helped me on this journey from the discovery of the manuscript through the editing process to publication, I am eternally grateful.

Thank you so much to Bruce Muldoon, who was my dad's faithful and indispensable law clerk during his judicial years. An early reader of the manuscript, Bruce offered wonderful advice. He helped with important research that allowed for meaningful updates. And he helped me get in touch with some of the key players in the book so that I could gather additional information and gain their insights into the stories my father told.

Among the players in the book that I had the chance to speak to, thank you to my dad's secretary and dear friend, Ann Hickey; his investigator, friend, and the funniest person my dad ever knew, Dick Van Zandt; and to Joe St. Lawrence Jr., the young man who helped bring a killer to justice in the first chapter. Their contributions to this book are immeasurable.

To my dear friend Holly Planells McKenna, a writer and educator who provided invaluable notes on the manuscript and helped steer me on the path toward publication. To Paul Salvo, a writer who never heard of my dad but upon reading the manuscript enthusiastically supported my efforts and helped me to believe that my goal was possible. To Nancy Sakaduski, a writer and publisher who offered great advice about the intricacies of the publishing world.

To M. Graham "Gray" Coleman and his assistant, Hope Bernhard, for the invaluable legal counsel and assistance in establishing ownership rights to my father's original manuscript.

To all my wonderful friends in Kennett Square, Pennsylvania, and Lewes, Delaware, for supporting me and my almost obsessive focus on the completion of this book.

I save my final thanks for my family. To my aunt, Carolyn Capstick Meehan, for helping me find the original manuscript and offering valuable assistance throughout the process. To my cousin, John Marino, another enthusiastic supporter who also provided important early legal advice. I am very grateful for the love and support of all of my aunts, uncles, cousins, nephews and nieces, particularly Jenn, Nancy, and Heather Rutishauser, who honored not only their grandfather but also their late mother, my sister, Laura Rutishauser, with their efforts to ensure publication of this book because they understood how important this would have been to their mom.

To my sons, Tim and Jeremy, who cheered me on and made me feel so proud to take this journey to honor my dad.

To my sisters and brothers, Pat Mangan, Mary Meehan Taylor, Tom Meehan, and Bob Meehan. A very special thank you for your help in digitizing the original manuscript, assisting in the editing process, searching for old photos, and offering up family stories. We came together as a team, each playing an important role in completing this final gift for our father.

And finally, to my husband, Hai. Like my parents before me, I am blessed to have my husband's unconditional love and support. His encouragement, advice, and belief in the ultimate success of this project provided the inspiration and confidence I needed to see *Confessions of a Hayseed DA* through to completion.

Notes

Confessions of a Hayseed DA contains a few references by the author to New York State legal statutes that he felt created challenges in his work as district attorney. As the book was originally written in the late 1970s and concerned cases that occurred from 1966 to 1974, the editor has provided updates on the status of these laws and rulings.

In chapter 5, "Boys' Night Out," the author cites two laws regarding corroboration: Corroboration of Accomplices and Corroboration of Rape Victims. The author expresses satisfaction and pride that the Corroboration of Rape Victims was changed in 1974. The author testified before committees in the New York State Senate and Assembly urging the change that was eventually enacted. According to the *New York Times* in a January 15, 1974, article, "the bill removes all need for corroboration by a witness, except in cases of consensual sodomy or of so-called statutory rape, where the victim is under the age of consent—18—or has a mental defect."

In regard to Corroboration of Accomplices, section 60.22 of the New York State Penal Code states: "A defendant may not be convicted of any offense upon the testimony of an accomplice unsupported by corroborative evidence tending to connect the defendant with the commission of such offense."

This law remains in effect, despite the author's wish: "I hope I am alive to see" the law changed.

In chapter 9, "That's Peggy O'Neil!," the author commented that a new penal law, enacted in 1967, had failed to include a penalty for the sale of prescriptions (the practice by which a doctor can write an illegal prescription for a fee). Penalties only existed for doctors who illegally sold the narcotics themselves. The law was later changed. Penal Law 220.65, enacted in 1986, made the sale of prescriptions a Class C felony, carrying a maximum penalty of five and a half years' imprisonment.

Index

Editor's Note: As stated in the Author's Preface, in most cases the
names of criminal defendants, victims and witnesses, as well
as some minor identifying details, were changed.
This Index does not include any fictitious names or details.